Mathematics

ONE

FOR COMMON ENTRANCE

Serena Alexander

GALORE PARK
AN HACHETTE UK COMPANY

About the author

Serena Alexander has taught mathematics since 1987, originally in both maintained and independent senior schools. From 1990 she taught at St Paul's School for Boys, where she was Head of mathematics at their Preparatory School, Colet Court, before moving first to Newton Prep as Deputy Head and then to Devonshire House as Head. She is now an educational consultant, with a focus on mathematics, and an ISI reporting inspector and in addition she helps to run regular mathematics conferences for prep school teachers.

Serena has a passion for maths and expects her pupils to feel the same way. After a lesson or two with her, they normally do!

The publishers would like to thank the following for permission to reproduce copyright material:

Photo credits Cover photo © alexvv – Fotolia **p1** © Elena Milevska – Fotolia **p2** © Getty Images/The Bridgeman Art Library **p16** © photomic – Fotolia **p128** © Maksym Yemelyanov – Fotolia **p128** © natrot – Fotolia **p166** © Mariusz Blach – Fotolia **p227** © Thinkstock/Getty Images/Hemera **p242** © Getty Images/iStockphoto/Thinkstock **p251** © BRAD – Fotolia **p262** © Marzanna Syncerz – Fotolia **p294** © Thinkstock/Getty Images/iStockphoto **p324** © Imagestate Media (John Foxx) **p327** © pixelrobot – Fotolia **p337** © Thinkstock/Getty Images/Dorling Kindersley RF **p339** © InaPandora – Fotolia

Acknowledgements p253, 254, 260 © Crown copyright 2015. Ordnance Survey Licence number 150001477

Every effort has been made to trace all copyright holders, but if any have been inadvertently overlooked the publishers will be pleased to make the necessary arrangements at the first opportunity.

Although every effort has been made to ensure that website addresses are correct at time of going to press, Galore Park cannot be held responsible for the content of any website mentioned in this book. It is sometimes possible to find a relocated web page by typing in the address of the home page for a website in the URL window of your browser.

Hachette UK's policy is to use papers that are natural, renewable and recyclable products and made from wood grown in sustainable forests. The logging and manufacturing processes are expected to conform to the environmental regulations of the country of origin.

Orders: please contact Bookpoint Ltd, 130 Milton Park, Abingdon, Oxon OX14 4SB. Telephone: +44 (0)1235 827827. Lines are open 9.00a.m.–5.00p.m., Monday to Saturday, with a 24-hour message answering service. Visit our website at www.galorepark.co.uk for details of other revision guides for Common Entrance, examination papers and Galore Park publications.

Published by Galore Park Publishing Ltd

An Hachette UK company

338 Euston Road, London, NW1 3BH

www.galorepark.co.uk

Typeset in 11.5/13pt ITC Officina Sans Std by Integra Software Services Pvt. Ltd., Pondicherry, India

Printed in Italy

New illustrations by Integra software services Pvt.Ltd

Some illustrations by Graham Edwards were re-used. The publishers will be pleased to make the necessary arrangements with regard to these illustrations at the first opportunity.

A catalogue record for this title is available from the British Library.

ISBN: 9781471846632

Contents

Introduction

This book is for pupils working towards their 13+ ISEB Common Entrance. It is intended for pupils in Year 7 who will be taking either Level 1 or Level 2 papers at the end of Year 8. It may also be suitable for pupils in Year 6 who will eventually be sitting either Level 3 Common Entrance or Scholarship papers. It has been written in line with the National Curriculum and the ISEB syllabus.

The book provides a sound and varied foundation on which pupils can build in the future. There is plenty of material to support this and many possibilities for extending the more able mathematicians. It provides a variety of approaches, ranging from the relatively modern 'mental' to the more historical 'traditional', leaving plenty of scope to adopt the most appropriate method for each pupil. There is no prescribed teaching order and topics may be visited more than once during the year.

It is understood that at Year 7 it may not be possible to determine which Level is most suitable for each individual. For this reason, questions in each exercise are graded with straightforward Level 1 type questions at the beginning leading to Level 2 type questions towards the end.

Algebra is introduced but the main emphasis is on sound number work with carefully written pencil-and-paper methods, geometry, probability and data handling. The problem-solving exercises are intended to develop pupils' reasoning skills. Worked examples demonstrate methods and techniques and at the end of each chapter there is an extension exercise designed to stretch the most able. A final summary exercise tests understanding and retention. Teachers should use their discretion over the use of calculators. The aim is to develop good written and mental arithmetic methods.

Pupils entering Year 7 who have not followed the revised Primary National Curriculum (2014) may benefit from more practice before embarking on the exercises here. New later Key Stage 2 Primary National Curriculum is covered comprehensively in Galore Park's *Mathematics Year 5* (ISBN: 9781471829383) and *Mathematics Year 6* (ISBN: 9781471829369).

Notes on features in this book

Words printed in **blue and bold** are keywords. All keywords are defined in the Glossary at the end of the book.

Example

Worked examples are given throughout to aid understanding of each part of a topic.

Exercise

Exercises are provided to give pupils plenty of opportunities to practise what they have learned.

Extension Exercise

Some exercises contain questions that are more challenging. These extension exercises are designed to stretch more able pupils.

Summary Exercise

Each chapter ends with a summary exercise, containing questions on all the topics in the chapter.

Useful rules and reminders are scattered throughout the book.

Activity

The National Curriculum for Mathematics reflects the importance of spoken language in pupils' development across the whole curriculum – cognitively, socially and linguistically. Activities to develop these skills are interspersed between the chapters. These are essential for developing pupils' mathematical vocabulary and presenting a mathematical justification, argument or proof.

1 Back to basics

In the beginning

People learning to count are very likely to use their fingers. Prehistoric humans almost certainly used their hands to communicate numbers. An early human could show three fingers on one hand and say: 'three sabre-tooth tigers', just as you hold up yours and say: 'three glasses of water'.

Roman numbers

For many years the Roman system for numbers was used throughout Europe. The system was derived from that of the Etruscans, who had derived their system from the Phoenicians. They used the symbols I, II, III, ... up to ten, which was X, and then XX, XXX, ... until C for a hundred and M for a thousand. Later, they introduced 'one-hand counting' and used V for five, L for fifty and D for five hundred. These symbols can be made with one hand. (D would look more like O.)

Finally the Romans introduced the idea of the inverted four – IV – which means one less than five. In the same way XL means ten less than 50. It is easiest to understand the system if you look at the first ten numbers in groups of five.

    I   II   III   IV V   VI   VII   VIII   IX X

and then the tens:

    X XX XXX XL L   LX LXX LXXX XC C

and the hundreds:

    C CC CCC CD D   DC DCC DCCC CM M

You can combine these three sets, to form the numbers that come between.

*   CCXLIV is two hundred and forty-four.

* MDCCXLIV breaks down into M 1000

        DCC   700

        XL   40

        IV   4

So   MDCCXLIV is 1744

Roman numerals are still used, both as upper-case letters, as above, and as lower-case: i, ii, iii, iv, v.

British kings and queens are also given Roman numerals. Look at this contemporary portrait of Henry VIII. Try to work out his age from the numbers in the background.

Exercise 1.1

Write these Roman numbers as decimal numbers.

1 iii

2 IX

3 viii

4 XX

5 MCC

6 ix

7 xxiv

8 CCL

9 DCXX

10 CLV

11 XLV

12 MCMXV

13 CMXLIX

14 DCCXCIV

15 MCMXIV

16 MMXII

17 LV (BCE)

18 MCDLV

19 MDLXXXVIII

20 MCMLXIX

21 Which historical events do you associate with the numbers in questions 15–20?

Exercise 1.2

Write these decimal numbers in Roman numerals.

1 5

2 10

3 25

4 120

5 1005

6 540

7 56

8 2016

9 301

10 2500

11 1110

12 607

13 417

14 867

15 1066

16 1776

17 1815

18 1666

19 1215

20 1945

21 Which historical events do you associate with the numbers in questions 15–20?

From Roman numbers to the decimal system

The Roman system is a system of **symbols**. The Arab world used a completely different system in which the position of a number, or **digit**, represented its value. The name 'digit' comes from the Latin word, *digiti*, for fingers.

This **decimal** system was slowly introduced to Europe by Muslim scholars and is now used worldwide. It gets its name from the Latin for ten: *decem*.

Place value

The value of any digit within a number is represented by its relative position within the number: units, tens, hundreds or thousands. Note the use of zero, or a nought, to indicate where there are no units or tens, for example.

	Th	H	T	U
Nine thousand	9	0	0	0
Five hundred		5	0	0
Thirty (3 tens)			3	0
Six				6
Four thousand and twelve	4	0	1	2

○ Larger numbers

As the numbers you need to represent get larger, the place values extend to ten thousand, hundred thousand. Instead of thousand thousands, you use millions, then ten millions and hundred millions.

This number is four hundred million, three hundred and four thousand and fifteen.

	HM	TM	M	HTh	TTh	Th	H	T	U
	4	0	0	3	0	4	0	1	5

When you write numbers with five or more digits, you generally leave a small space between the hundreds and the thousands and between the thousands and the millions.

400 304 015

○ Smaller numbers

Most numbers less than one may be represented as **fractions** of a whole. When you write **decimal fractions**, the decimal point separates the fractional part from the whole number.

	Th	H	T	U .	t	h	th
Nine tenths				0 .	9		
Four hundredths				0 .	0	4	
Two thousandths				0 .	0	0	2
Twenty-five thousandths				0 .	0	2	5
One thousand and five	1	0	0	5 .			
Four and three hundredths				4 .	0	3	
Five hundred and four and seven thousandths		5	0	4 .	0	0	7

Exercise 1.3

Write each number in figures.

1 Six thousand and nine

2 Eight thousand and thirteen

3 Fifteen and six tenths

4 Eight hundred and one and five thousandths

5 Four and six hundredths

6 Twenty-five thousand and six

7 Five million, six hundred and three thousand and twenty

8 Fifty-three thousand, four hundred and eight and seventeen thousandths

9 Five hundred and four million, sixty thousand and eight

10 Twelve million and sixteen hundredths

Exercise 1.4

Write these numbers in words.

1 21070

2 405012

3 1005030

4 0.05

5 12.004

6 30070011

7 2067005

8 40060

9 56.4

10 30.007

11 5720000

12 5720

13 103.16

14 3.025

15 5734105

16 13500543

17 750060400

18 7560004

19 7056040

20 7.506

◯ Comparing numbers

When you need to compare two or more numbers, you can study the place values of the digits.

Consider 3050 and 3005

Both numbers start with three thousand but the 5 in 3050 represents 5 tens whilst the 5 in 3005 represents 5 units, therefore 3050 is larger than 3005

Write this as: 3050 > 3005

By the same argument, 3005 is smaller than 3050

Write this as: 3005 < 3050

Note > means larger than and < means smaller than.

Exercise 1.5

1 Copy each pair of numbers and write < or > between them.

(a) 4900   4090

(b) 25007   25070

(c) 305107   350017

(d) 1030500   1003500

(e) 174908   174809

(f) 5403540   5430504

2 Copy each pair of numbers and write < or > between them.

(a) 0.303   0.330

(b) 0.4   0.004

(c) 7.01   7.001

(d) 0.13   0.103

(e) 5.205   5.25

(f) 10.05   10.015

3 Write these numbers in order of size, smallest first.

(a) 6070   6700   6007

(b) 25040   20540   25045

(c) 1060050   1600500   1060005

4 Write these numbers in order of size, largest first.

(a) 9809   9890   9089

(b) 106045   160450   106405

(c) 10200730   12700300   1060005

5 Write these numbers in order of size, smallest first.

(a) 0.3   0.003   0.303

(b) 4.5   4.05   4.505

(c) 12.702   1.207   12.07

6 Write these numbers in order of size, largest first.

(a) 14.06   1.604   16.4

(b) 100.5   105.05   100.05

(c) 2.07   2.7   2.007

7 Write down a number that lies between 107 and 110

8 Write down a number that lies between 0.4 and 0.5

9 Find a number that is larger than 0 but less than 1

10 Find a number that is larger than 0.05 but less than 0.055

The number line

Have you ever looked at significant dates on a timeline?

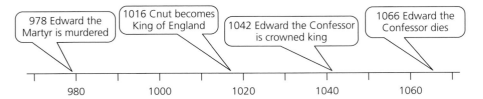

The dates on this line are labelled **A.D.** (Anno Domini), and used in our calendar to refer to the current era. **B.C.** (Before Christ) is used for dates earlier in history.

Note that there is no year 0 on a timeline.

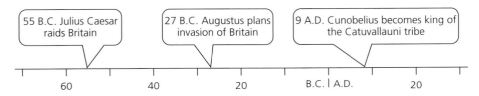

When you use a number line to show numbers, zero is included. The numbers below or to the left of zero are **negative numbers**.

You can also show decimal fractions on a number line.

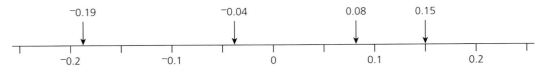

Exercise 1.6

1 Draw a number line from ⁻20 to 20. Let 2 cm represent each step of 10

   Mark these numbers on your number line: ⁻5   14   ⁻12   8

2 Draw a number line from ⁻0.2 to 0.2. Let 2 cm represent each step of 0.1

   Mark these numbers on your number line: 0.18   ⁻0.16   0.04   ⁻0.07

3 Draw a number line from ⁻4 to 12. Let 2 cm represent each step of 4

   Mark these numbers on your number line: 11   ⁻3   5   ⁻0.5   10.5

4 Draw a number line from ⁻8 to 2. Let 2 cm represent each step of 2

Mark these numbers on your number line: 1.5   ⁻7   ⁻4.5   0.5   ⁻2.5

5 Draw a number line from ⁻1 to 1 with 2 cm representing each step of 0.5

Mark these numbers on your number line: ⁻0.2   0.4   ⁻0.9   0.75

◯ Rounding

Look back at the number lines and you can see that 22 lies very close to 20 and that ⁻0.19 lies very close to ⁻2

Imagine you are working with a number with lots of digits, before or after the decimal point. You may not need to use all of those digits. It can be more convenient to work with a simpler number that has been **rounded** up or down.

You could say that   22 is 20   to the nearest ten (rounding down)

and   0.19 is 0.2   to one **decimal place** (1 d.p.).
                                                           (rounding up)

Notice that 0.15 lies exactly halfway between 0.1 and 0.2

The rule here is that you round up.

> You can also use the symbol ≈, which means 'approximately equal to'.
>
> $0.15 \approx 0.2$

                      0.15 is 0.2   to 2 d.p.

Examples

(i)   Round 25 750 489 to the nearest million.

   25 750 489 lies between 25 million and 26 million but is nearer to 26 million.

   $25\,750\,489 \approx 26$ million to the nearest million

(ii) Round 25 755 000 to the nearest ten thousand.

   25 755 000 lies halfway between 25 750 000 and 25 760 000, so round up.

   $25\,755\,000 \approx 25\,760\,000$ to the nearest ten thousand.

(iii) Round 750 489 to the nearest ten.

   750 489 lies between 750 480 and 750 490 but is nearer to 750 490.

   $750\,489 \approx 750\,490$ to the nearest ten

(iv) Round 0.7845 to two decimal places.

   0.7845 lies between 0.78 and 0.79 but is nearer to 0.78

   0.7845 = 0.78 to 2 d.p.

(v)   Round 0.7845 to three decimal places.

   0.7845 lies exactly halfway between 0.784 and 0.785, so round up.

   0.7845 = 0.785 to 3 d.p.

Can you see a simple rule developing?

1 Find the digit in the place-value position to which you are rounding.

2 Look at the value of the digit to its right.

3 If it is 5, 6, 7, 8 or 9, round up.

4 If it is 4, 3, 2, 1 or 0, leave the digit as it is.

Exercise 1.7

1 Round these numbers to the nearest hundred.

(a) 545
(c) 674
(e) 253 428

(b) 1450
(d) 34 650
(f) 19 999

2 Round these numbers to one decimal place.

(a) 0.195
(c) 12.309
(e) 16.750

(b) 4.25
(d) 105.035
(f) 3.099

3 Round these numbers to the nearest million.

(a) 6 750 000
(c) 12 500 000
(e) 1 500 000

(b) 9 075 999
(d) 956 000
(f) 9 945 890

4 Round these numbers to two decimal places.

(a) 15.2307
(c) 0.0150
(e) 1.8739

(b) 30.755
(d) 17.095
(f) 0.9999

5 Round these numbers to the nearest hundred thousand.

(a) 1 505 600
(c) 1 517 500
(e) 4 094 583

(b) 13 250 000
(d) 950 000
(f) 19 950 000

6 Round these numbers to three decimal places.

(a) 5.1045
(c) 0.0056
(e) 15.0106

(b) 14.0078
(d) 0.0095
(f) 4.0999

7 Round these numbers to the nearest thousand.

(a) 25 095
(c) 245 250
(e) 1 450 500

(b) 6500
(d) 109 095
(f) 19 500

8 Round these numbers to the nearest whole number.

(a) 1.005
(c) 0.524
(e) 0.253

(b) 35.645
(d) 14.535
(f) 4.075

9 What is the smallest whole number that can be written as 24 million to the nearest million?

10 What is the largest whole number that can be written as 450 000 to the nearest ten thousand?

11 What is the smallest whole number that can be written as 230 to the nearest ten?

12 What is the largest number that can be written as 0.9 to one decimal place?

13 What is the smallest number that can be written as 1.75 to two decimal places?

14 What is the largest number that can be written as 10 to the nearest whole number?

15 What is the smallest number that can be written as 5 to the nearest whole number?

Fractions and decimal fractions

A whole number may be divided into equal parts, with numerator 1, called **unit fractions**.

$\frac{1}{2}, \frac{1}{3}, \frac{1}{6}$ and $\frac{1}{13}$ are examples of unit fractions.

Unit fractions can be combined to form other fractions such as $\frac{2}{3}, \frac{3}{4}$ or $\frac{9}{10}$

$$\frac{2}{3} = \frac{1}{2} + \frac{1}{6}$$

Think again about decimal fractions, in which there are digits after the decimal point.

You can write these, without the decimal point, as normal fractions.

0.7 is 7 tenths or $\frac{7}{10}$

0.09 is 9 hundredths or $\frac{9}{100}$

Sometimes you may combine fractions with whole numbers.

5.25 is 5 and 25 hundredths or $5\frac{25}{100} = 5\frac{1}{4}$

7.125 is 7 and 125 thousandths or $7\frac{125}{1000} = 7\frac{1}{8}$

> You should always write fractions in their **lowest terms**. To reduce a fraction to its lowest terms, keep dividing the top and bottom numbers of the fraction by a number that divides exactly into both of them, until you cannot go any further.
>
> $$\frac{125}{1000} = \frac{25}{200} = \frac{5}{40} = \frac{1}{8}$$

You can use a number line to find fraction and decimal equivalents.

Look at this number line from 0 to 1. It is divided into tenths.

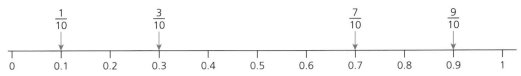

Notice that: $0.1 = \frac{1}{10}$ $0.3 = \frac{3}{10}$ $0.7 = \frac{7}{10}$ $0.9 = \frac{9}{10}$

This number line from 0 to 1 is divided into quarters.

Notice that: $0.25 = \frac{1}{4}$ $0.5 = \frac{1}{2}$ $0.75 = \frac{3}{4}$

This number line from 0 to 1 is divided into fifths.

Notice that: $0.2 = \frac{1}{5}$ $0.4 = \frac{2}{5}$ $0.6 = \frac{3}{5}$ $0.8 = \frac{4}{5}$

This number line from 0 to 1 is divided into eighths.

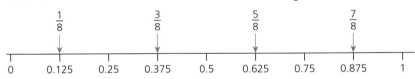

Notice that: $0.125 = \frac{1}{8}$ $0.375 = \frac{3}{8}$ $0.625 = \frac{5}{8}$ $0.875 = \frac{7}{8}$

> Number lines can be useful when you need to answer questions about fractions and decimals. Remember that the number line can extend below zero.

Examples

Draw a number line from ⁻1 to 1 and divide it into eighths. Mark on it the fraction and decimal equivalents for $\frac{-1}{4}, \frac{1}{2}$ and $\frac{3}{4}$

Then copy these pairs of numbers and write <, > or = between them.

(i)   0.25 and $\frac{1}{2}$ (ii)   0.75 and $\frac{3}{4}$ (iii) $\frac{-1}{4}$ and ⁻0.2

> Mark any additional decimal values on the number line.

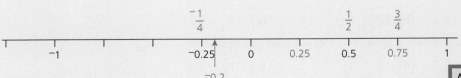

(i) $0.25 < \frac{1}{2}$ (ii) $0.75 = \frac{3}{4}$ (iii) $\frac{-1}{4} < {}^{-}0.2$

> Any number is greater than the numbers to its left on the number line.

11

Exercise 1.8

1 Draw a number line from $^-1$ to 1 and divide it into tenths. Mark on it the fraction and decimal equivalents for $\frac{^-3}{5}, \frac{^-2}{5}, \frac{1}{5}$ and $\frac{4}{5}$. Then copy these pairs of numbers and write <, > or = between them.

   (a) $\frac{^-2}{5}$ $\frac{1}{5}$ (b) 0.5 $\frac{1}{5}$ (c) $\frac{^-3}{5}$ $^-0.8$

2 Draw a number line from 7 to 8 and divide it into eighths. Mark on it the fraction and decimal equivalents for $7\frac{1}{8}, 7\frac{1}{2}, 7\frac{3}{4}$ and $7\frac{7}{8}$. Then copy these pairs of numbers and write <, > or = between them.

   (a) 7.25 $7\frac{1}{8}$ (b) 7.75 $7\frac{7}{8}$ (c) $7\frac{3}{4}$ 7.75

3 Draw a number line from 9 to 10 and divide it into tenths. Mark on it the fraction and decimal equivalents for $9\frac{1}{5}, 9\frac{3}{10}, 9\frac{1}{2}$ and $9\frac{4}{5}$. Then copy these pairs of numbers and write <, > or = between them.

   (a) 9.2 $9\frac{1}{5}$ (b) 9.75 $9\frac{4}{5}$ (c) $9\frac{3}{10}$ 9.25

4 Draw a number line from 3 to 4 and divide it into eighths. Mark on it the fraction and decimal equivalents for $3\frac{1}{4}, 3\frac{3}{8}, 3\frac{5}{8}$ and $3\frac{7}{8}$. Then copy these pairs of numbers and write <, > or = between them.

   (a) 3.5 $3\frac{3}{8}$ (b) 3.4 $3\frac{1}{4}$ (c) $3\frac{7}{8}$ 3.75

5 Draw a number line from $^-2$ to 0 and divide it into eighths. Mark on it the fraction and decimal equivalents for $^-1\frac{3}{4}, ^-1\frac{1}{4},$ and $\frac{^-3}{4}$. Then copy these pairs of numbers and write <, > or = between them.

   (a) $^-1\frac{1}{4}$ $^-0.5$ (b) $^-1.75$ $^-1\frac{3}{4}$ (c) $\frac{^-1}{2}$ $^-0.2$

You can use a number line to help you with the following questions.

6 Copy these pairs of numbers and write <, > or = between them.

   (a) $6\frac{1}{4}$ 6.4   (b) 6.8 $6\frac{7}{8}$ (c) $6\frac{3}{8}$ 6.3

7 Copy these pairs of numbers and write <, > or = between them.

   (a) $1\frac{1}{4}$ $^-1.2$ (b) $^-1.25$ $^-1\frac{2}{5}$ (c) $\frac{3}{4}$ $^-0.75$

8 Copy these pairs of numbers and write <, > or = between them.

   (a) $5\frac{1}{4}$ $^-5.2$ (b) 5.75 $5\frac{3}{4}$ (c) $^-5\frac{7}{8}$ 5.8

9 Copy these pairs of numbers and write <, > or = between them.

   (a) $^-1\frac{1}{5}$ 1.2   (b) 1.6 $^-1\frac{3}{5}$ (c) $^-1\frac{4}{5}$ $^-1.4$

10 Copy these pairs of numbers and write <, > or = between them.

   (a) $^-3\frac{1}{4}$ $^-3.4$ (b) $^-3.8$ $^-3\frac{5}{8}$ (c) $^-3\frac{7}{8}$ $^-3.7$

11 Write down the number that lies exactly halfway between $2\frac{1}{4}$ and $2\frac{3}{4}$

12 Write down the number that lies exactly halfway between $^-1\frac{1}{4}$ and $1\frac{1}{4}$

13 Write down the number that lies exactly halfway between $\frac{^-1}{4}$ and $\frac{3}{4}$

14 Write down the number that lies exactly halfway between $\frac{^-2}{5}$ and $1\frac{3}{5}$

15 Write down the number that lies exactly halfway between $^-2\frac{5}{8}$ and $1\frac{3}{8}$

◯ Sequences

A **sequence** is a list of numbers that is written in a special order. Each number in a sequence is a **term**.

The terms in a sequence follow a rule.

In a **linear sequence**, the **difference** between one term and the next is constant.

Example

Find the difference between the terms in this sequence. Then work out the next two terms.

$$\frac{1}{4}, \quad 1\frac{1}{2}, \quad 2\frac{3}{4}, \quad 4, \quad 5\frac{1}{4}$$

Method 1: Using the number line

First, draw the sequence on a number line.

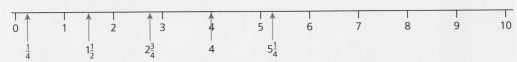

Next, work out the difference between the terms.

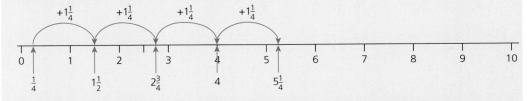

Now extend the sequence by two more 'jumps' and mark the next two terms.

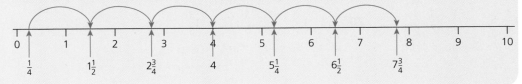

Method 2: Calculation

To find the difference, subtract one term from the one after it.

$$\text{Difference} = 1\tfrac{1}{2} - \tfrac{1}{4}$$

$$= 1\tfrac{1}{4}$$

Mentally check this works for the other terms in the sequence, for example, $5\tfrac{1}{4} - 4 = 1\tfrac{1}{4}$

$$\text{Next term (1)} = 5\tfrac{1}{4} + 1\tfrac{1}{4}$$

$$= 6\tfrac{1}{2}$$

$$\text{Next term (2)} = 6\tfrac{1}{2} + 1\tfrac{1}{4}$$

$$= 7\tfrac{3}{4}$$

Exercise 1.9

Work out the missing terms in these sequences. You will need to find the difference between terms first. Write the fractions in their lowest terms.

Remember to write fractions in their lowest terms.

$$\frac{125}{1000} = \frac{25}{200} = \frac{5}{40} = \frac{1}{8}$$

1 5, 8, 11, 14, ..., ...

2 1.2, 2.5, 3.8, 5.1, ..., ...

3 $^-$1.8, $^-$0.9, 0, 0.9, ..., ...

4 ..., ..., 0, 0.7, 1.4, 2.1

5 ..., $^-$1.3, $^-$0.6, 0.1, 0.8, ...

6 $\dfrac{1}{4}$, $\dfrac{3}{4}$, $1\dfrac{1}{4}$, $1\dfrac{3}{4}$, ..., ...

7 $\dfrac{2}{5}$, $\dfrac{4}{5}$, $1\dfrac{1}{5}$, $1\dfrac{3}{5}$, 2, ..., ...

8 $^-1\dfrac{1}{2}$, $\dfrac{^-3}{4}$, 0, $\dfrac{3}{4}$, $1\dfrac{1}{2}$, ..., ...

9 $^-1\dfrac{3}{4}$, $^-1$, $\dfrac{^-1}{4}$, $\dfrac{1}{2}$, $1\dfrac{1}{4}$, ..., ...

10 $\dfrac{1}{2}$, $\dfrac{3}{4}$, ..., $1\dfrac{1}{4}$, $1\dfrac{1}{2}$, ...

11 $1\dfrac{1}{5}$, $1\dfrac{3}{5}$, ..., $2\dfrac{2}{5}$, ..., $3\dfrac{1}{5}$

12 $\dfrac{^-3}{4}$, $\dfrac{^-1}{4}$, $\dfrac{1}{4}$, ..., $1\dfrac{1}{4}$, ...

13 ..., ..., 0, $\dfrac{3}{5}$, $1\dfrac{1}{5}$, $1\dfrac{4}{5}$

14 ..., $^-1\dfrac{1}{5}$, $\dfrac{^-3}{5}$, 0, ..., $1\dfrac{1}{5}$

15 $^-2\dfrac{1}{2}$, $^-1\dfrac{3}{4}$, ..., $\dfrac{^-1}{4}$, $\dfrac{1}{2}$, ...

16 $\dfrac{3}{8}$, 1, $1\dfrac{5}{8}$, $2\dfrac{1}{4}$, ..., ...

17 $1\dfrac{1}{2}$, $1\dfrac{7}{8}$, ..., $2\dfrac{1}{4}$, ..., $3\dfrac{3}{8}$

18 $\dfrac{^-7}{10}$, $\dfrac{^-2}{5}$, ..., $\dfrac{1}{5}$, $\dfrac{1}{2}$, ...

19 ..., ..., $\dfrac{7}{10}$, $1\dfrac{2}{5}$, $2\dfrac{1}{10}$, $2\dfrac{4}{5}$

20 ..., $^-1\dfrac{1}{5}$, $\dfrac{^-1}{2}$, $\dfrac{1}{5}$, ..., $1\dfrac{3}{5}$

Summary Exercise 1.10

1 Write these Roman numbers as ordinary decimal numbers.

   (a) iv

   (b) XII

   (c) xxiii

   (d) MDCX

   (e) MDCXL

   (f) MCMXCIV

2 Write these numbers in Roman numerals.

   (a) 7

   (b) 15

   (c) 38

   (d) 206

   (e) 1445

   (f) 1859

3 Copy each pair of numbers and write < or > between them.

   (a) 3010   3001

   (b) 2.5   ⁻1.4

   (c) 405 105   401 501

   (d) 3 055 007   3 054 700

   (e) 0.706   0.76

   (f) 20.4   20.004

4 Round these numbers to the nearest: (i) hundred (ii) ten thousand (iii) million.

   (a) 7 545 678   (b) 13 500 799   (c) 45 097 605

5 Round these numbers to: (i) 1 decimal place (ii) 2 decimal places
   (iii) 3 decimal places.

   (a) 5.6074   (b) 0.9639   (c) 9.9784

6 What is the largest whole number that can be written as 5000 to the
   nearest thousand?

7 What is the smallest number that can be written as 2.5 to one decimal place?

8 Copy these pairs of numbers and write <, > or = between them. Use a
   number line to help you, if you wish.

   (a) $7\frac{1}{4}$ 7.3

   (b) $⁻1\frac{2}{5}$ ⁻0.5

   (c) ⁻1.4 $⁻1\frac{2}{5}$

   (d) $⁻1\frac{1}{10}$ ⁻1.3

9 By drawing a number line or otherwise, write down the number that comes
   exactly halfway between:

   (a) $1\frac{1}{5}$ and $2\frac{4}{5}$

   (b) $\frac{⁻3}{4}$ and $1\frac{1}{4}$

10 Find the missing terms in each sequence.

   (a) ⁻2.4,   ⁻1.6,   ⁻0.8,   0,   ...,   ...,

   (b) ...,   ...,   0.1,   0.6,   1.1,   1.6

   (c) $⁻1\frac{1}{4}$, $\frac{⁻3}{4}$,   ...,   ..., $\frac{3}{4}$, $1\frac{1}{4}$

   (d) $\frac{⁻9}{10}$,   ...,   ..., $\frac{3}{10}$, $\frac{7}{10}$, $1\frac{1}{10}$

> You should always
> write fractions in
> their lowest terms. To
> simplify the fraction
> to its lowest terms,
> divide the top and
> bottom numbers
> of the fraction by
> numbers that divide
> into them exactly,
> until you cannot go
> any further.
> $$\frac{125}{1000} = \frac{25}{200} = \frac{5}{40} = \frac{1}{8}$$

Activity: Roman numeral investigations

You know that the Roman system of numerals was based on symbols.

I	1	V	5	X	10	L	50
C	100	D	500	M	1000		

You can add these symbols to each other (for example, XXX = 30) or combine them with other symbols to build numbers of any size.

When you are increasing the value of a symbol, the smaller number is always placed after the bigger number.

VI = 6   XXI = 21   LV = 55

The three symbols I, X and C may be written before a symbol of higher value to reduce its value.

I (1)	may be written before	V (5) to make	IV (4)
	may be written before	X (10) to make	IX (9)
X (10)	may be written before	L (50) to make	XL (40)
	may be written before	C (100) to make	XC (90)
C (100)	may be written before	D (500) to make	CD (400)
	may be written before	M (1000) to make	CM (900)

Note that:

- I can be written on its own, or before or after V or X
- X can be written on its own, or before or after L or C
- C can be written on its own, or before or after D or M

You may find variations to this rule but these are the essential principles on which the system is based.

You will frequently see years written in Roman numerals on buildings and memorials. This is Admiralty Arch in London.

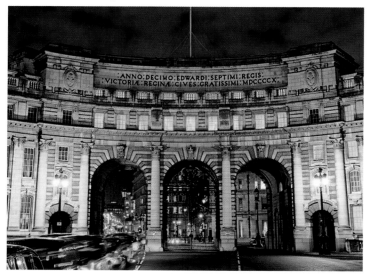

Longest years

1 Find the number between 1 and 2000 that is the longest, when written in Roman numerals. The longest is the number with the most numerals.

2 How many years after the year 2000 will there be a year with a longer number (when written in Roman numerals) than the one you found in question1?

3 What is the lowest-value Roman number with six letters, between 1 and 2000?

4 What is the highest-value Roman number, with six letters, between 1 and 2000?

How many numbers?

5 How many valid Roman numbers can you make, using just the numerals I, V and X? How many of these use each numeral once and once only?

6 How many valid Roman numbers can you make, using just the numerals I, V, X and L? How many of these use each numeral once and once only?

7 How many valid Roman numbers can you make, using just the numerals I, V, X, L, C once and once only? Which is the largest and which the smallest? What is the difference between them?

8 How many valid Roman numbers can you make, using just the numerals I, V, X, L, C and D once and once only? Which is the largest and which the smallest? What is the difference between them?

9 How many valid Roman numbers can you make, using just the numerals I, V, X, L, C, D and M once and once only? Which is the largest and which the smallest? What is the difference between them?

10 Copy the table below and complete it, using your results. Can you see a pattern? If you were to invent another letter for another number after M, what would it be? Use this number and continue your table.

No. of numerals	No. of numbers	Highest	Lowest	Difference
2	2	VI	IV	2 or II
3	2	XVI	XIV	2 or II
4				
5				
6				
7				

2 Mental calculations

One of the most common uses for numbers is to calculate answers to problems. It is important that you can do this quickly and accurately.

Mental arithmetic

You could use a calculator, but it can be much quicker to do basic arithmetic in your head, particularly if you use number bonds to break down the calculations into easily managed stages. There is no one correct way to do calculations mentally but here are some tips that may be useful. Visualising the number line can help.

Addition and subtraction

How will you add 14 to 29?

Add the units, then add the tens.

$14 + 9 = 23$ then $23 + 20 = 43$

How will you calculate $43 - 29$?

You can use a similar method to that you used for addition.

Subtract the units then subtract the tens.

$43 - 9 = 34$ then $34 - 20 = 14$

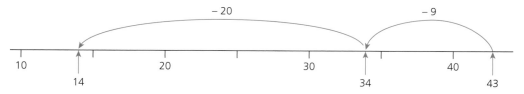

After any subtraction, you should quickly check your answer by doing the **inverse** addition.

$1401 - 367 = 1034$ Check: $1034 + 367 = 1401$

You can use mental arithmetic to solve everyday problems.

> **Example**
>
> There is a plague of frogs in my back garden. I collect 54 and my sister collects another 27. How many frogs do we have in total?
>
> 54 + 27 = 81

Exercise 2.1

For this exercise, write down the calculation you are going to do, but then do it in your head.

1 I have 46 stickers and I am given another 29. How many do I have now?

2 We drive 178 km before lunch and then 62 km after lunch. How far do we go in total?

3 There are 85 children due to go on today's trip but 27 are away. How many go?

4 The snail climbed up 47 cm but then slid down 19 cm. How far has it climbed in total?

5 I saved £152 but then spent £95 on a new tablet. How much do I have left?

6 On my new tablet I played a new game. I scored 428 points in the first round and 624 on the second. What is my total score?

7 134 people got on an empty train. At the next station 37 people got on and 54 got off. How many people are there on the train now?

8 There are 1431 pupils in our school. 725 of them are girls. How many are boys?

9 There are 211 pupils in Year 7. 89 of them walk to school, how many do not?

10 In Year 8 there are 79 girls and 124 boys. How many pupils are there in Year 8?

Multiplication and division

Just as with addition and subtraction, it is important to be able to multiply and divide mentally. This means that you need to know your times tables really well.

When you learn the times tables, you are learning four number bonds each time.

Subtraction is the inverse of addition. Division is the inverse of multiplication.

If you know that $8 \times 9 = 72$

you also know $9 \times 8 = 72$

and $72 \div 8 = 9$

and $72 \div 9 = 8$

Those four calculations were all exact, but suppose you had been asked to work out 75 ÷ 8

8 does not go exactly into 75, but 8 × 9 = 72

So, from 75 you can make 9 groups of 8 and have 3 left over. The 3 is the **remainder**.

Therefore you write: 75 ÷ 8 = 9 r 3

> Here, r stands for 'remainder'.

Exercise 2.2

Calculate the answers to these problems.

When you are doing a calculation in your head, write it down like this.

54 + 63 = 117

1 Oak House from Year 7 are going on a trip to the wildlife park. There are four teachers going and each teacher has a group of six pupils. How many pupils are there in Year 7?

2 Ash House from Year 7 are going on a trip to the museum. There are 50 pupils and each teacher accompanies a group with a maximum of 8 pupils. How many teachers will need to go?

3 The upper school are going on a trip to the theatre. There are 125 pupils and no teacher can have more than 11 in their group. What is the lowest number of teachers that can go on the trip?

4 The headmaster separated the upper school into girls and boys for a special talk. There are 76 boys and 74 girls. How many children are there in the upper school?

5 Fort Grange School has been collecting tokens from the supermarket to win some free software. Year 7 have 42 tokens, Year 8 have double the number of Year 7, Year 9 have one third the total of Year 7 and Year 8. How many tokens does the school have in all?

6 From Monday to Thursday every week the milkman delivers 7 loaves of bread. On Friday he delivers 2 extra. How many loaves does he deliver each week?

7 In the week he also delivers 6 trays of eggs, with 12 eggs in each tray. How many eggs is that?

8 There are normally 5 days in a school week. This term, there are 11 full weeks and one week of 3 days. For how many days am I at school this term?

9 The 45 pupils in the Year 7 have to go for an eye test. They go in groups of 8 How many groups go for the eye test?

10 Glue sticks come in boxes of 16. The school has ordered 12 boxes and these are shared among 8 classes. How many does each class receive?

Extension Exercise 2.3

Thorn House scored 129 points more than Beech. They scored 375 points altogether. How many did Beech have?

If you worked out 246, then you probably thought like this.

$$375 - 129 = 246$$

So Beech has 246 and that means that Thorn has 246 + 129, which is 375 – but that does not fit the question, because you're told they scored 375 altogether!

What you are told is that:

	Beech plus 129 equals Thorn
and	Thorn plus Beech equals 375
therefore	Beech plus 129 plus Beech equals 375
	Beech plus Beech equals 246 (as 375 – 129 = 246)

Beech has 123 points.

Therefore	Thorn equals 123 + 129

Thorn has 252 points.

Now try these questions. As in the example, these questions need more thought. Remember to write down all the calculations that you are doing, even if you are working mentally. That way you can check what you have done.

1   I pay 95p for a pen and a pencil. The pen costs 15p more than the pencil. How much does the pencil cost?

2   There are 21 children in my class. There are 5 more boys than girls. How many boys are there?

3   My father is 35 years older than I am. Together, our ages add up to 59. How old am I?

4   I spend £3.48 on a sandwich and a drink. The drink costs 72p less than the sandwich. How much does the sandwich cost?

5   My sister has saved £52 more than I have. Together we have £238. How much have I saved?

6   I scored a total of 167 marks in my two mathematics tests. I scored 19 marks more in the second test than in the first. How many marks did I score in the first test?

7   I have 55 more house points than my best friend and together we have 321. How many house points does my friend have?

8   I bought a pencil and a sharpener. The sharpener cost 15p more than the pencil. I spent 97p. How much did the sharpener cost?

9 I bought two pencils and a sharpener. The sharpener cost 12p more than one pencil. I spent 96p. What was the price of one pencil?

10 I bought three pencils and a pen. The pen cost £2.41 more than one pencil. I spent £4.13. What was the price of one pencil?

Suppose you had to fill in the missing numbers in this question.

$$57 \div \ldots = \ldots \, r\, 3$$

You can see that, as 57 − 3 = 54, the answer could have been:

$$57 \div 6 = 9 \, r\, 3$$

or $57 \div 9 = 6 \, r\, 3$ as $6 \times 9 = 54$

Although 6×9 is the only number bond in the times tables up to 12×12, it is worth noting that 54 is also equal to 2×27 and 3×18.

$57 \div 2 = 27 \, r\, 3$ and $57 \div 27 = 2 \, r\, 3$

$57 \div 18 = 3 \, r\, 3$ but $57 \div 3 = 19$ with no remainder

You may need to use the same reasoning for some of these questions. Remember that there may be more than one answer. Try to find all the possibilities.

11 Year 6 are going on a trip to a nature reserve. There are 54 pupils and each of the 6 teachers going with them has the same number of pupils in their group. How many pupils are there in each group?

12 Year 7 are going on a trip to the museum. Each teacher will lead a group with a maximum of 8 children. The smallest number of teachers was needed when there were four groups, all the same size, and one group of only four children. How many children are there in Year 7?

13 The upper school are going on a trip to the theatre. Each teacher will accompany a group with a maximum of 11 pupils. The smallest number of teachers was needed when there were eight groups, all the same size, and one group of only seven pupils. How many children are in the upper school?

14 I use a £2 coin to buy several snack bars. I receive 74p change. Mum asks me how much the snack bars were. I cannot remember exactly but am sure they were about 20p each. What is the possible price of a snack bar?

15 The baker delivers the same number of loaves every day for five days except on Friday when he delivers 4 extra. If he delivers 139 loaves altogether in a week, how many does he deliver on Friday?

16 Milk is delivered in 4-litre bottles and deliveries to a boarding school are made every day from Monday to Saturday. Fewer bottles are delivered on Saturdays than on the other days. If the school has 132 litres a week, how many litres are delivered on Saturday?

17 The school chef ordered enough eggs to make 351 pancakes for pancake day. If one egg makes 9 pancakes and eggs come in trays of 12, how many trays of eggs did the chef order and how many eggs will he not need?

18 There are 49 school days in the spring term. How many full weeks of 5 days is that? If the first day of term is a Thursday, what day of the week is the last day of term?

19 39 pupils are organised into groups. Most of the groups are the same size but there are only 3 pupils in the smallest group. How many groups are there? How many pupils are there in each group? Is there more than one answer?

20 A baker has 76 buns to pack in boxes. Each box will hold the same number of buns. The baker has four buns left over. What are the possible numbers of buns he could have packed in each box?

Activity: Number puzzles – using symbols

In the questions you have been answering, you were given some numbers. Sometimes you only have an answer. You can answer questions such as:

If the cost of three snack bars is 54p, what is the cost of one bar?

But what if the question looks like this?

■ + ■ + ■ = 54

You solve this in the same way as before, by dividing by 3 and so the answer is:

■ = 18

Example
Find the value of ●, ■ and ▲ in these questions.

● + ● = 38

● + ■ = 64

● + ■ + ▲ = 78

● = 38 ÷ 2 = 19

Then 19 + ■ = 64

■ = 64 − 19 = 45

And 19 + 45 + ▲ = 78

64 + ▲ = 78

▲ = 14

Find the value of each symbol in these questions.

1 ♥ × ♥ = 5 × ♥

2 ♡ + ♡ + ♡ = 48

3 ● + ● = 24

   ● + ▲ = 19

4 ▲ + ▲ + ▲ = 51

   ● + ▲ = 30

5 ▲ + ▲ + ▲ + ▲ = 64

   ▲ + ■ = 48 − ▲

6 ♡ + ♡ = ♥ − ♡

   ♥ + ♡ = 64

7 ♡ × ♡ = ♡ + ♡

8 ♡ × ♥ = 57

   ♡ − ♥ = 16

9 ▲ + ▲ + ■ = 54

   ▲ + ■ = 38

   ● + ▲ = 43 − ■

10 ■ + ■ + ▲ = 42

   ■ + ▲ + ▲ = 48

   ▲ + ■ = ● + ● + ●

3 Angles, triangles and bearings

What is geometry?

Geometry is the study of shapes, both **two-dimensional** (**2D**) and **three-dimensional** (**3D**). To study geometry well, you will need to make careful drawings. As you work through this chapter you will need a sharp pencil, a ruler, a **protractor** or angle measurer and a good eraser.

In this chapter you will learn about shapes that are bounded by straight lines. When you are working in two dimensions, these shapes are called **plane figures**.

Geometry is the basis of two-dimensional design, both artistic and technical, and three-dimensional construction. A sound understanding of geometry is necessary in many aspects of engineering, physics and architecture.

First, here are some reminders of the vocabulary you will need to use.

Angles

Angles are formed when two straight lines meet or cross. The angle is marked with an arc unless it is a right angle, in which case it is marked by a small square.

There are four types of angle. They fall into four categories, depending on their size.

Acute angle between 0° and 90°

Right angle of 90°

Obtuse angle between 90° and 180°

Reflex angle between 180° and 360°

To measure the size of an angle, you will need an angle measurer or protractor.

A protractor can look very confusing as it has two scales, each numbered from 0 to 180, but marked in opposite directions.

This is because you can measure an angle from either arm.

To measure an angle, place the protractor so that the centre is directly over the point or **vertex** of the angle and the base line is along one arm of the angle.

Then read the angle from the scale. Start at 0 and follow the scale round.

An acute angle of 55°   An obtuse angle of 125°

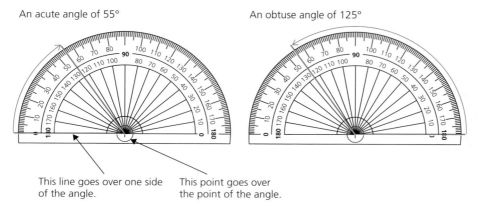

This line goes over one side of the angle.   This point goes over the point of the angle.

As there are two scales on the protractor, start by asking yourself: 'Is this angle more or less than 90°?' Then you can be sure to read the correct scale.

Reflex angles are slightly more tricky because they are greater than 180°. To measure a reflex angle, you will need to measure the non-marked angle. Then you take your answer away from 360°

Example

Measure the reflex angle ABC

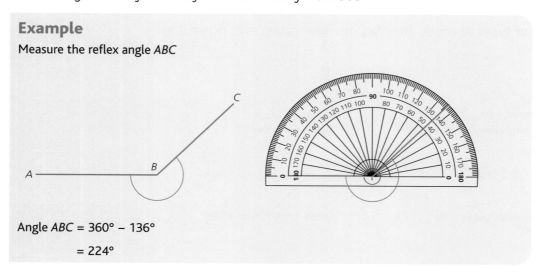

Angle ABC = 360° – 136°

= 224°

Note that the angle in the example is called **angle ABC**. It is formed by line *AB* meeting line *BC*. In this case, you could also refer to it as ∠*B,* as there is no confusion about which angle you are describing. In shapes made from several lines you can identify each angle with three letters.

Drawing angles

When you are drawing angles, remember to **estimate** the size of the angle first.

Examples

(i)   Draw ∠*BAC* = 124°

   Step 1:   Draw the line *AB*. Use a sharp pencil.

   A ——————————————— B

   Step 2:   Use your protractor to mark off ∠*CAB*. Draw a line from point *A* through the mark.

   Step 3:   Label the angle.

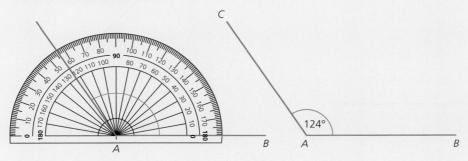

(ii)   Draw ∠*XYZ* = 236°

   236° is a reflex angle. The associated obtuse angle is 360° − 236° = 124°

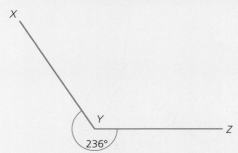

1 For each angle:

   (i)   write down the correct angle category: acute, right, obtuse or reflex

   (ii) estimate the angle – if it is acute your estimate should be between 0 and
         90°, if it is obtuse your estimate should be between 90° and 180°, if it is
         reflex your estimate should be between 180° and 360°

   (iii) measure the angle.

(a) ∠ ABC

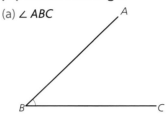

(e) ∠ ABC

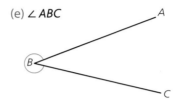

(b) ∠ XYZ

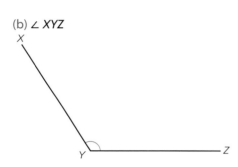

(f) ∠ PQR

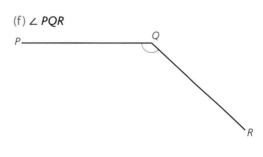

(c) ∠ DEF

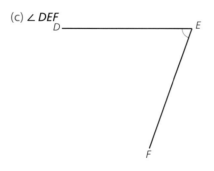

(g) ∠ RST

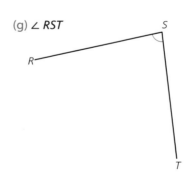

(d) ∠ GHI

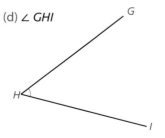

(h) ∠ XYZ

2 Draw these angles. For each one, start by drawing a line about 6 centimetres long and label it *AB*. Before drawing reflex angles you need to calculate the associated acute or obtuse angle first.

(a) ∠*BAC* = 70°   (e) ∠*ABC* = 212°

(b) ∠*ABC* = 130°   (f) ∠*BAC* = 56°

(c) ∠*BAC* = 35°   (g) ∠*ABC* = 193°

(d) ∠*ABC* = 300°   (h) ∠*BAC* = 264°

Triangles

A triangle is a closed plane figure with three sides. A triangle has three corners (or points or vertices). At each corner there is an angle.

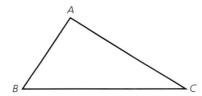

In the triangle *ABC*, the three sides of the triangle are all of different lengths and the three angles are all different, and all less than 90°. This is a **scalene triangle**.

A triangle with one angle that is equal to 90° is a **right-angled triangle**.

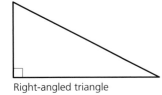   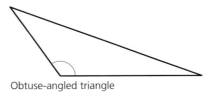

Right-angled triangle   Obtuse-angled triangle

A triangle with one angle that is greater than 90° is an **obtuse-angled triangle**.

A scalene triangle may be right-angled or obtuse-angled.

A triangle with two equal angles, and two equal sides, is an **isosceles triangle**. An isosceles triangle may be right-angled or obtuse-angled.

A triangle with all its angles equal to 60° and all its sides equal is an **equilateral triangle**.

To show that two or more lines are equal in length, you can mark them like this.

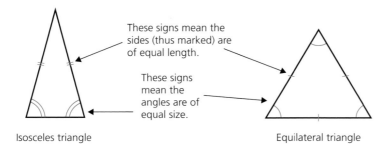

These signs mean the sides (thus marked) are of equal length.

These signs mean the angles are of equal size.

Isosceles triangle

Equilateral triangle

Drawing triangles

A triangle has three angles and three sides, but you do not need to know the measurements of all the sides and all the angles to draw it accurately. You only need to know three facts about a triangle:

- the lengths of three sides

- the sizes of two angles and the length of the enclosed side (this is the side between the two known angles)

- the lengths of two sides and the size of the enclosed angle (this is the angle between the two known sides).

1   When you know the lengths of three sides

Draw triangle ABC in which $AB = 8\,cm$, $BC = 6\,cm$ and $AC = 5\,cm$.

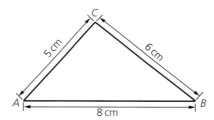

Make sure your pencil is sharp.

Step 1: Draw side AB accurately, measuring its length carefully.

Step 2: Open your compasses to a **radius** of 6 cm (because the length of BC is 6 cm). Put the compass point on point B and draw an arc above line AB, as shown.

Step 3: Open your compasses to a radius of 5 cm (the length of side *AC*). Put the compass point on point *A* and draw an arc that cuts the first arc. Mark the point where the arcs cross as *C*.

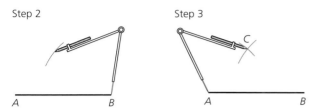

Step 4: Draw lines between the points *A* and *C* and the points *B* and *C*. You have now drawn your triangle *ABC*.

Step 5: Finally, write the lengths on the sides *AB*, *AC* and *BC*.

Then measure all the angles of the triangle and write them underneath the triangle like this:

∠*ABC* = 40°, ∠*BCA* = 92°, ∠*CAB* = 48°

Note the way the letters are ordered. The middle letter always represents the point of the angle you are measuring.

Write the **given** angles on the triangle and write **measured** angles underneath or beside the triangle.

Exercise 3.2

Draw these triangles accurately. Label them and measure all the angles. Write underneath whether they are scalene, obtuse-angled, right-angled, isosceles or equilateral.

1

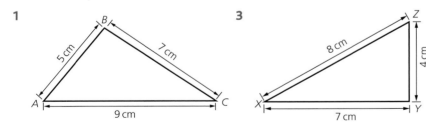

3

2

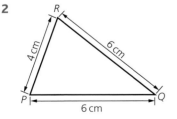

Make sketches of the next three triangles before you attempt to draw them accurately. It is sensible to make the longest side the horizontal base.

4 Construct triangle *ABC*, in which *AB* = 8 cm, *BC* = 7 cm and *AC* = 6 cm

5 Construct triangle *RST* in which *RS* = 7.5 cm, *RT* = 6 cm and *ST* = 4.5 cm

6 Construct triangle *PQR* in which *PQ* = 4 cm, *QR* = 7.5 cm and *PR* = 7.5 cm

2   When you know two angles and the enclosed side

Step 1: First draw the side accurately.

Step 2: Then measure one of the angles from one end of the line you have just drawn. Make sure you draw a long line.

Step 3: Then measure the other angle from the other end of the line you drew in step 1. Make sure this line cuts the long line you drew in step 2

You have drawn your triangle.

3   When you know two sides and the enclosed angle

Step 1: First draw one of the sides accurately.

Step 2: Then draw the angle from the end of the line drawn in step 1. Make sure you draw a long line.

Step 3: Open your compasses to the length of the second line you know. Then put the compass point on the point (vertex) of the angle you drew in step 1. Draw an arc that cuts the line of the angle from step 2.

Step 4: Now you can draw the last side of your triangle by drawing a line from the end of your first line to the point where the arc crosses the angle line.

> Leave the construction lines and arcs on your drawing. Do not try to rub them out; they are part of your answer.

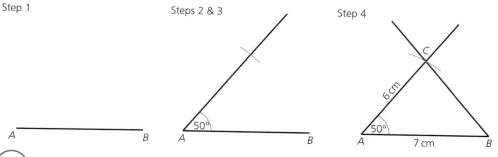

Draw these triangles accurately. Measure any angles and lengths that you have not been given and write these underneath your drawing. Write underneath whether they are scalene (obtuse-angled or right-angled), isosceles (obtuse-angled or right-angled) or equilateral.

1

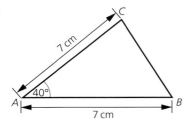

3

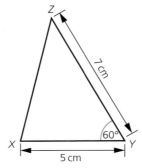

2

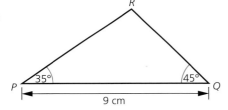

Make sketches of the next three triangles before you attempt to draw them accurately.

4 Construct triangle *ABC* in which *AB* = 6 cm, *AC* = 7 cm and ∠*BAC* = 45°

5 Construct triangle *XYZ* in which *YZ* = 8 cm, *XYZ* = 40° and ∠*XZY* = 65°

6 Construct triangle *PQR* in which *QR* = 7 cm, *PQR* = 60° and ∠*PRQ* = 60°

7 Construct triangle *LMN* in which *LM* = *LN* = 6 cm and ∠*MLN* = 40°

Constructing the angle bisector
Now you can learn how to use a pair of compasses to **bisect** an angle.

> To **bisect** is to divide something exactly in two.

Example
Draw an acute angle *ABC* with arms of length 6 cm.

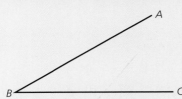

Step 1: Open your compasses to a radius of about 4 cm. Place the compass point on *B* and draw two arcs, one on *AB* and one on *BC*. These are the first arcs.

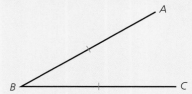

Step 2: Without changing the setting of your compasses, place the compass point on the place where the first arc cuts *AB* and draw another arc. Then put the compass point on the place where the first arc cuts *BC* and draw an arc to cut the arc you have just drawn. These are your second arcs.

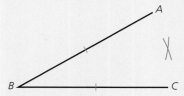

Step 3: Draw a line from *B* through the point of intersection of the second arcs. Label this line *BD*. *BD* bisects ∠*ABC*, so ∠*ABD* = ∠*DBC*

Exercise 3.4

You can check that each construction is accurate by measuring with a protractor.

1 Draw ∠*XYZ* = 40° and construct the angle bisector *XP*

2 Draw ∠*ABC* = 72° and construct the angle bisector *BD*

3 Draw ∠*PQR* = 136° and construct the angle bisector *QS*

4 Draw ∠*LMN* = 48° and construct the angle bisector *MP*

5 Construct triangle *PQR* in which *PQ* = 7 cm, *QR* = 6 cm and *PR* = 5 cm.
   Bisect ∠*RPQ* and mark the point where the bisector meets *RQ* as *S*

6 Construct triangle *LMN* in which *LM* = *LN* = 7 cm and ∠*MLN* = 64°
   Bisect ∠*LMN* and mark the point where the bisector meets *LN* as *P*

⬭ Angles of a triangle

Look back at each of the triangles that you have drawn in the last two exercises. Add up all three angles. What do you notice about the angle **sum** of each triangle?

You should find that the angle sum is 180° every time.

Therefore it seems as if the angles of a triangle always add up to 180°

Draw a triangle in your book. It can be any triangle and you can draw more than one if you wish.

Step 1: Trace over the triangle and cut out the tracing, so that you have a cut-out triangle.

Step 2: Draw an arc on each angle of your cut-out.

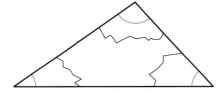

Step 3: Next tear off the three angles of your tracing.

Step 4: Draw a straight line under your original triangle.

Now fit your three angles together on the line. They should fit along the line exactly.

You know that the number of degrees on a straight line is 180°

Therefore you have demonstrated that the angles of **any** triangle add up to 180°

⬭ Facts about angles

Now you know that the angles of a triangle add up to 180°

Here are some more facts you already know about angles.

Angles on a straight line
The number of degrees on a straight line is 180

Angles on a straight line add up to 180°

Vertically opposite angles

Look at this diagram.

Measure angles *AED*, *AEB*, *BEC*, *CED*.

What do you notice?

The opposite angles are equal!

As 'opposite' is a confusing term when you look at polygons, these angles are called **vertically opposite** angles.

Vertically opposite angles are equal.

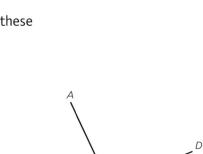

Angles at a point

Look at this diagram.

The number of degrees in a full turn is 360

Since the angles *AEB*, *BEC*, *CED*, *DEA* form a full turn, they must add up to 360°

These are **angles at a point**.

Angles at a point add up to 360°

Sometimes you will meet problems that include two special triangles, isosceles and equilateral triangles.

They give you two more angle facts.

Base angles of an isosceles triangle are equal.

All angles of an equilateral triangle are equal to 60°

Perpendicular lines

Perpendicular means 'at right angles to'. The right angle is marked with a square.

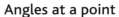

Perpendicular lines meet at 90°

Parallel lines

Parallel lines are lines that will never meet, however far they are extended.

To show that lines are parallel, you mark them with one or more arrows.

Parallel lines and angles

Look at this pair of parallel lines, *AB* and *CD*, **intersected** by the line *PQ*.

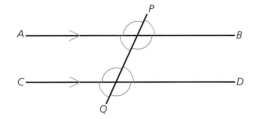

If you measure the acute angles you will see they are all equal and if you measure the obtuse angles you will see that they are all equal.

Alternate angles

The angles made by a line crossing a pair of parallel lines in the shape of a letter Z are **alternate angles**.

Alternate angles are equal.

Corresponding angles

The angles made by a line crossing a pair of parallel lines in the shape of a letter F are **corresponding angles**.

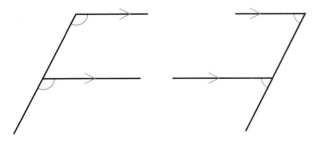

Corresponding angles are equal.

Co-interior angles

The angles made by a pair of parallel lines in the shape of a letter U are **co-interior angles**. Co-interior angles add up to 180°

You have now noted several facts about angles that you can use to solve problems with unknown angles.

When you solve angle problems, you should follow these rules.

1 Always draw the diagram.

2 Write down the working in the order that you do it, on the left-hand side of the page.

3 Write down the reasons on the right-hand side of the page.

Examples

(i) Find the sizes of the angles marked by letters. Give reasons for your answers.

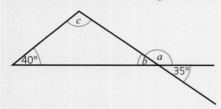

$a = 180° - 35°$ Angles on a straight line add up to 180°

   $= 145°$

$b = 35°$ Vertically opposite angles are equal.

$c = 180° - (40° + 35°)$ Angles in a triangle add up to 180°

   $= 105°$

(ii) Find the sizes of the angles marked by letters. Give reasons for your answers.

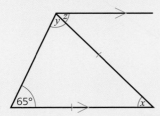

$y = 65°$ Base angles of an isosceles triangle are equal.

$x = 180° - (65° + 65°)$ Angles in a triangle add up to 180°

   $= 50°$

$z = 50°$ Alternate angles are equal.

Exercise 3.5

Find the sizes of the angles marked by letters. Give reasons for your answers.

1

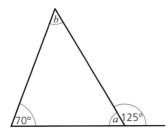

3

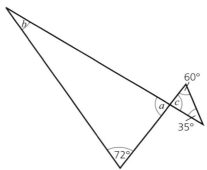

2

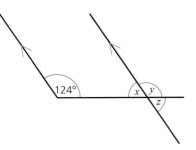

4

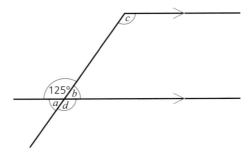

5

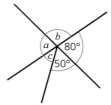

8

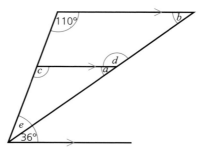

6

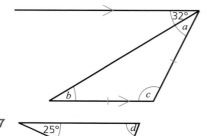

9

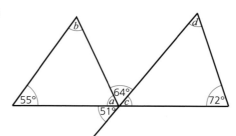

7

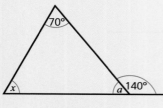

10

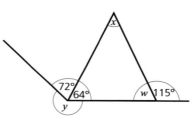

In the last exercise all the angles that you needed to find were represented by letters. In the next exercise you are only asked to find one angle, but you may need to find some other angles first.

You must show other angles clearly on your diagram. You can choose letters to represent them.

Example

Find the value of angle x.

Mark the unknown angle a.

$a = 180° - 140°$ (angles on a straight line add up to 180°)

   $= 40°$

$x = 180° - (70° + 40°)$ (angles in a triangle add up to 180°)

   $= 70°$

Exercise 3.6

Find the size of each unknown angle, labelled x.

1
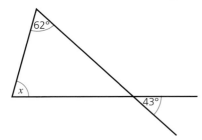

5
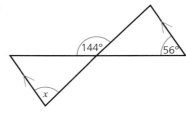

2
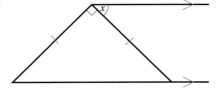

6
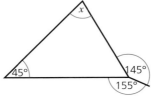

3
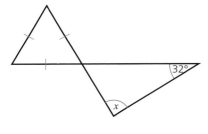

7
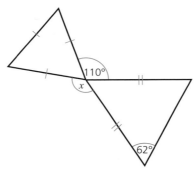

4
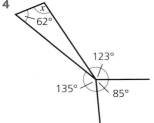

8
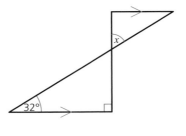

⬤ Bearings

Navigators use angles all the time. If you have done any map reading, or any serious sailing, you will probably be used to looking at the points of the **compass**.

Measuring the bearing

Bearings are always measured clockwise from north.

In the diagram on the left, you can see that the bearing of point *B* from point *A* is being measured with a protractor.

In the diagram on the right you can see that the bearing of point *C* from point *A* is being measured with a protractor.

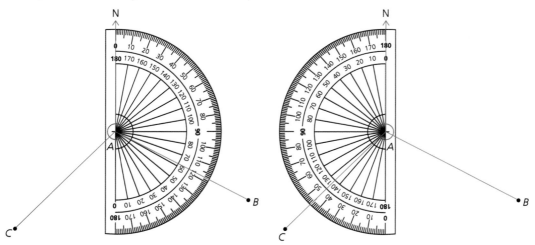

The bearing of *B* from *A* is 118°

The bearing of *C* from *A* = 180° + 45°

= 225°

Exercise 3.7

1 Copy this compass and fill in the missing directions.

The angle in a full turn is 360°. Taking the north point as 0°, then east will be 90°, but all bearings have three figures, and so you say 090° (oh-nine-oh).

2 Copy this compass and fill in all the missing bearings.

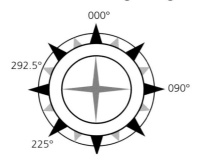

3 This diagram is a plan of Milo standing in the middle of a field. Around him are a cow, a sheep, a farmer and a tree. Measure the bearing of each one from Milo's position.

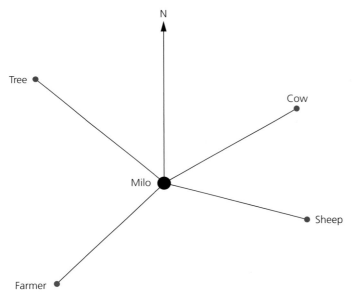

4 Mark a point *P* in the middle of your page. Draw the position of these points from *P*.

Point *A*, 5 cm away from *P* on a bearing of 072°

Point *B*, 4.5 cm away from *P* on a bearing of 135°

Point *C*, 3.8 cm away from *P* on a bearing of 212°

Point *D*, 5.2 cm away from *P* on a bearing of 336°

1 The hands of a clock move at different speeds. In one hour the minute hand turns through a full circle, an angle of 360°, but the hour hand will have only turned through one twelfth of a full circle, an angle of 30°

Through how many degrees will:

(i) the minute hand   **(ii)** the hour hand turn in:

(a) 20 minutes   **(b)** 15 minutes   **(c)** 5 minutes?

2 What will be the angle between the hands at:

(a) 10 past six   **(b)** quarter past three   **(c)** 20 to four?

3 A regular hexagon is made up from equilateral triangles.

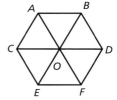

Find the size of:

(a) ∠EOD   **(c)** ∠DEC

(b) ∠DEO   **(d)** ∠DEA

4 The equilateral triangle ABC touches the square CDEF at C.   AC = CD

Note: The triangle can move whilst still touching the square CDEF at C

(a) If ∠ACF = 90°, find the size of ∠CAF

(b) If ∠BCD = 120°, find the size of ∠BAF

(c) If ∠BCD = 90°, find the size of ∠BAF

(d) If ∠ACE = 180°, find the size of ∠BCD

(e) If ∠BCD = 120°, find the size of ∠BFD

(f) If ∠BFD = 90°, find the size of ∠BCD

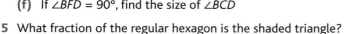

5 What fraction of the regular hexagon is the shaded triangle?

Summary Exercise 3.9

1 **(a)** Construct the triangle ABC in which AB = 6.5 cm, BC = 5.5 cm and ∠ABC = 54°. Measure AC. What type of triangle is triangle ABC?

(b) Construct the triangle XYZ in which XY = 8 cm, YZ = 6.5 cm and XZ = 5.5 cm. Construct the bisector of ∠XYZ and mark the point where it meets XZ as P. Measure ∠ZYP.

2 Find the sizes of the angles marked x, y and z in each diagram. Give reasons for your answers.

(a)

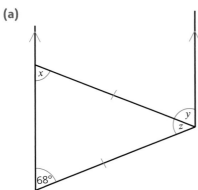

(c)

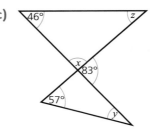

(d)

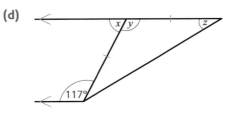

(b)

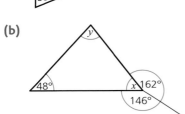

3 (a) Find the size of the angle marked x on this diagram. Mark any other angles that you have to find clearly and give reasons for each calculation.

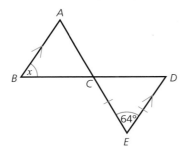

(b) What type of triangle is triangle ABC?

4 Mark a point P in the middle of your page. Draw the position of these points from P.

Point X, 4.5 cm away from P on a bearing of 303°

Point Y, 3.7 cm away from P on a bearing of 029°

Point Z, 5.8 cm away from P on a bearing of 164°

Written calculations

4

It is useful to be able to calculate accurately in your head but you will often need to work out the answers to more difficult or complicated calculations on paper.

This chapter starts with a review and some revision exercises to remind you of the correct methods and to give you some practice. Use the rows and columns in your exercise book to line up the digits properly, using what you know about place value.

Addition and subtraction

Addition

Example

Add: 15 835 + 307 + 42

	TTh	Th		H	T	U
	1	5		8	3	5
				3	0	7
+					4	2
	1	6		1	8	4
		1			1	

Note the small carried numbers here. Write them under the line then remember to add them into the column above.

If the numbers you are adding include decimal fractions, remember to line up the decimal points. Draw them on the grid line, between the units and the tenths, in a neat column.

Example

Add: 2.056 + 356 + 4.25

	H	T	U .	t	h	th
			2 .	0	5	6
	3	5	6 .	0	0	0
+			4 .	2	5	0
	3	6	2 .	3	0	6
			1		1	

Write 0s in the gaps and include any missing decimal points before you start the addition.

Exercise 4.1

Complete these additions, writing the digits in the correct columns. Show all your working, including carried numbers.

1 537 + 121

2 3146 + 2535

3 12 345 + 789

4 51 329 + 4519

5 7534 + 14 328

6 3.45 + 3.26

7 19 + 4.532

8 34.6 + 0.329

9 2.875 + 1.9

10 0.543 + 6.06

11 27 + 0.451 + 8.9

12 2477 + 9.1 + 0.465

13 3.503 + 1.576 + 0.375

14 19.65 + 18.52 + 6.746

15 56.4 + 7.89 + 5.642

16 7.899 + 8.76 + 9.341

17 35.5 + 567 + 1.923

18 4.562 + 1.5 + 34.87 + 17

19 0.56 + 7.346 + 41 + 63.8

20 19 + 7.899 + 916.38

Subtraction

Think about mental calculations.

You know that it is simpler to work out 27 − 4 = 23 than 27 − 9 = 18

This is because 7 − 4 = 3 is easy and the 2, representing 20, is unchanged.

In the second calculation, you cannot take 9 from 7, so you have to split the 20 into two 10s.

When working on paper, you need to make sure the top number is greater than the bottom number, for each column. Then you subtract in columns.

If in a column the top number is smaller than the bottom number you take 1 from the digit to the left and add ten to the top number. This is called **exchanging**. Sometimes this is called borrowing but you should always pay back anything you borrow!

Examples

(i) Subtract: 453 − 127

	H	T	U
	4	⁴5̶	¹3
−	1	2	7
	3	2	6

You cannot take 7 from 3. Take 1 ten from 50 to leave 40 and add the ten to 3 to make 13

Then subtract.

Always check your answer mentally by doing the inverse calculation.

127 + 326 = 453

(ii) Subtract: 2642 − 1369

	Th	H	T	U
	2	⁵6̶	¹³4̶	¹2
−	1	3	6	9
	1	2	7	3

In the units column you cannot take 9 from 2. Take 1 ten from 40 to leave 30 and add the ten to 2 to make 12

In the tens column you cannot take 6 from 4. Take 1 hundred from 600 to leave 500 and add 100 to the 3 (which represents 30) to make 130 (13 tens).

Check your answer mentally by using the inverse calculation: 1369 + 1273 = 2642

Just as with addition, if there are decimal points in the numbers you must align them vertically, between the units and tenths. Write in the decimal points and 0s before you start your calculation.

Example

Subtract: 43.745 − 1.9

	T	U	.	t	h	th
	4	$^2\cancel{3}$	.	^{1}7	4	5
−		1	.	9	0	0
	4	1	.	8	4	5

Write 1.9 as 1.900 to fill in the gaps.

In the tenths column, you cannot take 9 from 7 so take 1 unit from 3 to leave 2 and add this unit (10 tenths) to 7 tenths to make 17 tenths.

Check mentally that 1.9 + 41.845 = 43.745

Exercise 4.2

Complete these subtractions. Take care to write the digits in the correct columns. Show all your working, including exchanged numbers.

1 548 − 127
2 4368 − 1235
3 352 − 125
4 3532 − 1718
5 3146 − 2452

6 16.352 − 3.67
7 8.156 − 3.8
8 62.92 − 4.54
9 73.51 − 65.29
10 34.89 − 7.34

When there is a 0 in the top line, it is hard to see what to exchange. You cannot take 1 away from 0. Look along the number, to the left, until you find a non-zero number, then take 1 away from that.

Examples

(i) Subtract: 503 − 147

	H	T	U
	^{4}5	$^9\cancel{0}$	^{1}3
−	1	4	7
	3	5	6

You cannot take 7 from 3. You cannot take ten from 0. So take 10 from 500 to leave 490 and add the ten to 3 to make 13 Then subtract.

Remember to check mentally that 147 + 356 = 503

(ii) Subtract: 6004 − 4139

	Th	H	T	U
	^{5}6	$^9\cancel{0}$	$^9\cancel{0}$	^{1}4
−	4	1	3	9
	1	8	6	5

In the units column you cannot take 9 from 4 You cannot take 1 ten from 0 tens, so keep looking left. Take 1 ten from 6000 to leave 5990 and add the ten to 4 to make 14

Then subtract and remember to check your answer.

The same applies with decimals.

Example

Subtract 13.5 – 4.312

H	T	U	.	t	h	th
	$\not{1}$	^{1}3	.	^{4}5 $\quad$ ^{9}0		^{1}0
–		4	.	3	1	2
		9	.	1	8	8

In the thousandths column, you cannot take 2 from 0. In the hundredths column you cannot take 1 from 0 so take 1 hundredth from 5 tenths to leave 49 hundredths and add 10 to the 0 to make 10 thousandths.

In the units column you cannot take 4 from 3 so take 1 ten from the tens column and add it to the 3 to make 13

Write 13.5 as 13.500 to fill in the gaps.

Check mentally that 4.312 + 9.188 = 13.5

Exercise 4.3

Calculate the answers to these subtractions. Showing all the working, including exchanged numbers.

1 405 – 167

2 302 – 188

3 790 – 345

4 6007 – 2148

5 5040 – 3427

6 45.06 – 17.8

7 8.06 – 3.72

8 1.9 – 0.36

9 34.5 – 1.725

10 34.2 – 17.56

11 40 500 – 16 799

12 300 235 – 18 307

13 75 – 19.625

14 260 – 19.19

15 37 – 1.024

16 24 000 – 3543

17 402 – 30.89

18 25 – 19.95

19 104 – 65.56

20 170 – 89.909

Exercise 4.4

Each question requires two calculations, first an addition and then a subtraction.

1 4.4 + 12.6 – 7.2

2 0.712 + 5 – 3.06

3 42.1 + 6.75 – 0.865

4 123 + 6.75 – 99

5 41.3 + 6.7 – 3

6 34.55 + 15.41 – 0.076

7 1.7 + 9.437 – 3.18

8 43.6 + 5.4 – 21.75

9 183 + 4.07 – 0.47

10 99 + 9 – 9.99

Money, money, money: £££

You use decimals all the time, often without realising it. Over most of the world, the currency, for example, is based on decimals.

There are 100p to the pound.

Therefore   1p is one hundredth of a pound.

or   1p is £0.01

and   75p is £0.75

                £3.50 is 350p

> Note that you always write amounts of money with two decimal places, even if the digit in the second decimal place is a zero. When solving problems with money, be sure to calculate either in pounds or in pence; do not mix the two.

Exercise 4.5

Calculate the answers to these problems. You may use any methods of calculation that you like but write down all of your working. If you are doing a calculation in your head, write it down like this:

$$54 + 63 = 117$$

If you need to use written methods, show all your working carefully. There is no need to be ashamed of working out – it helps you to get the correct answer.

1 I had £5 but spent 84p. How much do I have left?

2 Last term, Mrs Merry awarded 635 house points and Mr Frown awarded 356 house points.

   (a) How many house points did they award between them?

   (b) How many more house points did Mrs Merry award than Mr Frown?

3 We are driving from Southampton to London and then on to Norwich. It is 81.3 miles from Southampton to London and 133.5 miles from London to Norwich.

   (a) What is the total length of our journey?

   (b) How much greater is the distance between London and Norwich than that between London and Southampton?

4 I pay £15.75 for a new game and 95p for a bag to carry it in. How much do I spend in total?

5 On a trip to the zoo, I spend £17.59 on a ticket, £1.72 on a bus fare and £5 on a guide book.

   (a) How much do I spend in total?

   (b) How much change do I have from £30?

6 Mount Everest, the highest mountain in the world, is 8844 m high and Mont Blanc is 4815 m high. How much higher is Mount Everest than Mont Blanc?

7 I have saved £35.95, my brother has saved £28.15 and my sister has saved £15

(a) How much have we saved altogether?

(b) How much more have I saved than my brother?

8 This table shows the population one of the UK's smallest territories, the Saint Helena group of islands, in 2014

Island	Population
Saint Helena	5809
Ascension	1532
Tristan da Cunha	382
Gough Island	6

(a) How many more people live on Saint Helena than on all the other islands together?

(b) What is the total population of the territory?

9 Our school has been collecting tokens from the supermarket to win some free software. Year 5 have 412 tokens, Year 6 have 1096, Year 7 have 3198 and Year 8 have a miserable 95. How many tokens does the school have in all?

10 The school's tokens earned them £1050 worth of software. They buy £299.95 worth of mathematical software, £535.50 worth of graphics software and spend the rest on games. How much do they spend on games?

Multiplication and division

Multiplication

As with addition, it is important when multiplying to put the numbers in the correct columns before you start. Then work with units first, then tens, then hundreds.

Remember to put the carried numbers under the line.

Examples

(i) Multiply: 127×4
Estimate: $100 \times 4 = 400$

H	T	U
1	2	7
	×	4
5	0	8
1	2	

The small numbers under the line show that $4 \times 7 = 28$ and that $4 \times 2 = 8; 8 + 2 = 10$

(ii) Multiply: 3428×7
Estimate: $3000 \times 7 = 21\,000$, so you will need an extra column.

TTh	Th		H	T	U
	3		4	2	8
				×	7
2	3		9	9	6
	2		1	5	

The small numbers under the line show that $7 \times 8 = 56$
$7 \times 2 = 14;$ $14 + 5 = 19$
$7 \times 4 = 28;$ $28 + 1 = 29$
$7 \times 3 = 21;$ $21 + 2 = 23$

(iii) Multiply: 1.65×8
Estimate: $2 \times 8 = 16$, so you will need an extra column.

T	U .	t	h
	1 .	6	5
	×	8	
1	3 .	2	0
1	5	4	

$8 \times 5 = 40$

Write the 0 in the answer and carry the 4 by writing it under the line.

For decimal numbers, multiply as before but remember to put the decimal point in the answer line.

$1.65 \times 8 = 13.20$
$1.65 \times 8 = 13.2$ When you write your final answer you can leave out the 0

Calculate the answers to these multiplications. Show all your working, including the carried digits.

Remember to estimate first, to make sure you put the right number of columns in the frame. Then check your answer.

1	32×3		6	2043×7
2	28×2		7	3246×8
3	417×4		8	4368×9
4	256×5		9	5032×5
5	132×6		10	8036×7
11	3.1×6		16	31.85×6
12	32.4×5		17	4.125×8
13	1.95×8		18	1.424×5
14	2.02×9		19	52.95×9
15	21.65×6		20	184.5×7

Division

Many people find division the hardest of all the four mathematical operations. Make sure that you know the times tables and can work out the remainders. Writing the calculation on paper can help.

The number columns are still important in division. Make sure that your answer is in the correct place. The first example is worked out step by step, the second is done all in one process, as you would write it out. The third reminds you how remainders can be calculated as decimals.

> Remember that division is the only operation for which you work from the highest place value down to the smallest, instead of starting with units and then going up through tens to hundreds.

Examples

(i) Divide: $1536 \div 4$

Step 1 You cannot divide 4 into 1; carry the 1. Then $15 \div 4 = 3$ r 3; write 3 in the answer line, carry the remainder 3

	Th	H	T	U
		3		
4	1	$^1 5$	$^3 3$	6

Step 2 33 ÷ 4 = 8 r 1. Write 8 in the answer line, carry the remainder 1

	Th	H	T	U
		3	8	
4	1	¹5	³3	¹6

Step 3 16 ÷ 4 = 4. Write 4 in the answer line. There is no remainder.

	Th	H	T	U
		3	8	4
4	1	¹5	³3	¹6

(ii) Divide: 3219 ÷ 8

	Th	H	T	U	
		4	0	2	r 3
8	3	³2	1	¹9	

Step 1 You cannot divide 8 into to 3 so, carry the 3

Step 2 32 ÷ 8 = 4 Write 4 in the answer line. There is no remainder to carry.

Step 3 1 ÷ 8 = 0 r 1 Write 0 in the answer line and carry the 1

Step 4 19 ÷ 8 = 2 r 3 Write 1 in the answer line and then r 1

Remember that you can write a remainder as a fraction.

$3219 ÷ 8 = 402 \text{ r } 3$ or $402\frac{3}{8}$

If the number is a decimal, you may need to write some extra 0s at the end, to find the exact answer – but only if you are dividing by 2, 4, 5, or 8 and sometimes 6
If you are dividing by 3, 7 or 9, you will not get an exact answer by writing extra 0s

(iii) Divide: 4.2 ÷ 8

	U	.	t	h
	0	.	5	2
8	4	.	⁴2	²0

Step 1 4 ÷ 8 = 0 r 4   Write 0 in the answer line and carry the 4

Step 2 42 ÷ 8 = 5 r 2   Write 5 in the answer line. Add a 0 in the hundredths column and carry the 2

	U	.	t	h	th
	0	.	5	2	5
8	4	.	⁴2	²0	⁴0

Step 3 20 ÷ 8 = 2 r 4   Write 2 in the answer line. Write a 0 in the thousandths column and carry the 4

Step 4 40 ÷ 8 = 5   Write 5 in the answer line.

So, 4.2 ÷ 8 = 0.525

Exercise 4.7

Calculate the answers to these. Show all your working, including the carried numbers.

1	69 ÷ 3	6	1.542 ÷ 6
2	164 ÷ 2	7	1424 ÷ 4
3	384 ÷ 3	8	48.51 ÷ 9
4	48.5 ÷ 5	9	653.5 ÷ 5
5	1.324 ÷ 4	10	6.237 ÷ 3

These may have remainders. Write each remainder as a fraction or a decimal fraction.

11	196 ÷ 6	16	8926 ÷ 8
12	921 ÷ 7	17	400.8 ÷ 8
13	1618 ÷ 8	18	8.214 ÷ 6
14	5319 ÷ 9	19	9263 ÷ 9
15	4516 ÷ 6	20	73.85 ÷ 7

If necessary, write extra 0s at the end, to find the exact answers to these.

21	1.9 ÷ 2	26	6.92 ÷ 8
22	8.7 ÷ 5	27	1.3 ÷ 4
23	1.2 ÷ 8	28	3.6 ÷ 5
24	13.5 ÷ 9	29	2.97 ÷ 6
25	8.16 ÷ 6	30	7.16 ÷ 8

Working with remainders

Doughnuts are packed in boxes of six. If the bakery bakes 410 doughnuts, how many boxes will they fill?

$410 ÷ 6 = 68 \text{ r } 2 \text{ or } 68\frac{1}{3}$

The answer is 68 because you must round down. The bakery will fill 68 boxes and have 2 doughnuts left over.

Now consider this seating problem.

Dining tables seat 8 pupils. If there are 250 pupils sitting down to lunch, how many tables will they need?

$250 ÷ 8 = 31 \text{ r } 2 \text{ or } 31\frac{1}{4}$

The answer is 32 tables because you must round up. You cannot have 2 pupils with nowhere to sit.

When answering these problems think carefully about whether to round any remainders up or down.

Exercise 4.8

Calculate the answers to these problems. You may use any methods of calculation that you like but you must write down all of your working. If you are doing a calculation in your head, write it down like this:

$$54 + 63 = 117$$

If you are using written methods, show all your working carefully.

1   I have £5, which is exactly enough to buy four notebooks. What is the price of one notebook?

2   Pupils receive a house point for every five merits. I have collected 124 merits. How many house points have I earned?

3   The school has bought 7 packs of homework diaries, costing £12.24 per pack.

   (a) What is the total cost?

   (b) If there are eight diaries in each pack, what is the cost of one diary?

4   A coil of rope is 124.5 metres long. How many 6 metre lengths can I cut from the coil? What length is left over?

5   (a) What is the cost of 8 roses costing £2.35 each?

   (b) The roses are a present for our teacher. Six of us share the cost. How much do we each pay?

6   237 children need packed lunches on sports day. The school chef buys oranges in bags of eight and biscuits in packs of 6. She must buy how many:

   (a) bags of oranges   (b) packs of biscuits?

7   I buy two magazines costing £2.24 each and a drink costing 95p. How much change do I receive from a £10 note?

8   I have saved £15.46. My brother has saved half as much as I have and my sister has saved twice as much as my brother and I together. How much has my sister saved?

9   A farmer sells eggs in boxes of 8. In a week, she has collected 2543 eggs. How many boxes can she fill?

10 (a) There are 19 children in our class and we want to be sure everyone has the same amount of food. Copy and complete this shopping list for the class party.
       ... multipacks of crisps (6 bags in each pack) @ £1.40 each
       ... multipacks of fruit juice (3 carton in each pack) @ 95p each
       ... boxes of assorted sandwiches (4 sandwiches in each box) @ £3.50 each
       ... bags of oranges (8 oranges in each bag) @ £1.25 each

   (b) What is the total cost?

   (c) We give all the extra food to our teacher. How many bags of crisps, cartons of juice, sandwiches and oranges does our teacher receive?

These questions are just like those you have been working on in this chapter, but some of them have numbers missing. Copy and complete the questions, replacing the question marks with the missing numbers to make the calculations correct. Check your answers by considering the inverse.

1

	H	T	U
	4	?	8
+	1	7	?
	?	5	5

5

	H	T	U
	4	?	7
+	?	3	?
	7	1	3

2

	H	T	U
	6	?	5
−	?	3	?
	4	4	8

6

	H	T	U
	5	?	3
−	3	4	?
	?	6	5

3

H	T	U
1	?	1
	×	?
5	4	3

7

Th	H	T	U
?	?	4	?
		×	4
7	3	?	8

4

	H	T	U
	2	4	?
4	?	6	8

8

	H	T	U
	1	?	8
7	?	6	?

Summary Exercise 4.10

1 Calculate the answers.

   (a) 245 + 457   (c) 3478 + 672 + 19

   (b) 15.6 + 7.054   (d) 435 + 0.726 + 29.8

2 Calculate the answers.

   (a) 367 − 148   (c) 5.005 − 1.437

   (b) 15 − 0.65   (d) 20.04 − 9.734

3 Calculate the answers.

   (a) 146 × 4   (c) 3468 × 8

   (b) 24.3 × 7   (d) 1.995 × 6

4 Calculate the answers. Write any remainders as fractions.

   (a) 476 ÷ 4   (b) 6019 ÷ 3

5 Calculate the answers. Write in extra 0s to get the exact answer.

   (a) 18 ÷ 4   (b) 1.4 ÷ 8

6 Take four hundred and twelve from six hundred and two.

7 A florist buys 285 roses and makes them into bunches, each with nine roses. How many bunches does she make?

8 Mr Black has a collection of 3025 stamps and Mr Red has a collection of 1985 stamps.

   (a) How many stamps do they have altogether?

   (b) How many more stamps does Mr Black have than Mr Red?

9 One cake can be cut into eight slices. How many cakes will we need so that each of the 3251 visitors at Speech Day has a slice?

10 I share 316 chocolates with my five friends.

(a) How many do we each get?

(b) The dog eats the left over chocolates. How many does the dog eat?

11 Replace the question marks with numbers to make these calculations correct.

(a)

	H	T	U
	?	4	5
+	5	6	?
	7	?	3

(b)

	H	T	U
	?	3	?
		×	6
	8	?	4

Activity: What's in the box?

The boxes here represent number-cruncher machines.

Each machine changes the number that goes in so that a new number comes out. This is a '× 2' machine.

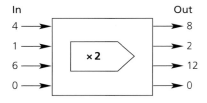

1 What comes out of these machines?

(a)

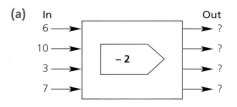

(b)

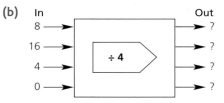

2 What went in these machines?

(a)

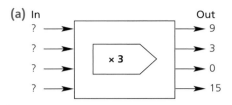

In		Out
?	× 3	9
?		3
?		0
?		15

(b)

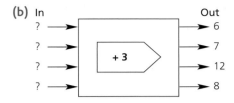

In		Out
?	+ 3	6
?		7
?		12
?		8

3 What machine is in these boxes?

(a)

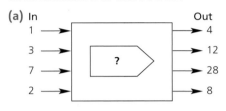

In		Out
1	?	4
3		12
7		28
2		8

(c)

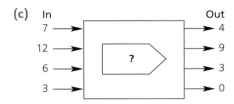

In		Out
7	?	4
12		9
6		3
3		0

(b)

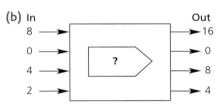

In		Out
8	?	16
0		0
4		8
2		4

(d)

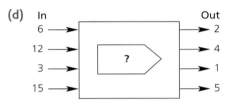

In		Out
6	?	2
12		4
3		1
15		5

Some boxes have two machines in them. This is a + 1 × 2 box.

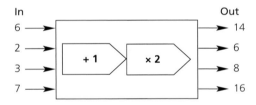

In			Out
6	+ 1	× 2	14
2			6
3			8
7			16

4 What comes out of these boxes?

(a)

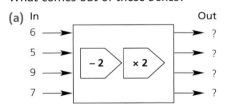

In			Out
6	− 2	× 2	?
5			?
9			?
7			?

(b)

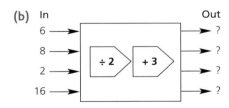

In			Out
6	÷ 2	+ 3	?
8			?
2			?
16			?

5 What went into these machines?

(a)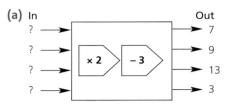

(b)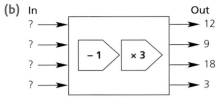

6 What machines are in these boxes? There may be more than one answer.

(a)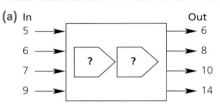

(c)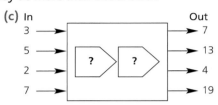

(b)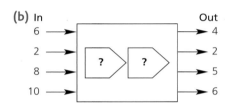

(d)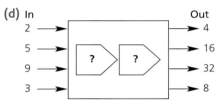

 # More about ten

The number system that we use is based on the number ten. In this chapter, you will look at how that helps you with calculations.

⬭ Powers of ten

You know that when you write out numbers in full, the value of each digit is shown by the column in which it is written.

A number may be more than 1:

Millions			Thousands			HTU		
HM	TM		HTh	TTh		H	T	U

These columns come after the decimal point.

tenths	hundredths	thousandths	ten thousandths
t	h	th	tth

You also know that:

$$10 \times 10 = \quad 100$$
$$10 \times 10 \times 10 = \quad 1000$$
$$10 \times 10 \times 10 \times 10 = 10\,000$$

You can write these numbers in a more compact manner.

10 is 10   or 10^1 (ten to the **power** one, but just write 10)

100 is 10×10 or 10^2 (ten to the power two or ten squared)

1000 is $10 \times 10 \times 10$ or 10^3 (ten to the power three or ten cubed)

10 000 is $10 \times 10 \times 10 \times 10$ or 10^4 (ten to the power four) and so on...

> Notice that the number that **indicates** the **power of ten** is the same as the number of 0s in the number. It is called an **index number**.

From the pattern in the numbers it follows that you can write 10^7 as 1 followed by 7 0s, that is 10 000 000 (ten million).

So instead of thinking of 700 as a 7 in the hundreds column, you could think of it as a 7 in the 10^2 column.

10^2 is called **ten squared**. If you were to draw a pattern of ten rows of ten dots, in two dimensions it would form a square.

10^3 is **called ten cubed**. If you were to make a block from small **cubes**, in three dimensions, that was 10 wide, 10 long and 10 high the result would also be a cube.

You cannot make 10^4 into any two- or three-dimensional shape, so you say: 'ten to the power 4'

Similarly, 10^5 is ten to the power 5

> You will learn more about powers in the next chapter.

Example

Write 700 as a single digit multiplied by a power of ten.

$$700 = 7 \times 10 \times 10$$
$$= 7 \times 10^2$$

Exercise 5.1

Write each number as a single digit multiplied by a power of ten.

1   20

2   300

3   4000

4   5000

5   30 000

6   40

7   3000

8   400 000

9   60 000

10   900

> Take care to put spaces in the places between hundreds and thousands and between thousands and millions.

A number written as a single digit multiplied by a power of 10 can be expanded into a full number.

Example

Write the number 8×10^4 in full.

$$8 \times 10^4 = 8 \times 10 000$$
$$= 80 000$$

Exercise 5.2

Write each number in full. Take care to put spaces in the right places.

1 10^3

2 7×10^4

3 8×10^2

4 9×10^6

5 2×10^5

6 5×10^6

7 3×10^8

8 7×10^7

9 10^9

10 10^{10}

Multiplying and dividing by powers of 10

Consider $30 \times 10 = 300$

It looks as if you are making the number larger by placing a 0 on the right-hand side but, in fact, what is happening is that the digits in the numbers are moving one place to the left and the empty space at the end is filled with a 0

Th	H	T	U		
		3	0		
				×	10
	3	0	0		
				×	10
3	0	0	0		

The same is true for numbers less than one.

0.3×1000

Th	T	H	U	. t		
			0	. 3		
				×	1000	
	3	0	0			

The answer is 1000 times larger than 0.3, so all the digits move three places to the left. The gaps in the tens and units columns are filled with 0s. There is now no need to write the decimal point as all the digits are in the columns to the left of it.

When you divide by powers of ten, the digits all move to the right.

Consider 450 ÷ 10

Th	T	H	U		
	4	5	0		
				÷	10
		4	5		

The answer is a tenth of 450, so all the digits move one place to the right. The 0 in the units column disappears.

Therefore 450 ÷ 10 = 45

The same is true with numbers less than one.

Consider 10.2 ÷ 100

Th	T	H	U .	t	h	th		
		1	0 .	2				
						÷	100	
			0 .	1	0	2		

The answer is 100 times smaller than 10.2, so all the digits move two places to the right. The empty digit space in the units column is filled by 0

Therefore 10.2 ÷ 100 = 0.102

The decimal number system makes multiplying and dividing by powers of ten very simple. This is why so many units of measurement are **powers** of ten.

$$100p = £1$$
$$10\,mm = 1\,cm$$
$$1000\,g = 1\,kg$$

Examples

(i) Multiply: 450 × 10 000

450 × 10 000 = 4 500 000

> There are 4 0s in 10 000 so the numbers all move 4 places to the left. Do not forget the 0 from 450 so there are 5 '0's in all.

(ii) Multiply: 0.304 × 1000

0.304 × 1000 = 304 (there is no need to write 304.0)

> There are 3 0s in 1000 and therefore the 3 moves from tenths to hundreds. The other numbers follow behind in the same order as before.

(iii) Divide: 35 500 ÷ 1000

35 500 ÷ 1000 = 35.5

> All the digits move three places right so the 5 is now in the tenths column, to the right of the decimal point.

(iv) Divide: 7060 ÷ 10 000

7060 ÷ 10 000 = 0.706

> The 7 moves from thousands to tenths. The other numbers follow behind in the same order as before.

Exercise 5.3

You should be able to do these calculations quickly. For whole numbers with more than four digits, make sure that you put the small spaces in the right places between thousands and hundreds and between millions and thousands. Do not include the spaces when you count how many places to move the digits.

1 40 × 10

2 60 × 100

3 400 ÷ 10

4 400 ÷ 100

5 200 × 1000

6 625 × 100

7 2 ÷ 10

8 7020 × 100

9 60 ÷ 10

10 7000 ÷ 100

11 0.4 × 1000

12 30 ÷ 100

13 8 ÷ 100

14 0.05 × 100

15 0.007 × 1000

16 400 000 ÷ 100

17 0.15 × 10

18 6 000 000 ÷ 1000

19 0.45 × 100

20 7 ÷ 1000

21 0.4 × 10

22 4.5 × 100

23 2.4 ÷ 100

24 0.034 × 1000

25 3465 ÷ 1000

26 2635 × 100

27 45.3 ÷ 100

28 23 045 × 1000

29 820.7 × 100

30 30.15 ÷ 10

Multiplying and dividing by multiples of 10, 100, 1000

Multiplying by multiples of 10, 100, 1000

You can use the same principles for multiplying by multiples of tens, hundreds and thousands.

Examples

(i) Multiply: 400×20

   $400 \times 20 = 8000$

(ii) Multiply: 0.6×20

   $0.6 \times 20 = 0.6 \times 10 \times 2$

   $\quad\quad\quad\quad = 6 \times 2$

   $\quad\quad\quad\quad = 12$

> Note that the three 0s in the question become three 0s in the answer.

When working with larger numbers you may need to put them in a frame.

Examples

(i) Multiply: 613×700

   Estimate: $600 \times 700 = 420\,000$ you will need a HTh column.

HTh	TTh	Th		H	T	U
				6	1	3
			×	7	Ø	Ø
4	2	9		1	0	0
		2				

> As you are multiplying by 700 you start by writing the 0s in the T and U columns.

(ii) Multiply: 85×600

   Estimate $80 \times 600 = 48000$, you will need a TTh column.

TTh	Th		H	T	U
			8	5
		×	6	Ø	Ø
5	1		0	0	0
	3				

> You need to take care when the last digit of either number is a 5

> The two red 0s are because you are multiplying by 600, the blue 0 is because
> $6 \times 5 = 30$

Exercise 5.4

Complete these multiplications.

1   40 × 30

2   60 × 700

3   200 × 90

4   0.4 × 600

5   0.07 × 400

6   30 × 8000

7   0.8 × 30

8   1.3 × 200

9   400 × 500 × 300

10   5000 × 40 × 900

11   24 × 50

12   315 × 200

13   72 × 500

14   47 × 300

15   627 × 400

16   500 × 39

17   542 × 700

18   600 × 52

19   408 × 800

20   80 × 465

Dividing by multiples of 10, 100, 1000

When you are dividing by a multiple of 10, 100 or 1000, divide by the non-zero digit first and then by 10, 100 or 1000. Always check your answer by multiplying.

Examples

(i)   Divide: 9000 ÷ 200

$$9000 ÷ 200 = 9000 ÷ 2 ÷ 100$$

$$= 4500 ÷ 100$$

$$= 45 \qquad \text{(Check: } 45 × 200 = 9000)$$

(ii)   Divide: 0.3 ÷ 60

$$0.3 ÷ 60 = 0.3 ÷ 6 ÷ 10$$

$$= 0.05 ÷ 10$$

$$= 0.005 \qquad \text{(Check: } 0.005 × 60 = 0.03 × 10 = 0.3)$$

Complete these divisions.

1	$120 \div 30$	6	$32 \div 80$
2	$4200 \div 700$	7	$18 \div 200$
3	$18\,000 \div 90$	8	$12 \div 200$
4	$1600 \div 4$	9	$16 \div 20$
5	$7200 \div 800$	10	$40 \div 500$
11	$0.6 \div 30$	16	$320 \div 40$
12	$2.1 \div 700$	17	$18\,000 \div 900$
13	$18 \div 90$	18	$120 \div 600$
14	$1600 \div 40$	19	$18 \div 200$
15	$72\,000 \div 800$	20	$8000 \div 500$

◯ Long multiplication

What happens when you want to multiply 52×23?

$$52 \times 23 = 52 \times (3 + 20)$$

$$= 52 \times 3 + 52 \times 20$$

Now put these numbers into frames.

First estimate $50 \times 20 = 1000$, you will need a Th column.

You could do this in three stages.

52×3

H	T	U
	5	2
×		3
1	5	6

52×20

Th	H	T	U
		5	2
	×	2	0
1	0	4	0

$52 \times 3 + 52 \times 20$

	Th	H	T	U
			1	5	6
+		1	0	4	0
			1	1	9	6

Note that the 0 from × 20 is written in the units column.

It can be quicker to combine these stages in one frame.

Th	H	T	U	
		5	2	
	×	2	3	
	1	5	6	× 3
1	0	4	0	× 20 Write the 0 in the units column.
1	1	9	6	

If you need to do working out to answer a problem, write the calculation clearly and make sure that the answer is written clearly.

Remember these steps for **long multiplication**.

1 Estimate the answer in order to work out how many columns you will need.

2 Set up the frame.

3 Write down the side what you are multiplying by.

4 Cross off the nought from the multiple of 10 and write it in the units column.

5 Multiply by the units digit. Write any carried numbers carefully in that row.

6 Multiply by the tens digit. Write any carried numbers carefully in that row.

7 Add the two rows. Write any carried numbers below the answer line.

8 Check your final answer is similar to your estimate.

Example

Multiply: 1738×68

Estimate: $2000 \times 60 = 120\,000$

	HTh	TTh	Th		H	T	U	
			1		7	3	8	
×						6	8	
		1	3_5		9_3	0_6	4	× 8 The carried numbers from × 8 are in this row.
+	1	0_4	4_2		2_4	8	0	× 60 The carried numbers from × 60 are in this row
	1	1	8		1	8	4	The carried numbers from + are here.
			1					

Write down, next to each row, what you are multiplying by.

Exercise 5.6

Use a formal written method to work these out.

1	36 × 27	6	415 × 35
2	68 × 54	7	304 × 72
3	73 × 78	8	806 × 68
4	23 × 83	9	612 × 35
5	32 × 46	10	256 × 91

11	673 × 45	16	2356 × 38
12	325 × 29	17	6089 × 45
13	426 × 47	18	45 123 × 58
14	1406 × 78	19	32 654 × 89
15	1923 × 63	20	23 453 × 37

Now use a calculator to check your answers.

Problem solving

In the next exercise you are going to solve problems. You may be able to work them out mentally or you may need to write the calculation in a frame. Always start by writing down the actual calculation on one line, then decide how you are going to calculate. Remember to estimate first, this helps you set up the frame with the correct number of columns and also helps you to check your answer.

Exercise 5.7

1 There are 365 days in a year and 24 hours in a day. How many hours are there in a year?

2 There are 60 seconds in a minute, 60 minutes in an hour and 24 hours in a day. How many seconds are there in a day?

3 There are 31 days in January. How many hours are there?

4 In our school there are 28 classes with 29 children in each class. How many children are there in the school?

5 My parents say they spend £135 per week on food. There are 52 weeks in a year. How much is this per year?

6 My father's car does 14 miles to the litre. If he fills up with 37 litres, how far will he be able to go before he needs to fill up again?

7 The school needs to buy new computers. If the cost of one computer is £545, what is the cost of 24 computers?

8 36 children are going on an adventure holiday. If the cost for one child is £526, what is the cost for the whole group?

9 One train can carry 584 passengers. If the company runs 36 trains a day, what is the maximum number of passengers that can travel with the company?

10 A party of 37 business executives each pay £1576 for a flight to New York. What is the total cost?

Multiple multiplications!

The next few questions need more than just one multiplication calculation. Make sure your work is clear and that you do not run calculations together.

> **Example**
>
> One Shoppa Shuttle bus takes 23 passengers. Its journey to the shops and back takes 20 minutes. What is the maximum number of passengers one bus can take in ten hours?
>
> If each journey takes 20 minutes, the bus can do 3 journeys per hour. So far, so good. But what next?
>
> Number of journeys = 3×10
>
> $\qquad = 30$
>
> Number of passengers = 30×23
>
> $\qquad = 690$

It is important to use the equals sign correctly.

Exercise 5.8

1 One Star Tours cabin takes 48 passengers per ride. Each ride takes 15 minutes. How many passengers will 6 cabins take in twelve hours?

2 MacPizza can produce 23 pizzas in every 12 minutes. How many pizzas can they produce between 07:30 when they open and 23:30 when they close?

3 I reckon that I spend 45 minutes on homework every night, six nights a week. If this term is 14 weeks long, how many minutes do I spend on homework? How many hours and minutes is this?

4 We go on a school trip with 7 buses. Four buses take 49 passengers and 3 take 55. How many people go on the trip?

5 In a school down the road there are 14 classes with 32 pupils in each class and 16 classes of 29 pupils. How many pupils are in the school?

6 I am saving £1.60 a week. I have been saving for 24 weeks. How much more money do I need to buy a computer program costing £49.99?

7 A ferry to Spain carries 2349 passengers and makes two return trips a week every week of the year. How many passengers does it carry in a year?

8 On a flight to China an aeroplane has 48 first class passengers paying £1645 and 226 economy passengers paying £645. How much money have the passengers paid in total?

◯ Long division

Before looking at **long division** remember what happens in simple division.

$992 \div 4$

	H	T	U
	2	4	8
4	9	^{1}9	^{3}2

First: 9 divided by 4 is 2 remainder 1   4 x 2 = 8   9 – 8 = 1

write 2 above the 9, carry the 1 and write it before the 9 in the tens column.

Then: 19 divided by 4 is 4 remainder 3   4 x 4 = 16   19 – 16 = 3

write 4 above the 19, carry the 3 and write it before the 2 in the units column.

Then: 32 divided by 4 is 8 with no remainder,

write 8 above the 32

You can use exactly the same principle for long division. Generally, you only use long division when you are dividing by a number greater than 12

Examples

(i) Divide: 851 ÷ 23   You can check by multiplying over here.

	Th	H	T	U
			3	7
2	3	⁷8	¹5	1
		6	9	
		1	6	1
		1	6	1
				0

Divide.

Multiply.

Subtract, pull down the number.

Divide, multiply.

2	3
×	3
6	9

	2	3
	×	7
1	6	1

(ii) Divide: 8670 ÷ 27

		Th	H	T	U	
			3	2	1	r 3
2	7	8	6	7	0	
		8	1			
			5	7		
			5	4		
				3	0	
				2	7	
					3	

Divide.

Multiply.

Subtract, pull down

Divide, multiply

Subtract, pull down

Divide, multiply

Subtract

2	7
×	3
8	1

2	7
×	2
5	4

8670 ÷ 27 = 321 r 3

Exercise 5.9

Complete these calculations by long division. The first five questions have no remainders, but the rest may have.

1 832 ÷ 26

2 703 ÷ 19

3 936 ÷ 39

4 966 ÷ 23

5 408 ÷ 17

6 938 ÷ 27

7 839 ÷ 71

8 917 ÷ 38

9 568 ÷ 41

10 840 ÷ 65

11	2538 ÷ 54	16	8208 ÷ 27
12	2523 ÷ 87	17	4507 ÷ 71
13	5704 ÷ 46	18	3906 ÷ 38
14	9135 ÷ 63	19	2056 ÷ 41
15	9633 ÷ 39	20	1910 ÷ 65

Round up or round down?

Some divisions have remainders. When they are in real-life contexts, you need to decide whether to round up or down. You can't have half a person, for example. You will need to make this decision in the next exercise.

Exercise 5.10

Complete these questions by long division. Then decide whether you should round the answer up or down to answer the question correctly.

1 I have bought a battery that says it will run for 3900 hours. How many whole days is that?

2 One Star Tours coach takes 48 people. How many coaches will be needed for 2418 people are to go on the tour?

3 Mercury takes 88 Earth days to complete one revolution around the Sun. How many complete revolutions will it make in three Earth years of 365 days?

4 There are 14 pounds in one stone. How much does a 179 pound man weigh in stones and pounds?

5 There are approximately 39 inches in one metre. Approximately how many metres are there in 100 yards, given that there are 12 inches in one foot and 3 feet in one yard?

6 My car does about 9 miles to the litre. Approximately how much will it cost me to travel 420 miles if petrol costs £1.36 per litre?

7 If an average man weighs 69 kg, how many men can travel on a plane whose maximum passenger load is 30 600 kg? Is this an exact answer?

8 A businessman works out that he will have to pay £9000 in tax at the end of the year. How much should he save each week to make sure that he has enough?

Extension Exercise 5.11

You have seen several patterns emerging from multiplying and dividing. The first is the powers of ten.

$$10 = 10$$
$$10 \times 10 = 100$$
$$10 \times 10 \times 10 = 1000 \text{ and so on.}$$

The number one is also very interesting.

$$1 = 1$$
$$1 \times 1 = 1$$
$$1 \times 1 \times 1 = 1$$

1   Can you find another number that gives the same answer, however many times it is multiplied by itself?

2   Consider the following pattern.

$$1 = 1$$
$$1 + 1 = 2$$
$$1 + 1 + 1 = 3$$

Form a similar pattern to this, based on 2. A special series of numbers is produced. What are these numbers called?

3   Copy and complete these sentences.

(a)   If you multiply an even number by an even number, you always get...

(b)   If you multiply an even number by an odd number, you always get...

(c)   If you multiply an odd number by an even number, you always get...

(d)   If you multiply an odd number by an odd number, you always get...

4   From your answers to question 3, does it follow that there must be more even numbers than odd numbers?

5   Copy and complete these sentences.

(a)   If you add an even number to an even number, you get...

(b)   If you add an even number to an odd number, you get...

(c)   If you add an odd number to an even number, you get...

(d)   If you add an odd number to an odd number, you get...

6 Copy and complete these patterns of numbers. Say whether there is a regular adding rule, a regular multiplying rule or neither of these.

(a) 2, 4, 8, 16, …, … .

(d) 2, 5, 8, 11, … , … .

(b) 1, 5, 25, … , … .

(e) 11, 101, 1001, … , … .

(c) 1, 2, 4, 7, … , … .

Summary Exercise 5.12

1 (a) Write each of these as a single digit multiplied by a power of ten.

(i) 60 000

(ii) 300

(iii) 400 000

(b) Write these out in full.

(i) 4×10^2

(ii) 8×10^6

(iii) 7×10^7

2 Complete these calculations.

(a) 30×10

(c) $7\,000\,000 \div 1000$

(b) 3.5×1000

(d) $0.9 \div 100$

3 Complete these calculations.

(a) 300×600

(c) 0.6×200

(b) $720\,000 \div 800$

(d) $1.8 \div 300$

4 Use a formal written method to complete these multiplications.

(a) 24×37

(c) 2314×46

(b) 163×45

(d) 3548×75

5 Use a formal written method to complete these divisions.

(a) $784 \div 49$

(c) $8820 \div 36$

(b) $706 \div 26$

(d) $2675 \div 58$

6 One school minibus takes 17 pupils. How many minibuses do we need to take the whole year of 92 children on an outing?

7 The cartridge for my printer will print 1000 A4 pages. I print three dozen pages per day. How many days will my printer cartridge last?

8 My school wants to buy 34 computers. If each computer costs £690, how much will they cost altogether?

9 A long-distance lorry driver drives 450 miles every day. If he works 24 days each month, how many miles does he drive in a year?

10 It costs £76 per computer to upgrade the school's word-processing package. If the school has 24 computers, how much will this cost in total?

The school has only budgeted for £1000. How many computers can the school upgrade for this amount?

11 Write down 1. Multiply it by 21 and write down the answer. Multiply that answer by 22 and write it down.

Continue until you have a number greater than 10 000. Did you expect the result you got?

Try to explain it. Think about powers of ten.

12 Write down the number that is the digit 9 written 18 times. Divide it by 19 (It does go exactly!)

6 More about numbers

Rules of divisibility

You probably know your multiplication tables without even having to think about them. This will include all of the inverses relating to division. You often need to recall which numbers divide exactly into a given number. Looking at patterns can help you discover rules.

The two times table
Consider the sequence of results in the two times table. This gives:

2, 4, 6, 8, 10, 12, 14, 16, ...

These numbers all result from a multiplication by two and they are all even. Therefore you can say:

All numbers that are even can be divided by two.

The three times table
The sequence of results in the three times table is:

3, 6, 9, 12, 15, 18, 21, 24, 27, 30, ...

These numbers go up in threes and are alternately odd and even, but the most interesting thing about them is their digit sum. Adding the digits for each term gives the series:

3, 6, 9, 3, 6, 9, 3, 6, 9, ...

The three times table does not stop at 36. You can find the digit sum for the larger numbers like this.

39:	$3 + 9 = 12 \rightarrow 1 + 2 = 3$
42:	$4 + 2 = 6$
45:	$4 + 5 = 9$
390:	$3 + 9 + 0 = 12 \rightarrow 1 + 2 = 3$
393:	$3 + 9 + 3 = 15 \rightarrow 1 + 5 = 6$
396:	$3 + 9 + 6 = 18 \rightarrow 1 + 8 = 9$

If the sum of the digits of a number is a **multiple** of 3, the number can be divided by 3

The four times table

The sequence starts:

4, 8, 12, 16, 20, ...

and if you extend it, you find it continues to:

100, 104, 108, 112, ...

As 100 can be divided by four, you can ignore the number in the hundreds column.

If the last two digits of a number can be divided by four, however big the number, then the whole number can be divided by four.

So, for example, the numbers 724, 948 and 1 572 604 can all be divided by four.

The five times table

This is very straightforward, giving the sequence:

5, 10, 15, 20, 25, 30, 35, 40, ...

Any number that ends in 5 or 0 can be divided by five. Again, this applies, however large the number.

The six times table

This gives the sequence:

6, 12, 18, 24, 30, 36, 42, 48, ...

You know that $6 = 3 \times 2$, and so the numbers in the six times table have the properties of the two times table and the properties of the three times table.

All even numbers with a digit sum that is a multiple of three can be divided by six.

So for an even number such as 342:

$3 + 4 + 2 = 9$

Since 9 is divisible by 3, and 342 is an even number, so therefore 342 is divisible by 6

The seven times table

The seven times table has a number of interesting patterns, but they are not obvious.

There are rules that can help you to check if a number is divisible by seven but they are complicated and the quickest way is usually to do the division. It therefore helps to know your seven times table really well.

The eight times table

This gives the pattern:

8, 16, 24, 32, 40, ...

This is very similar to the four times table. It is very easy to get the two patterns confused and so, to keep things simple, divide by four first and then see if you can divide again by two.

The nine times table

The nine times table is possibly the most interesting of all these sequences from the times tables. The simplest pattern is similar to the three times table. Look at the digit sum:

9, 18, 27, 36, 45, 54, ...

The digit sum is always 9, or a multiple of 9

If the digits of a number can be added up to make 9 or a multiple of 9, then that number can be divided by 9

The ten times table

This is very straightforward. Numbers in the ten times table are:

10, 20, 30, 40, 50, ...

Any number that ends in 0 can be divided by 10

So there are very clear rules for dividing by 2, 3, 4, 5, 6, 8, 9 and 10

These are called the **rules of divisibility**.

There are also rules for dividing by other numbers, but these are so complicated that it is probably quicker to do the division.

Factors and multiples

Numbers that divide exactly into another number are factors.

For example, 3 and 6 are two of the factors of 12

Numbers that are the result of multiplying one whole number (or factor) by another whole number are multiples. For example:

12 is a multiple of 6 (and also a multiple of 4 and of 3 and of 2)

Without knowing it, when you learnt your times tables you were studying factors and multiples.

Multiples give you the result of a multiplication.

Factors give you the result of a division.

As $7 \times 8 = 56$ then 56 is a multiple of 7 and of 8; and 7 and 8 are factors of 56

Examples

Is 9 a factor of these numbers?

(i) 1242

The digit sum of 1242 is:

$1 + 2 + 4 + 2 = 9$

9 is a factor of 1242

(ii) 7146

The digit sum of 7146 is:

$7 + 1 + 4 + 6 = 18$

18 is a multiple of 9

9 is a factor of 7146

Exercise 6.1

1 Which of these numbers are multiples of 3?

(a) 36

(b) 81

(c) 147

(d) 297

(e) 434

2 Can 12 345 be divided by:

(a) 2

(b) 3

(c) 4

(d) 5

(e) 6?

3 Which of these numbers have 9 as a factor?

(a) 495

(b) 365

(c) 1760

(d) 7534

(e) 12 906

4 List all the factors that you can of 1260

5 Is 7 a factor of:

   (a) 147   (c) 315

   (b) 203   (d) 1043?

6 What is the highest number that is a factor of both 12 and 16?

7 What is the lowest number that can be divided by both 5 and 7?

8 What is the lowest number that can be divided by both 6 and 8?

9 Make a list of the first fifteen multiples of:

   (a) 4   (b) 6

   and the first ten multiples of:

   (c) 9   (d) 12

   Put a box round any number that occurs in all four lists.

10 List all the factors that you can of each of these numbers.

   (a) 7   (d) 23

   (b) 11   (e) 83

   (c) 13

   What do you notice?

Index numbers

Here is a quick summary of what you have learnt about powers of 10

$$10^2 = 10 \times 10 \qquad\qquad = \quad 100$$

$$10^3 = 10 \times 10 \times 10 \qquad = \quad 1000$$

$$10^4 = 10 \times 10 \times 10 \times 10 = 10000$$

Each line above starts with a power of 10. The small, raised numbers, such as the 4 in 10^4, are index numbers. The index number indicates the **power**.

When the index number is 2, the number is squared.

So 2^2 is 2 squared, 3^2 is 3 squared, and so on.

When the index number is 3, the number is cubed.

So 2^3 is 2 cubed, 3^3 is three cubed, and so on.

Seven cubed is:

$$7^3 = 7 \times 7 \times 7 = 343$$

For index numbers over 3, you say 'to the power of':

Thus, three to the power four is:

$$3^4 = 3 \times 3 \times 3 \times 3 = 81$$

10^4 is 10 to the power of 4

Exercise 6.2

1 Copy and complete these calculations, then write down the next three rows.

$$2 \qquad\qquad\quad = 2$$
$$2^2 = 2 \times 2 \qquad = \dots$$
$$2^3 = \dots \times \dots \times \dots = \dots$$
$$2^4 = \qquad\qquad = \dots$$

2 Write these multiplications as powers, for example, write $2 \times 2 \times 2 \times 2$ as 2^4 and calculate the resulting numbers.

(a) $3 \times 3 \times 3$

(b) 4×4

(c) $5 \times 5 \times 5 \times 5$

(d) $3 \times 3 \times 3 \times 3 \times 3$

(e) 7×7

(f) $6 \times 6 \times 6$

3 Evaluate each of these numbers.

(a) 4^3

(b) 3^4

(c) 5^3

(d) 4^2

(e) 4^4

(f) 3^3

4 Evaluate each expression.

(a) $2^2 + 3^3$

(b) $2^3 - 3^3$

(c) $4^3 - 4^3$

(d) $3^3 + 4^2$

(e) $6^3 + 4^2$

(f) $5^3 + 5^3$

5 Evaluate each expression.

(a) $4^2 + 3^3$

(b) $5^2 - 2^3$

(c) $5^3 - 4^3$

(d) $3^3 - 4^2$

(e) $5^3 + 3^2$

(f) $5^3 + 4^3$

Square numbers and triangular numbers

Pythagoras was a famous mathematician who was alive from c.560 B.C. to c.480 B.C. His followers, the Pythagoreans, experimented with numbers, representing them as dots and arranging them in patterns such as triangles and squares.

1 Copy these patterns. Add the next three patterns and write the number of dots under each pattern.

$1 \times 1 = 1$ $2 \times 2 = 4$ $3 \times 3 = 9$ $4 \times 4 = 16$

The numbers you have worked out are the square numbers. They are the results of multiplying a number by itself.

You can always arrange these numbers of dots (1, 4, 9, ...) into a square.

2 Copy these patterns. Add the next three patterns and write the number of dots under each pattern.

1   3   6

The numbers you have written above are the **triangular** (or triangle) numbers. You can always arrange these dots into a right-angled isosceles triangle. There are other methods of working them out.

3 Copy and complete this number series.

    1   = ...

    1 + 2   = ...

    1 + 2 + 3   = ...

    1 + 2 + 3 + ... = ...

Add the next three rows.

4 Now try adding one triangular number to the next triangular number. Draw the next three patterns in this sequence and write the total number of dots under each pattern, as in the examples below.

1     $3 + 1 = 4$ $6 + 3 = 9$ $10 + ...$ $= ...$

What do you notice?

5 Copy and complete this table of numbers, made by adding consecutive odd numbers. Add the next three rows of the pattern.

    1   = ...

    1 + 3   = ...

    1 + 3 + 5   = ...

    1 + 3 + 5 + 7   = ...

Square numbers again!

> **Consecutive** means one follows the other.

6 What happens if you add up consecutive even numbers? Copy and complete these calculations and add the next three rows.

2 = 2

2 + 4 = 6

2 + 4 + 6 = ...

2 + 4 + 6 + ... = ...

How would you describe this pattern?

> Try dividing it by two.

7 You know that a number to the power 3 is that number cubed.

Therefore 3 cubed is $3^3 = 3 \times 3 \times 3 = 27$

Copy and complete this pattern.

$2^3 = 2 \times 2 \times 2 \quad =$

$3^3 = ... \times ... \times ... =$

$4^3 = 4 \times 4 \times 4 \quad =$

$5^3 = ... \times ... \times ... =$

$6^3 = ... \times ... \times ... =$

$7^3 = ... \times ... \times ... =$

$8^3 = ... \times ... \times ... =$

$9^3 = ... \times ... \times ... =$

$10^3 = ... \times ... \times ... =$

8 **(a)** Copy and complete this pattern.

$2^3 - 1^3 =$

$3^3 - 2^3 =$

$4^3 - 3^3 =$

$5^3 - 4^3 =$

(b) Add the next three rows.

(c) Your answers are all odd numbers. Try to explain why.

(d) Write each of the answers as the sum of consecutive numbers like this:

$3^3 - 2^3 = 27 - 8$

$= 19$

$= 9 + 10$

(e) You should notice that the first number in each of your consecutive numbers is a multiple of 3

(i) List these multiples of three and write them as a multiplication i.e. $9 = 3 \times 3$

(ii) What do you call the numbers that you have multiplied by 3?

◯ The table square

Some numbers have lots of factors and are multiples of several different pairs of numbers. Other numbers have very few factors. To look at these in more detail, consider a table square.

Exercise 6.4

You have seen a table square like this before. Each number is the result of multiplying the number on the top row by the number in the left-hand column.

The first few are done for you.

×	2	3	4	5	6	7	8	9	10	11	12
2	4	6	8	10	12	14	16	18			
3	6	9	12	15	18	21					
4	8	12	16	20	24						
5											
6											
7											
8											
9											
10											
11											
12											

1   Copy and complete the table square. Note that the numbers in the top row and left-hand column go up to 12

2   Look at the numbers that you have written. Some numbers occur once, some twice and some a great many times. Choose four different colours and colour:

   (a) all the numbers that occur twice and only twice in the first colour

   (b) all the numbers that occur exactly four times in the next colour

   (c) all the numbers that occur six or more times in the third colour

   (d) all the numbers that occur an odd number of times (once, three times, five times) in the fourth colour.

3   Copy and complete these sentences using the words 'odd', 'factors', 'symmetrical' and the correct numbers.

   (a) The numbers in the table square are … about one **diagonal**.

   (b) All the numbers down that diagonal occur are … number of times. They are square numbers.

(c) The numbers that occur most often are: ...., ... and ... .These numbers have lots of ... .

(d) Some numbers do not occur on the table square at all. These numbers have as factors only 1 and the number itself. Examples of these are ... and ... .

Prime numbers and prime factors

> The number 1 itself is not a prime number because it does not have exactly two factors.

Prime numbers

When you looked at factors of numbers, you found some numbers had exactly two factors: the number itself and 1. These are **prime numbers**.

Exercise 6.5

Eratosthenes was a Greek astronomer who was alive about 275–195 B.C. Although the Greeks knew about prime numbers before this time, astronomers had a particular interest in them as they used prime numbers to carry out complex calculations.

1 Draw a 1 to 100 square, with ten rows and ten columns. Since you know that a prime number has only two factors, itself and 1, you can use this square to find all the prime numbers up to 100.

(a) Put a square round 1 because it is a square number, but not a prime number because it does not have exactly two factors.

(b) Put a circle round 2. This is the first prime number. Now cross off any number that is a multiple of 2. You will have to go beyond your times tables to include all multiples of 2 on the square.

(c) The next prime number is 3. Put a circle round 3 and cross off all the multiples of 3 that have not already been crossed off.

(d) The next prime number is 5. Put a circle round 5 and cross off all the multiples of 5

Your square should look like this.

1	2	3	4	5	6	7	8	9	10
11	12	13	14	15	16	17	18	19	20
21	22	23	24	25	26	27	28	29	30
31	32	33	34	35	36	37	38	39	40

Check that it does and then continue in this way until you have nothing but prime numbers with circles round them in the square.

2 List all the prime numbers between one and one hundred.

Finding factor pairs

When you were filling in your table square, you may have noticed that some numbers, such as 36 and 24, occurred in several places. This is because they have several factors.

When numbers have several factors, you may need to find all of them. One way to do this is by finding the **factor pairs**.

Start by dividing by small numbers. Each small factor will have a corresponding larger factor. Work your way up by dividing by increasingly large factors, until you have found them all.

For example, the factor pairs of 6 are:

1 and 6

2 and 3

The factors are therefore 1, 2, 3 and 6

When you list factors, enclose them in special brackets. For example:

Factors of 6 = {1, 2, 3, 6}

When you are looking for factors of a number, it can be helpful to use a T-shaped frame, as shown in the next example. Start with 1 at the top left and the number itself top right. Then work through all the numbers to find the factors, until you start repeating numbers. The numbers in the T-shaped frame are all the factors, neatly assembled in pairs.

Example

Find the factors of 12

```
        12
  1  ×  12
  2  ×  6
  3  ×  4
```

Note that you stop at this stage, because the next calculation, 4 × 3, is identical to 3 × 4 which you have already found. Similarly, 6 × 2 is the same as 2 × 6

Now you can read all four factors from the T-shape, starting at the top left and moving down the left-hand side, round the bottom and up the other side: 1, 2, 3, 4, 6, 12

Reading across the T-shape gives the factor pairs: 1 × 12, 2 × 6, 3 × 4

Exercise 6.6

1 Copy and complete this frame to find all the factors of 36

	36	
1	×	36
2	×	18
3	×	12

Factors of 36 = {..., ..., ..., ..., ..., ..., ..., ..., ...}

2 Use a frame to find all the factor pairs and hence all the factors of 72

3 Use a frame to find all the factor pairs and hence all the factors of 100

4 Use a frame to find all the factor pairs and hence all the factors of 360

5 List all the factors of 128. What do you notice about them?

6 List all the factors of 243. What do you notice about them?

7 List all the factors of each of these numbers.

(a) 4   (d) 25

(b) 9   (e) 36

(c) 16   (f) 49

What do you notice about them?

8 Copy and complete these sentences, using some of these words: odd, even, square, factors, triangle, multiples.

(a) 24, 72 and 360 each have an ... number of factors.

(b) 36 and 100 each have an ... number of factors. This is because they are ... numbers.

(c) 360 can be a more useful number than 100 because it has more ... .

More about factors and multiples

Any number that is not a prime number (or 1) can be written as the **product of prime numbers**. A **product** is the result of a multiplication. For example, the product of 3 and 4 is 12

Here are the first dozen numbers, written as products of their **prime factors**. A prime factor is a factor that is also a prime number.

1 = 1   7 = 7 and is prime

2 = 2 and is prime   8 = 2 × 2 × 2

3 = 3 and is prime   9 = 3 × 3

4 = 2 × 2   10 = 2 × 5

5 = 5 and is prime   11 = 11 and is prime

6 = 2 × 3   12 = 2 × 2 × 3

The numbers that are multiplied together are the prime factors.

You can find prime factors for any number apart from 1

Method 1: Use a factor tree

This is especially useful when you are working with low numbers.

Find a factor pair, but try not to start with 1 × something or 2 × something.

For the first pair, try to avoid prime numbers.

Example

Express the number 24 as the product of prime factors. Use indices to write the final answer.

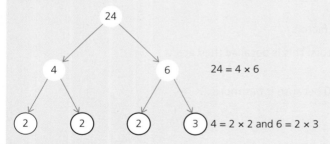

24 = 4 × 6

4 = 2 × 2 and 6 = 2 × 3

$24 = 2 \times 2 \times 2 \times 3$

$\quad = 2^3 \times 3$

2 and 3 are both prime; the tree stops when the numbers at the ends of the 'branches' are all prime.

> **Indices** is the plural of index. 'Using indices' means writing numbers as powers.

Exercise 6.7

Use the factor tree method to express each number as the product of prime factors. Use indices in your answers.

1	36		6	45
2	25		7	28
3	18		8	32
4	27		9	44
5	40		10	42

Method 2: Divide by prime numbers

To find the prime factors of a number, divide it by a succession of prime numbers until you reach 1

Use this method for larger numbers and numbers that you expect to have a large number of factors.

The successive division looks a bit like a ladder, so this is sometimes called the 'ladder method'.

Examples

(i) Find the prime factors of 24

2	2	4
2	1	2
2		6
3		3
		1

24 is even and so can be divided by 2

12 is even and so can be divided by 2

6 is even and so can be divided by 2

3 is a prime number.

$$24 = 2 \times 2 \times 2 \times 3$$
$$= 2^3 \times 3$$

(ii) Find the prime factors of 78

	2	7	8
	3	3	9
1	3	1	3
			1

78 is even and so can be divided by 2

39 is odd but 3 + 9 = 12 so 39 can be divided by 3

13 is a prime number.

$$78 = 2 \times 3 \times 13$$

Use successive division, as in the examples above, to find the prime factors.

1 Express each number as the product of prime factors. Use indices.

(a) 36   (g) 400

(b) 49   (h) 162

(c) 56   (i) 144

(d) 65   (j) 230

(e) 72   (k) 360

(f) 125   (l) 365

2 (a) Find the prime factors of 24 and 54

(b) What prime factors do they have in common?

3 Find the prime factors of 125 and 100. What prime factors do they have in common?

4 Find the prime factors of 12, 30 and 48. What prime factors do they have in common?

5 (a) Look back at the prime factors of 24 and 54. List them all. If a factor occurs twice in one number you must include it twice; if it occurs once in each, just include it once.

(b) Multiply all the factors together. Do both 24 and 54 divide exactly into this number?

(c) Is there a lower number that they both divide exactly into?

6 Repeat question 5 for:

(a) 125 and 100

(b) 12, 30 and 48

7 Which numbers that are less than 100 have the most factors? How many different prime factors do these numbers have?

8 Which numbers that are less than 500 have the most factors? How many different prime factors do these numbers have?

Now try this the other way round.

9 Which numbers that are less than 100 have the greatest number of different prime factors? How many factors do these numbers have?

10 Which numbers that are less than 500 have the greatest number of different prime factors? How many factors do these numbers have?

Highest common factors

A number that will divide exactly into two numbers is a **common factor** of the two numbers. You found common factors in questions 2, 3 and 4 of Exercise 6.8. The largest number that will divide exactly into two or more other numbers is their **highest common factor** or **HCF**.

To find the highest common factor of two or more numbers, you need to find the factors that are common to each of the numbers and multiply them together.

Example

Find the HCF of 36 and 42

2	3	6				2	4	2
2	1	8				3	2	1
3		9				7		7
3		3						1
		1						

$36 = 2 \times 2 \times 3 \times 3 \qquad 42 = 2 \times 3 \times 7$

The HCF of 36 and 42 is $2 \times 3 = 6$

Exercise 6.9

1 Find the HCF of each set of numbers.

(a) 15 and 12

(b) 8 and 28

(c) 360 and 100

(d) 18, 24 and 36

(e) 18 and 24

(f) 25 and 60

(g) 72 and 90

(h) 130, 360 and 100

(i) 14 and 16

(j) 104 and 56

(k) 12, 15 and 18

(l) 72, 100 and 120

> If you have already found the prime factors in an earlier question, you do not have to work them out again.

You will need to work out the HCF of two or more numbers, to answer the remaining questions.

2 What is the highest number that is a factor of 24, of 45 and of 60?

3 I have a box of 48 eggs and Sam has a box of 84 eggs. We can both fill an exact number of identical egg boxes. What is the maximum number of eggs that an egg box can hold?

4 I have 15 pink stickers and 24 blue stickers. I want to arrange them in patterns so that each pattern has the same number of pink and blue stickers. How many patterns will I make?

5 My Dad is 54 and my Mum is 36. I can divide both their ages exactly by my big brother's age and by my little sister's age.

   (a) What is the oldest that my brother could be?

   (b) How old is my little sister? Is there more than one possible answer?

Lowest common multiples

A number that appears in the multiplication tables of two different numbers is a **common multiple** of the two numbers. In questions 5 and 6 of Exercise 6.8 you used prime factors to find the lowest number into which two numbers would both divide exactly. This is the **lowest common multiple** or **LCM**.

To find the lowest common multiple of two or more numbers, you need to include all the prime factors of one number and any extra factors that are in the other numbers but not the first.

Example

Find the LCM of 36 and 42

2	3	6			2	4	2
2	1	8			3	2	1
3		9			7		7
3		3					1
		1					

$36 = 2 \times 2 \times 3 \times 3$
$42 = 2 \times 3 \times 7$

The LCM of 36 and 42 is $2 \times 2 \times 3 \times 3 \times 7 = 252$

Exercise 6.10

1 Find the LCM of each set of numbers.

   (a) 9 and 12

   (b) 18 and 14

   (c) 100 and 80

   (d) 4 and 7

   (e) 6 and 15

   (f) 25 and 40

   (g) 24 and 18

   (h) 30 and 75

   (i) 8 and 12

   (j) 6, 9 and 10

   (k) 12, 15 and 18

   (l) 14, 15 and 16

You will need to work out the LCM of two or more numbers, to answer questions 2–5

2 Find the lowest number that 5, 8 and 10 will divide exactly into.

3 The alarm on my watch rings every 15 minutes. The alarm on my friend's watch rings every 20 minutes. If they both go off at the same time, how many minutes will pass before they both ring together again?

4 A smuggler set a light in his window. It flashed every 15 seconds. The local policeman set his light to flash every 25 seconds, in order to confuse the smuggler. If the two lights flashed together, after how many seconds did they flash together again?

5 A red frog and a green frog are on the same lily pad (number 1). They decide to have a race across the chain of 50 lily pads on the pond. The red frog can jump so high that he lands on every 8th lily pad. The green frog can only leap high enough to land on every 6th lily pad. Are there any lily pads on which both the red and green frogs will land? How many fewer leaps does the red frog make than the green?

Square roots and cube roots

The square root of a number is that smaller number which, if multiplied by itself, produces the original number. Thus the square root of 4 is 2 because $2 \times 2 = 4$. The square root of 9 is 3 because $3 \times 3 = 9$

The square root has a special symbol: $\sqrt{}$

You write the square root of 4 as $\sqrt{4} = 2$

The cube root of a number is that smaller number which, if multiplied by itself twice, produces the original number. Thus the cube root of 8 is 2 because $2 \times 2 \times 2 = 8$. The cube root of 27 is 3 because $3 \times 3 \times 3 = 27$

The cube root has a special symbol: $\sqrt[3]{}$

You write the cube root of 8 as $\sqrt[3]{8} = 2$

Exercise 6.11

1 Write down the square root of each number.

(a) 100   (b) 1   (c) 16

2 Give the answers to these.

(a) $\sqrt{121}$ (b) $\sqrt{64}$ (c) $\sqrt{25}$

3 Write down the cube root of each number.

(a) 1   (b) 64   (c) 125

4 Give the answers to these.

(a) $\sqrt[3]{8}$ (b) $\sqrt[3]{1000}$ (c) $\sqrt[3]{216}$

Extension | Exercise 6.12

If you break down numbers that are perfect squares into their prime factors, you can find their square roots.

> **Think back to negative numbers, and recall that the product of two negative numbers is positive. So any square number has two square roots. However, unless you are told to use the negative square root, you may assume that you need the positive root.**

Example

Find the square root of 36

$$36 = 2 \times 2 \times 3 \times 3$$
$$= (2 \times 3) \times (2 \times 3)$$
$$\sqrt{36} = 2 \times 3$$
$$= 6$$

1 Write each number as the product of its prime factors and hence find its square root.

(a) 144   (d) 2025

(b) 441   (e) 900

(c) 1225   (f) 1296

2 Write each number as the product of its prime factors and hence find its cube root.

(a) 729   (c) 3375

(b) 1728   (d) 2744

3 64 has both a square root and a cube root that are whole numbers. Write 64 as the product of its prime factors to explain why.

4 What is the next largest number to have both a square root and cube root that are whole numbers? What are the square root and the cube root of the number?

5 What power of ten has both a square root and cube root that are whole numbers? What are the square root and the cube root of the number?

Summary Exercise 6.13

1 Which of these numbers can be divided exactly by 3?

   (a) 225

   (b) 132

   (c) 134

   (d) 1023

   (e) 143

   (f) 6000

2 Which of the numbers in question 1 can be divided by:

   (a) 5

   (b) 6

   (c) 9?

3 List all the factors of each number.

   (a) 16

   (b) 40

   (c) 28

   (d) 50

4 Complete this pattern of numbers to find all the factors of 120

   $1 \times 120 = 120$

   $2 \times 60 \ = 120$

   $3 \times 40 \ = 120$

5 Consider the numbers from 1 to 100

   (a) What is the largest number that is both a multiple of 4 and of 5?

   (b) What is the smallest number that is both a multiple of 7 and of 2?

   (c) What is the largest number that has 13 as a factor?

   (d) What is the largest number that has 7 as a factor?

   (e) How many numbers contain the digit 5?

   (f) What is the largest number that has both 5 and 7 as factors?

   (g) Which numbers have only even numbers as factors?

   (h) Which numbers have only odd numbers as factors?

   (i) What is the largest number that is a factor of 500?

6 Write each number as a product of its prime factors.

   (a) 35

   (b) 21

   (c) 144

   (d) 156

7 Find the HCF and LCM of each pair of numbers.

(a) 24 and 45

(b) 16 and 42

8 There are two lighthouses off the coast of France. One flashes once every 24 seconds and the other flashes once every 40 seconds. If they start the evening flashing together, after how many seconds will they flash together again?

Activity: A 1–100 square investigation

This is a 1 to 100 square.

1	2	3	4	5	6	7	8	9	10
11	12	13	14	15	16	17	18	19	20
21	22	23	24	25	26	27	28	29	30
31	32	33	34	35	36	37	38	39	40
41	42	43	44	45	46	47	48	49	50
51	52	53	54	55	56	57	58	59	60
61	62	63	64	65	66	67	68	69	70
71	72	73	74	75	76	77	78	79	80
81	82	83	84	85	86	87	88	89	90
91	92	93	94	95	96	97	98	99	100

Consider a 3×3 square of numbers from the 1 to 100 square above.

12	13	14
22	23	24
32	33	34

Look at the corners.

You should see that $\qquad$ 12 + 34 = 46

and $\qquad$ 32 + 14 = 46

12	13	14
22	23	24
32	33	34

Look at the centres.

You should see that $\qquad$ 13 + 33 = 46

and $\qquad$ 22 + 24 = 46

Is this true of all 3×3 squares? If so, why?

1 (a) Copy out another 3 by 3 square.

   (b) Add the opposite corners. Record the answers.

   (c) Add the opposite centres. Record the answers.

   (d) Double the number in the middle square. What is the answer?

2 Repeat question 1 for more 3 by 3 squares. Do you get the same answers every time?

3 To explain your answer, copy out this 3 by 3 square. You see the middle number is called by the letter n. Thus the number before n must be $n - 1$ and the number after it must be $n + 1$

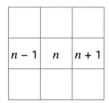

   (a) Write the numbers in the empty squares in relation to n.

   (b) Now explain your answers to questions 1 and 2

4 Now draw some 4 × 4 squares in your exercise book and investigate them. What do you notice about the corner and central numbers with these squares?

Fractions

From Chapter 1, you know that you can use **fractions** and **decimal fractions** to describe numbers that are not whole numbers.

In Chapter 4 you learnt how to calculate with decimal fractions just as you do with whole numbers. In this chapter you will be calculating with fractions, building on the work you have done with common factors and common denominators.

Equivalent fractions

This **rectangle** has been divided into twelfths.

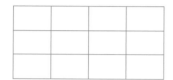

If you shade in six of those twelfths, you have actually shaded half of the rectangle.

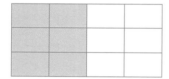

You can write this as: $\dfrac{6}{12} = \dfrac{1}{2}$

These are called **equivalent fractions**: six twelfths is equivalent to one half.

Lowest terms

When you write one half as $\dfrac{1}{2}$ the fraction is in its lowest terms because it cannot be rewritten as an equivalent fraction with smaller numbers. It is very important always to give fractions in your answers in their lowest terms.

You can simplify fractions by dividing the **numerator** (top number) and **denominator** (bottom number) by the same factor. This is called **cancelling**, or **simplifying**, the fraction. This will not alter the value of the fraction as $\dfrac{2}{2} = \dfrac{3}{3} = \dfrac{24}{24} = \dfrac{51}{51} = 1$

Examples

Write these fractions in their lowest terms.

(i) $\dfrac{16}{48}$

(ii) $\dfrac{36}{42}$

$\dfrac{16}{48} = \dfrac{8}{24} = \dfrac{1}{3}$

$\dfrac{36}{42} = \dfrac{18}{21} = \dfrac{6}{7}$

You do not have to change the fraction into its lowest terms in one – or even two – steps. Remember the rules of divisibility and keep cancelling until you can't cancel any more.

Exercise 7.1

1 Copy these squares and shade half of each of them.

(a)  (b) (c) (d)

2 Copy these squares and shade one quarter of each of them.

(a) (b) (c) (d)

3 What fraction of each rectangle is shaded? Give your answer as a fraction in its lowest terms.

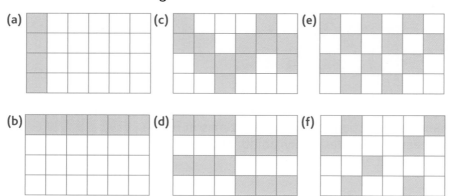

4 What fraction of each rectangle is shaded?

5 Draw four rectangles, each 4 cm by 5 cm.
   Shade these fractions.

(a) $\frac{1}{2}$ (b) $\frac{2}{5}$ (c) $\frac{3}{10}$ (d) $\frac{3}{4}$

6 Write each of these fractions in its lowest terms.

(a) $\frac{14}{24}$ (b) $\frac{24}{36}$ (c) $\frac{12}{46}$ (d) $\frac{33}{121}$ (e) $\frac{68}{100}$

7 These are the answers to Helena's homework. Sometimes she remembers to cancel her fractions to their lowest terms, but sometimes she forgets. Which of these are in their simplest form?

(a) $\frac{14}{21}$ (b) $\frac{24}{35}$ (c) $\frac{14}{22}$ (d) $\frac{8}{25}$ (e) $\frac{12}{75}$

8 Copy these statements and fill in the missing numbers to make these fractions equivalent.

(a) $\frac{1}{3} = \frac{4}{?} = \frac{?}{24} = \frac{33}{?}$ (c) $\frac{1}{4} = \frac{3}{?} = \frac{?}{24} = \frac{12}{?}$

(b) $\frac{3}{5} = \frac{9}{?} = \frac{?}{25} = \frac{33}{?}$ (d) $\frac{2}{9} = \frac{4}{?} = \frac{?}{27} = \frac{50}{?}$

Writing one quantity as a fraction of another

You use fractions to describe a part of a whole, for example, when you say: 'a quarter of an hour' or 'half the class'.

To calculate one quantity as a fraction of another, you write the fraction like this:

$$\frac{15 \text{ minutes}}{60 \text{ minutes}} \quad \text{or} \quad \frac{12 \text{ pupils}}{24 \text{ pupils}}$$

and then simplify the fraction until it is in its lowest terms.

$$\frac{15 \text{ minutes}}{60 \text{ minutes}} = \frac{15}{60} = \frac{1}{4} \quad \text{and} \quad \frac{12 \text{ pupils}}{24 \text{ pupils}} = \frac{12}{24} = \frac{1}{2}$$

You must take care to ensure that the units of the numerator and the denominator are the same.

Examples

(i) Write 20p as a fraction of £1

The fraction is $\frac{20}{100} = \frac{2}{10} = \frac{1}{5}$

(ii) There are 12 boys in our class of 20

What fraction of the class are boys?

The fraction is $\frac{12}{20} = \frac{3}{5}$

Exercise 7.2

1 (a) Write 15p as a fraction of 50p

(b) Write 28p as a fraction of 50p

(c) Write 45p as a fraction of 50p

(d) Write 17p as a fraction of 50p

2 (a) Write 25p as a fraction of £1

(b) Write 75p as a fraction of £1

(c) Write 72p as a fraction of £1

(d) Write 28p as a fraction of £1

3 (a) Write 300g as a fraction of 500g

(b) Write 400g as a fraction of 1kg

(c) Write 550g as a fraction of 1kg

(d) Write 840g as a fraction of 1kg

4 (a) Write 10cm as a fraction of a metre

(b) Write 8mm as a fraction of a metre

(c) Write 25cm as a fraction of 2 metres

(d) Write 150cm as a fraction of 5 metres

5 (a) Write 100 ml as a fraction of a litre

(b) Write 350 ml as a fraction of 2 litres

(c) Write 1250 ml as a fraction of 5 litres

(d) Write 3750 ml as a fraction of 10 litres

6 (a) Write 120 m as a fraction of 1 km

(b) Write 600 m as a fraction of 2 km

(c) Write 3250 m as a fraction of 4 km

(d) Write 2750 m as a fraction of 10 km

7 There are 250 pupils in a school. 100 of them play the piano, 80 of them play the violin and 24 of them are in the orchestra.

(a) What fraction of the school play the piano?

(b) What fraction of the school play the violin?

(c) What fraction of the school are in the orchestra?

8 There are 8 boys in our class of 18

(a) What fraction of the class are boys?

(b) What fraction of the class are girls?

9 There are 45 pupils in Year 7. 18 are girls

(a) What fraction of Year 7 are girls?

(b) What fraction of Year 7 are boys?

10 I have been given a £20 note. I spend £5 on a Merry Meal at McCambells, £2 on a new pen, £2.50 on some coloured pencils, £4.50 on a game and the rest on sweets for my friends.

What fraction of the £20 note do I spend on:

(a) the Merry Meal

(b) the new pen

(c) coloured pencils

(d) the game

(e) sweets?

Using equivalent fractions

It can be difficult to compare fractions, or to add or subtract fractions, when they have different denominators. You need to find **equivalent fractions** that all have the same denominator.

To keep the numbers as simple as possible, you need to find the lowest common multiple of the denominators.

This is called the **lowest common denominator.** If you spend a little time to do this, it can lead to easier calculations.

It is quite simple to find the common denominator when one denominator is a factor of the other. If you want to compare fractions with completely different denominators, you need to write them first as equivalent fractions with a common denominator. The lowest common denominator will be the lowest common multiple of the denominators.

Example

Which is greater, $\frac{7}{9}$ or $\frac{9}{11}$?

$$\frac{7}{9} = \frac{7}{9} \times \frac{11}{11} = \frac{7 \times 11}{9 \times 11} = \frac{77}{99} \qquad\qquad \frac{9}{11} = \frac{9}{11} \times \frac{9}{9} = \frac{9 \times 9}{11 \times 9} = \frac{81}{99}$$

$\frac{9}{11}$ is greater than $\frac{7}{9}$

You can write this as:

$$\frac{9}{11} > \frac{7}{9}$$

as > means 'is larger than' and < means 'is smaller than'.

Exercise 7.3

1 Work out the lowest common denominator for each pair of fractions.

(a) $\frac{1}{2}$ and $\frac{2}{3}$ (c) $\frac{1}{4}$ and $\frac{3}{8}$ (e) $\frac{2}{5}$ and $\frac{2}{3}$

(b) $\frac{3}{7}$ and $\frac{4}{9}$ (d) $\frac{7}{8}$ and $\frac{5}{6}$ (f) $\frac{7}{12}$ and $\frac{2}{3}$

2 Write each of the fraction pairs in question 1 with the same common denominator. Write < or > between them.

3 Work out equivalent fractions and then write < or > between each pair of fractions.

(a) $\frac{3}{5}$ and $\frac{2}{3}$ (c) $\frac{1}{3}$ and $\frac{3}{8}$ (e) $\frac{2}{15}$ and $\frac{2}{3}$

(b) $\frac{7}{15}$ and $\frac{5}{12}$ (d) $\frac{7}{12}$ and $\frac{5}{9}$ (f) $\frac{7}{9}$ and $\frac{2}{3}$

4 Work out equivalent fractions, then arrange these in order of size, smallest first.

$$\frac{4}{9} \qquad \frac{3}{7} \qquad \frac{2}{3} \qquad \frac{1}{2}$$

5 Work out equivalent fractions, then arrange these these in order of size, largest first.

$$\frac{1}{3} \qquad \frac{2}{15} \qquad \frac{4}{9} \qquad \frac{1}{12}$$

6 In each group of fractions, there is an odd one out. Which is it?

(a) $\dfrac{3}{6} \quad \dfrac{12}{24} \quad \dfrac{5}{9} \quad \dfrac{13}{26} \quad \dfrac{15}{30}$

(c) $\dfrac{3}{9} \quad \dfrac{6}{16} \quad \dfrac{9}{24} \quad \dfrac{15}{40} \quad \dfrac{75}{200}$

(b) $\dfrac{8}{12} \quad \dfrac{12}{18} \quad \dfrac{50}{75} \quad \dfrac{22}{36} \quad \dfrac{32}{48}$

(d) $\dfrac{16}{56} \quad \dfrac{4}{15} \quad \dfrac{10}{35} \quad \dfrac{8}{28} \quad \dfrac{24}{84}$

Proper and improper fractions

Any fraction in which the numerator is smaller than the denominator has a value between zero and one. Fractions like this are called **proper fractions**.

Any fraction in which the numerator is greater than the denominator has a value greater than one. Fractions like this are called **top-heavy** or **improper fractions**.

For example:

$$\frac{1}{5} \quad \frac{2}{5} \quad \frac{3}{5} \quad \frac{4}{5} \qquad \frac{5}{5} = 1 \qquad \frac{6}{5} \quad \frac{7}{5} \quad \frac{8}{5} \quad \frac{9}{5}$$

$\underbrace{\hspace{3cm}}$ proper fractions

$\underbrace{\hspace{3cm}}$ improper fractions

Mixed numbers
Consider these statements.

- 'It is a quarter past four.'

- 'I am eleven and three quarters.'

- 'I have grown two and a quarter centimetres.'

These are **mixed numbers** because they are each a mixture of a number and a fraction. If you turn mixed numbers into fractions, you get improper fractions.

Examples

(i) Write $\frac{23}{7}$ as a mixed number.

$$\frac{23}{7} = 3\frac{2}{7} \qquad (23 \div 7 = 3 \text{ remainder } 2)$$

(ii) Write $3\frac{2}{5}$ as an improper fraction.

$$3\frac{2}{5} = \frac{17}{5} \qquad (5 \times 3 + 2 = 17)$$

Exercise 7.4

1 Write each mixed number as an improper fraction.

(a) $1\frac{3}{4}$ (c) $3\frac{2}{5}$ (e) $2\frac{1}{7}$ (g) $6\frac{4}{5}$ (i) $10\frac{3}{10}$

(b) $7\frac{3}{7}$ (d) $2\frac{2}{5}$ (f) $4\frac{7}{12}$ (h) $15\frac{3}{4}$ (j) $8\frac{4}{9}$

2 Write each improper fraction as a mixed number.

(a) $\frac{13}{4}$ (c) $\frac{21}{6}$ (e) $\frac{19}{9}$ (g) $\frac{43}{7}$ (i) $\frac{93}{12}$

(b) $\frac{23}{8}$ (d) $\frac{29}{10}$ (f) $\frac{27}{2}$ (h) $\frac{25}{4}$ (j) $\frac{101}{5}$

Finding a fraction of an amount

Earlier in this chapter you coloured half of a rectangle.

If the rectangle had 24 squares, then you would have coloured 12 of them.

Finding a fraction of an amount is another way of thinking of division.

Example

Find $\frac{1}{3}$ of 24 cm

$\frac{1}{3}$ of 24 cm = $24 \div 3 = 8$ cm

1 Find $\frac{1}{3}$ of 24 cm

2 Find $\frac{1}{6}$ of 30 litres

3 Find $\frac{1}{2}$ of 10 m

4 Find $\frac{1}{4}$ of 16 squares

5 Find $\frac{1}{8}$ of 24 km

6 Find $\frac{1}{3}$ of £12

7 Find $\frac{1}{9}$ of 18 cm

8 Find $\frac{1}{8}$ of 160 mm

9 Find $\frac{1}{2}$ of 860 g

10 Find $\frac{1}{5}$ of 155 litres

Just as you can find one third, or one quarter, or one eighth of a number, so you might wish to find two-thirds, or three-quarters, or four-fifths.

Example

Find $\frac{2}{3}$ of 24 km

$\frac{1}{3}$ of 24 = 24 ÷ 3 = 8

$\frac{2}{3}$ of 24 km = 8 × 2 = 16 km

You can also consider dividing by common factors before you calculate. You can often get smaller numbers by doing this.

Example

Find $\frac{3}{8}$ of 360°

$\frac{3}{8}$ of 360° = $\frac{3}{{}_1 8} \times \frac{360^{\,45}}{1}$

$= 3 \times 45$

$= 135°$

Exercise 7.6

1 Find $\frac{3}{4}$ of 24 cm

2 Find $\frac{5}{6}$ of 30 kg

3 Find $\frac{3}{5}$ of 35 m

4 Find $\frac{3}{8}$ of 16 miles

5 Find $\frac{5}{6}$ of £24

6 Find $\frac{2}{3}$ of 120 mm

7 Find $\frac{4}{9}$ of 180 g

8 Find $\frac{3}{4}$ of 1600 ml

9 Find $\frac{3}{5}$ of 250 mg

10 Find $\frac{7}{10}$ of 3000 mm

11 Find $\frac{5}{9}$ of 54 kg

12 Find $\frac{7}{12}$ of 36 km

13 Find $\frac{11}{20}$ of 100 miles

14 Find $\frac{3}{7}$ of 63 m

15 Find $\frac{5}{8}$ of 56 litres

16 Find $\frac{4}{9}$ of 810 cm

17 Find $\frac{5}{16}$ of 640 mg

18 Find $\frac{5}{7}$ of 91 m

19 Find $\frac{13}{30}$ of 150 ml

20 Find $\frac{5}{24}$ of 360 km

In questions 21 to 24 say which is bigger.

21 $\frac{1}{4}$ of 24 or $\frac{1}{3}$ of 21

22 $\frac{3}{4}$ of 16 or $\frac{1}{2}$ of 20

23 $\frac{2}{3}$ of 24 or $\frac{3}{5}$ of 20

24 $\frac{5}{6}$ of 36 or $\frac{2}{3}$ of 45

Adding and subtracting fractions

Suppose you divide a square into four equal quarters.

From this is it easy to see that: $\quad \frac{1}{4} + \frac{1}{4} = \frac{2}{4} \quad \frac{1}{4} + \frac{1}{2} = \frac{3}{4} \quad \frac{1}{4} + \frac{3}{4} = 1$

Similarly: $\quad \frac{1}{2} - \frac{1}{4} = \frac{2}{4} - \frac{1}{4} = \frac{1}{4}$

> Some additions may give you an answer of more than one (an improper fraction). In this case, always write your final answer as a mixed number.

Example

Work out $\frac{4}{5} + \frac{3}{5}$

$$\frac{4}{5} + \frac{3}{5} = \frac{7}{5}$$

$$= 1\frac{2}{5}$$

Sometimes fractions are already mixed numbers. You need to add or subtract the whole numbers as well as the fractions. Make sure that your final answer does not contain an improper fraction.

Example

Add: $1\frac{5}{8} + 2\frac{7}{8}$

$$1\frac{5}{8} + 2\frac{7}{8} = 3\frac{12}{8}$$

$$= 4\frac{4}{8}$$

$$= 4\frac{1}{2}$$

Exercise 7.7

Calculate the answers to these. You may need to add another stage, so that your answer is in its lowest terms.

1 $\frac{1}{4} + \frac{1}{4}$

2 $\frac{3}{5} - \frac{1}{5}$

3 $\frac{3}{4} + \frac{3}{4}$

4 $\frac{7}{8} - \frac{3}{8}$

5 $\frac{2}{9} + \frac{2}{9}$

6 $\frac{5}{7} - \frac{2}{7}$

7 $\frac{5}{8} - \frac{3}{8}$

8 $\frac{5}{9} + \frac{4}{9} + \frac{8}{9}$

9 $\frac{5}{7} + \frac{4}{7} + \frac{6}{7}$

10 $\frac{5}{12} + \frac{7}{12} + \frac{11}{12}$

11 $1\frac{3}{4}+2\frac{3}{4}$

12 $2\frac{4}{5}-1\frac{1}{5}$

13 $2\frac{2}{3}+1\frac{2}{3}$

14 $3\frac{5}{8}-1\frac{1}{8}$

15 $1\frac{8}{9}+1\frac{2}{9}$

16 $4\frac{5}{12}-1\frac{1}{12}$

17 $2\frac{1}{6}+2\frac{5}{6}$

18 $4\frac{4}{5}+\frac{3}{5}$

19 $1\frac{3}{10}+3\frac{9}{10}$

20 $5\frac{11}{12}-2\frac{5}{12}$

Adding fractions with different denominators

You have seen that $\frac{1}{4}+\frac{1}{2}=\frac{3}{4}$

This is because $\frac{1}{2}=\frac{2}{4}$

You could have written the calculation like this.

$$\frac{1}{4}+\frac{1}{2}=\frac{1}{4}+\frac{2}{4}$$
$$=\frac{3}{4}$$

as 4 is the common denominator for $\frac{1}{2}$ and $\frac{1}{4}$

Remember to look for the lowest common denominator, which is the lowest common multiple of the denominators.

Example

Add: $\frac{3}{10}+\frac{5}{12}$

$\frac{3}{10}+\frac{5}{12}$ — 60 will be the lowest common denominator.

$\frac{3}{10}=\frac{18}{60}$ and $\frac{5}{12}=\frac{25}{60}$ — Find equivalent fractions.

$\frac{3}{10}+\frac{5}{12}=\frac{18}{60}+\frac{25}{60}$

$=\frac{18+25}{60}$ — Write the addition over the common denominator.

$=\frac{43}{60}$ — Add the numerators.

Sometimes your answer will be an improper fraction. You should turn this into a mixed number.

Example

Add: $1\frac{7}{8}+\frac{11}{12}$

$1\frac{7}{8}+\frac{11}{12}$ 24 will be the lowest common denominator.

$1\frac{7}{8}=1\frac{21}{24}$ and $\frac{11}{12}=\frac{22}{24}$ Find equivalent fractions.

$1\frac{7}{8}+\frac{11}{12}=1\frac{21+22}{24}$ Write the addition over the common denominator.

$=1\frac{43}{24}$ Add the numerators.

$=1+1\frac{19}{24}$ Turn the improper fraction into a mixed number.

$=2\frac{19}{24}$ Add the whole numbers.

Exercise 7.8

Add these fractions and mixed numbers.

1   $\frac{1}{8}+\frac{1}{2}$ 6 $\frac{2}{5}+\frac{1}{4}$

2   $\frac{1}{5}+\frac{2}{10}$ 7 $\frac{1}{7}+\frac{3}{5}$

3   $1\frac{2}{3}+\frac{1}{6}$ 8 $\frac{2}{3}+\frac{1}{5}$

4   $\frac{3}{10}+1\frac{1}{2}$ 9 $1\frac{5}{7}+\frac{3}{5}$

5   $1\frac{1}{4}+\frac{5}{12}$ 10 $\frac{3}{5}+1\frac{3}{4}$

11 $1\frac{1}{5}+\frac{2}{3}$

12 $2\frac{3}{7}+\frac{3}{5}$

13 $1\frac{2}{5}+\frac{1}{8}$

14 $2\frac{3}{8}+\frac{1}{5}$

15 $1\frac{4}{5}+\frac{2}{7}$

16 $1\frac{3}{4}+\frac{5}{7}$

17 $2\frac{1}{6}+\frac{7}{10}$

18 $1\frac{5}{6}+\frac{3}{4}$

19 $1\frac{7}{12}+\frac{2}{3}$

20 $2\frac{2}{9}+\frac{2}{15}$

Subtracting fractions with different denominators

When you have to subtract fractions with different denominators, you first need to write them as equivalent fractions with a common denominator.

Example

Subtract: $1\frac{3}{5}-\frac{1}{3}$

$1\frac{3}{5}-\frac{1}{3}$ 15 is the lowest common denominator.

$\frac{3}{5}=\frac{9}{15}$ and $\frac{1}{3}=\frac{5}{15}$ Find equivalent fractions.

$1\frac{3}{5}-\frac{1}{3}=1\frac{9-5}{15}$ Write the subtraction over the common denominator.

$=1\frac{4}{15}$ Subtract the numerators.

Exercise 7.9

Subtract these. Make sure the fractions in your answers are in their lowest terms.

1 $\frac{4}{5}-\frac{2}{3}$

2 $\frac{2}{3}-\frac{1}{4}$

3 $\frac{5}{8}-\frac{1}{6}$

4 $\frac{2}{3}-\frac{2}{7}$

5 $\frac{7}{8}-\frac{5}{6}$

6 $\frac{4}{5}-\frac{1}{3}$

7 $\frac{2}{5}-\frac{2}{9}$

8 $\frac{4}{9}-\frac{1}{3}$

9 $\frac{5}{7}-\frac{2}{3}$

10 $\frac{4}{5}-\frac{3}{4}$

11 $1\frac{4}{5} - \frac{1}{3}$

16 $1\frac{3}{5} - \frac{1}{3}$

12 $1\frac{2}{3} - \frac{1}{5}$

17 $1\frac{4}{5} - 1\frac{5}{9}$

13 $1\frac{11}{12} - 1\frac{5}{6}$

18 $1\frac{7}{9} - \frac{2}{3}$

14 $1\frac{1}{3} - \frac{2}{7}$

19 $1\frac{4}{7} - 1\frac{2}{5}$

15 $1\frac{5}{8} - 1\frac{1}{6}$

20 $1\frac{11}{12} - \frac{5}{8}$

As for any other subtraction there will be times when the first subtraction is not possible (for example, 5 − 9). Then you need to exchange with the next number on the left. Remember, however, that you are not exchanging ten units – you are exchanging 8 eighths, 12 twelfths, 16 sixteenths – depending on the denominator of the fraction. Sometimes it is easier to work with improper fractions.

Examples

(i) Subtract: $1\frac{1}{2} - \frac{5}{6}$

$1\frac{1}{2} - \frac{5}{6}$ 6 is the lowest common denominator.

$1\frac{1}{2} - \frac{5}{6} = 1\frac{3}{6} - \frac{5}{6}$ Find equivalent fractions. You cannot take 5 from 3

$= \frac{9}{6} - \frac{5}{6}$ Turn the mixed number into an improper fraction.

$= \frac{4}{6} = \frac{2}{3}$

(ii) Subtract: $1\frac{1}{3} - \frac{3}{4}$

$1\frac{1}{3} - \frac{3}{4}$ 12 is the lowest common denominator.

$\frac{1}{3} = \frac{4}{12}$ and $\frac{3}{4} = \frac{9}{12}$ Find equivalent fractions.

$1\frac{1}{3} - \frac{3}{4} = 1\frac{4-9}{12}$ You cannot take 9 from 4

$= \frac{16-9}{12}$ Turn 1 into $\frac{12}{12}$, add 12 to 4

$= \frac{7}{12}$ Take 9 from 16

Exercise 7.10

For the first ten questions, turn the first fraction into an improper fraction.

1 $1\frac{1}{5} - \frac{1}{3}$

6 $1\frac{1}{7} - \frac{3}{4}$

2 $1\frac{1}{3} - \frac{3}{5}$

7 $1\frac{1}{6} - \frac{4}{9}$

3 $1\frac{1}{8} - \frac{2}{3}$

8 $2\frac{2}{5} - \frac{2}{3}$

4 $1\frac{3}{8} - \frac{5}{6}$

9 $1\frac{3}{8} - \frac{2}{5}$

5 $1\frac{2}{5} - \frac{7}{10}$

10 $2\frac{1}{9} - \frac{7}{12}$

For the next ten questions, exchange 1 unit for a fraction.

11 $1\frac{1}{4} - \frac{2}{3}$

16 $1\frac{1}{9} - \frac{5}{6}$

12 $1\frac{3}{7} - \frac{4}{5}$

17 $2\frac{2}{7} - \frac{3}{4}$

13 $2\frac{1}{3} - \frac{7}{8}$

18 $1\frac{1}{6} - \frac{2}{3}$

14 $1\frac{2}{7} - \frac{2}{3}$

19 $3\frac{1}{8} - \frac{5}{6}$

15 $3\frac{1}{4} - \frac{5}{6}$

20 $1\frac{2}{15} - \frac{3}{10}$

Multiplying and dividing fractions

Multiplying a fraction by a whole number
You know that multiplying is the same as adding again and again.

$$4 \times \frac{2}{3} = \frac{2}{3} + \frac{2}{3} + \frac{2}{3} + \frac{2}{3}$$

See how this works with rectangles.

You can see there is a total of 8 thirds.

Putting them together to make whole rectangles gives:

Two wholes and two thirds

So $4 \times \dfrac{2}{3} = 2\dfrac{2}{3}$

You can set this out as a calculation.

Examples

(i) Multiply: $4 \times \dfrac{2}{3}$

$$4 \times \frac{2}{3} = \frac{4 \times 2}{3}$$

$$= \frac{8}{3}$$

$$= 2\frac{2}{3}$$

(ii) Multiply: $3 \times 1\dfrac{4}{5}$

If you have a mixed number, multiply the numbers and the fractions separately.

$$3 \times 1\frac{4}{5} = 3 \times 1 + 3 \times \frac{4}{5} \quad \text{Keep the multiplications separate.}$$

$$= 3 \times 1 + \frac{12}{5}$$

$$= 3 + \frac{12}{5}$$

$$= 3 + 2\frac{2}{5} \quad \text{Turn the improper fraction into a mixed number.}$$

$$= 5\frac{2}{5} \quad \text{Add the whole numbers.}$$

Exercise 7.11

Complete these multiplications. If the answer is an improper fraction, write it as a mixed number. Make sure your fractions are in their lowest terms.

1 $2 \times \dfrac{1}{5}$ 　　　　　　　　　4 $5 \times \dfrac{3}{4}$

2 $3 \times \dfrac{1}{2}$ 　　　　　　　　　5 $3 \times \dfrac{4}{5}$

3 $4 \times \dfrac{2}{5}$ 　　　　　　　　　6 $4 \times \dfrac{5}{6}$

7   $6 \times \frac{3}{8}$

8   $5 \times \frac{4}{9}$

9   $3 \times \frac{5}{6}$

10   $4 \times \frac{3}{7}$

11   $2 \times 1\frac{2}{3}$

12   $2 \times 2\frac{5}{7}$

13   $3 \times 2\frac{3}{4}$

14   $2 \times 1\frac{4}{5}$

15   $3 \times 2\frac{2}{5}$

16   $4 \times 2\frac{5}{6}$

17   $3 \times 1\frac{4}{9}$

18   $5 \times 3\frac{7}{10}$

19   $4 \times 2\frac{7}{12}$

20   $2 \times 3\frac{5}{8}$

Multiplying with fractions

This rectangle is $\frac{1}{4}$ m wide and $\frac{1}{2}$ m long.

$\frac{1}{4}$m

$\frac{1}{2}$m

Now look at it as part of a square metre.

$\frac{1}{4}$

$\frac{1}{4}$

$\frac{1}{4}$

$\frac{1}{4}$

$\frac{1}{2}$ $\frac{1}{2}$

You can see that the rectangle is $\frac{1}{8}$ of the whole square.

$$\frac{1}{2} \times \frac{1}{4} = \frac{1}{8}$$

This is like working out half of a quarter.

Now consider $\frac{2}{5} \times \frac{3}{4}$ This is like working out $\frac{2}{5}$ of $\frac{3}{4}$

To find $\frac{1}{5}$ of $\frac{3}{4}$ you would divide by 5 and that will be $\frac{3}{20}$

To find $\frac{2}{5}$ of $\frac{3}{4}$ you would multiply $\frac{3}{20}$ by 2 to find the answer of $\frac{6}{20} = \frac{3}{10}$

It is much simpler to do this all in one calculation.

To keep the calculation really simple, divide by any common factors first.

Examples

(i) Multiply: $\frac{2}{5} \times \frac{3}{4}$

$\frac{2}{5} \times \frac{3}{4} = \frac{\overset{1}{\cancel{2}}}{5} \times \frac{3}{\underset{2}{\cancel{4}}}$ Cancel by dividing by a common factor: 2

$= \frac{1 \times 3}{5 \times 2}$ Multiply the numerator and the denominator.

$= \frac{3}{10}$

(ii) Multiply: $1\frac{5}{9} \times \frac{3}{10}$

If you have a mixed number, turn it into an improper fraction first.

$1\frac{5}{9} \times \frac{3}{10} = \frac{\overset{7}{\cancel{14}}}{\underset{3}{\cancel{9}}} \times \frac{\overset{1}{\cancel{3}}}{\underset{5}{\cancel{10}}}$ Cancel by dividing by common factors: 2 and 3

$= \frac{7 \times 1}{3 \times 5}$ Multiply the numerator and the denominator.

$= \frac{7}{15}$

Exercise 7.12

Complete these calculations. Make sure your fractions are in their lowest terms.

1 $\frac{1}{3} \times \frac{1}{5}$

2 $\frac{1}{2} \times \frac{1}{3}$

3 $\frac{1}{5} \times \frac{1}{4}$

4 $\frac{1}{2} \times \frac{4}{5}$

5 $\frac{1}{2} \times \frac{6}{7}$

6 $\frac{3}{4} \times \frac{1}{9}$

7 $\frac{4}{5} \times \frac{1}{4}$

8 $\frac{3}{5} \times \frac{2}{3}$

9 $\frac{3}{4} \times \frac{4}{7}$

10 $\frac{5}{6} \times \frac{2}{5}$

11 $1\frac{5}{9} \times \frac{5}{8}$

16 $\frac{4}{5} \times 3\frac{1}{3}$

12 $1\frac{2}{3} \times \frac{5}{12}$

17 $2\frac{2}{5} \times \frac{5}{6}$

13 $1\frac{1}{3} \times \frac{3}{4}$

18 $\frac{3}{4} \times 1\frac{1}{9}$

14 $1\frac{4}{5} \times \frac{1}{3}$

19 $2\frac{4}{7} \times \frac{7}{9}$

15 $2\frac{1}{3} \times \frac{3}{7}$

20 $\frac{5}{6} \times 1\frac{5}{7}$

Dividing a fraction by a whole number

Suppose you had pizza last night for supper. This morning, there is $\frac{3}{4}$ of a pizza left, and there are two of you who have had no breakfast.

How much of the pizza will there be, for each of you?

You need to divide the pizza into two equal shares.

Mathematically:

$$\frac{3}{4} \div 2 = ?$$

To put it another way, each of you can have half of the remaining pizza.

Mathematically:

$$\frac{3}{4} \times \frac{1}{2} = ?$$

You know how to multiply fractions, so now you can work it out and each enjoy $\frac{3}{4} \times \frac{1}{2} = \frac{3}{8}$ of a pizza.

Now look at it mathematically.

Consider the division $\frac{1}{5} \div 2$

This can be shown as a diagram.

The fifth has been divided in two. Each part is one tenth of a full circle.

$$\frac{1}{5} \div 2 = \frac{1}{10}$$

This is exactly the same as $\frac{1}{5} \times \frac{1}{2} = \frac{1}{10}$ as division is the inverse of multiplication.

Similarly, for the division $\frac{3}{4} \div 5$, you can see that each quarter will be further divided into 5 parts so each part will be a twentieth.

$$\frac{3}{4} \div 5 = \frac{3}{20}$$

and this is the same as $\frac{3}{4} \times \frac{1}{5} = \frac{3}{20}$

Dividing a fraction by a fraction

Think again about pizzas. You have three pizzas in the freezer, and you know that your friends could each eat a quarter of a pizza. So how many of you could snack on three pizzas? The question is: 'How many quarter pizzas are there in 3 whole pizzas?'

Now look at it mathematically.

Consider the division $3 \div \frac{1}{4}$

You can see that in three whole pizzas there are 12 quarters.

So $3 \div \frac{1}{4} = 12$

When you divide a whole number by a fraction that is less than 1, the answer is larger than the original number.

You know that division is the inverse of multiplication.

So, since $12 \div 4 = 3$, then $12 \times \frac{1}{4} = 3$

For the same reason, $12 \div \frac{1}{4}$ is the same as $12 \times \frac{4}{1}$ or 12×4

The result of dividing 1 by a number is the **reciprocal** of the number.

When you find the reciprocal of a fraction, it looks as if you turn it upside down. You will learn more about why this happens in later studies.

The reciprocal of $\frac{1}{4}$ is $\frac{4}{1}$ or 4 and the reciprocal of 4 is $\frac{1}{4}$

The reciprocal of $\frac{3}{5}$ is $\frac{5}{3}$ and the reciprocal of $\frac{5}{3}$ is $\frac{3}{5}$

To divide by a fraction, multiply by its reciprocal.

This means that to divide by a fraction, you turn it upside down and multiply by the result.

Examples

(i) Divide: $4 \div \frac{1}{3}$

$$4 \div \frac{1}{3} = 4 \times \frac{3}{1}$$ Turn ÷ into × and multiply by the reciprocal.

$$= \frac{4 \times 3}{1}$$ Multiply.

$$= 12$$ This is a whole number.

(ii) Divide: $\frac{14}{15} \div \frac{2}{5}$

$$\frac{14}{15} \div \frac{2}{5} = \frac{14}{15} \times \frac{5}{2}$$ Turn ÷ into × and multiply by the reciprocal.

$$= \frac{7}{3}\frac{14}{15} \times \frac{5^1}{2_1}$$ Divide by common factors 2 and 5

$$= \frac{7}{3}$$ Multiply.

$$= 2\frac{1}{3}$$ This is a mixed number.

Exercise 7.13

Complete these divisions. Make sure your fractions are in their lowest terms.

1   $1 \div \frac{1}{4}$

2   $3 \div \frac{1}{5}$

3   $4 \div \frac{1}{3}$

4   $5 \div \frac{1}{5}$

5   $2 \div \frac{1}{9}$

6   $\frac{1}{3} \div \frac{1}{9}$

7   $\frac{1}{7} \div \frac{1}{14}$

8   $\frac{1}{9} \div \frac{1}{6}$

9   $4 \div \frac{1}{6}$

10   $6 \div \frac{1}{4}$

11   $\frac{3}{4} \div \frac{1}{8}$

12   $\frac{11}{15} \div \frac{3}{5}$

13   $\frac{3}{5} \div \frac{3}{8}$

14   $\frac{8}{9} \div \frac{2}{3}$

15   $\frac{3}{10} \div \frac{2}{5}$

16   $\frac{4}{7} \div \frac{3}{14}$

17   $\frac{11}{14} \div \frac{2}{7}$

18   $\frac{11}{24} \div \frac{3}{8}$

19   $\frac{15}{16} \div \frac{5}{8}$

20   $\frac{9}{10} \div \frac{3}{5}$

Write out the fraction calculation, then answer the question.

1 (a) I buy a packet of sweets. One third of them were stuck together; what fraction of the sweets in the packet was not stuck together?

(b) There are 24 sweets in a packet. How many of them were stuck together?

2 I leave home and walk for two-thirds of a mile. Then I realise that I am going to be late for school so I run the remaining tenth of a mile. How far is it from home to school?

3 I am twelve and a half and my little sister is seven and three-quarters. What is the difference between our ages?

4 I am eleven and three-quarters now. How old will I be in two and a half years' time?

5 My father buys a sack of seed potatoes but when he gets them home, he finds that one-tenth of them are rotten and two-fifths have already started sprouting so cannot be eaten. What fraction of the potatoes can he eat? (As you know, rotten potatoes do not sprout.)

6 The length of string wound into a ball is 4 metres. How many lengths of $\frac{2}{5}$ metre can I cut from the ball?

7 Nine children each ate $\frac{3}{8}$ of a pizza. How many whole pizzas were ordered?

8 In a class of children, one-quarter has only one pet and two-thirds have two pets. If no one has more than two pets, what fraction of the class has no pets at all?

9 In a school day we have 5 lessons of $\frac{3}{4}$ hour and three lessons of $1\frac{1}{3}$ hours. How many hours do I spend in lessons in a day?

10 I have a bottle that contains $1\frac{3}{4}$ litres of lemonade and I pour it out into cups so we each get $\frac{7}{16}$ litre. How many of us are there?

11 It is 5 miles from my house to my friend's house. I travel one half of the way by road and one-fifth by cycle track. The last part is across a field. What is the length of the journey across the field?

12 (a) My maths teacher is dividing my class into groups. She makes two groups, each with a quarter of the class, and three groups each with one-sixth of the class. How many are there in the class?

(b) My English teacher wants to divide our class into one-half, one-third and one-ninth but the division will not go exactly. He borrows a boy from the class next door, does the division (which works out exactly, with a whole number of us in each group) and then sends him back. How many are there in the class?

Extension Exercise 7.15

You can find number patterns and series in fractions too.

1 (a) Copy and complete this pattern.

$$\frac{1}{2} = \frac{1}{2}$$

$$\frac{1}{2} + \frac{2}{3} =$$

$$\frac{1}{2} + \frac{2}{3} + \frac{3}{4} =$$

Add the next three lines to the pattern and calculate the answers.

(b) Try the same series but with × instead of +

$$\frac{1}{2} \times \frac{2}{3} =$$

$$\frac{1}{2} \times \frac{2}{3} \times \frac{3}{4} =$$

2 (a) Add the next two lines to this pattern and calculate the answers.

$$\frac{1}{3} =$$

$$\frac{1}{3} + \frac{3}{5} =$$

$$\frac{1}{3} + \frac{3}{5} + \frac{5}{7} =$$

(b) Try the same series but with × instead of +

$$\frac{1}{3} \times \frac{3}{5} =$$

$$\frac{1}{3} \times \frac{3}{5} \times \frac{5}{7} =$$

3 Look at this series. Write the three next lines and calculate:

$$\frac{1}{2} =$$

$$\frac{1}{2} + \frac{1}{4} =$$

$$\frac{1}{2} + \frac{1}{4} + \frac{1}{8} =$$

If you continue the series, will the sum ever be equal to one?

Is there a point when the answer is so close to one that you can assume that it is equal to one? (For discussion.)

4 Study the series below. If you continue the series, will you ever get the answer $\frac{2}{10}$ or $\frac{1}{5}$?

$$\frac{1}{10} =$$

$$\frac{1}{10} + \frac{1}{100} =$$

$$\frac{1}{10} + \frac{1}{100} + \frac{1}{1000} =$$

Summary Exercise 7.16

1 What fraction of a metre is 25 cm?

2 Find $\frac{2}{3}$ of 36

3 Write these fractions in their lowest terms.

(a) $\frac{12}{26}$ (b) $\frac{35}{50}$ (c) $\frac{100}{75}$ (d) $\frac{125}{100}$

4 Fill in the missing numbers, so that these fractions are equivalent.

$$\frac{3}{4} = \frac{9}{\Box} = \frac{\Box}{24} = \frac{24}{\Box} = \frac{\Box}{120}$$

5 Which of these is the larger?

$\frac{7}{9}$ or $\frac{5}{7}$

6 Calculate the answers to these,

(a) $\frac{3}{5} + \frac{1}{4}$ (b) $\frac{3}{4} + \frac{2}{3}$ (c) $3\frac{5}{9} + 2\frac{7}{9}$ (d) $1\frac{3}{4} + \frac{7}{10}$

7 Calculate the answers to these.

(a) $\frac{3}{7} - \frac{1}{4}$ (b) $\frac{7}{8} - \frac{5}{6}$ (c) $1\frac{1}{6} - \frac{4}{5}$ (d) $2\frac{1}{4} - \frac{7}{10}$

8 Calculate the answers to these.

(a) $\frac{1}{3} \times \frac{3}{4}$ (b) $2 \times 3\frac{3}{4}$ (c) $1\frac{1}{3} \times \frac{2}{5}$ (d) $\frac{1}{3} \times 1\frac{7}{8}$

9 Calculate the answers to these.

(a) $5 \div \frac{1}{3}$ (b) $\frac{7}{8} \div \frac{1}{4}$ (c) $\frac{14}{15} \div \frac{2}{5}$ (d) $1\frac{3}{5} \div \frac{4}{15}$

10 Half of my class has brown hair, one-third has blonde hair, one-sixth has black hair and the rest have ginger hair. What fraction of the class has ginger hair?

11 Four bars of chocolate are divided equally among 18 children. What fraction of a bar does each receive? If there are 18 squares of chocolate in each bar, how many squares do they each receive?

12 A snail is at the bottom of a bucket with sides that are 40 cm high. The snail climbs at the rate of 10 cm every 50 minutes. After every 50 minute climb the snail rests for 10 minutes. During its rest the snail slips down one-tenth of the total distance that he has climbed from the bottom of the bucket. How long will it take him to climb out of the bucket?

Activity: The Fibonacci sequence

The series of numbers you generated at the end of Chapter 5 was:

1, 1, 2, 3, 5, 8, 13, 21, 34, 55, ...

Each new term is made by adding the two preceding numbers, so 8 + 5 = 13 and 8 + 13 = 21

This is called the **Fibonacci sequence** after Leonardo Fibonacci (1175–1250), also known as Leonardo of Pisa, who was the first mathematician to have written about it. He was also one of the first to adopt the Arabic numerals, which he learnt about from a Muslim teacher.

Fibonacci enjoyed playing with numbers. Here is one of his puzzles.

Arrange all the odd numbers in a triangular pattern and then add up each row. What do you notice?

$$1$$
$$3 \qquad 5$$
$$7 \qquad 9 \qquad 11$$
$$13 \qquad 15 \qquad 17 \qquad 19\,...$$

$$1 = 1 = 1 \times 1 \times 1$$
$$3 + 5 = 8 = 2 \times 2 \times 2$$
$$7 + 9 + 11 = 27 = 3 \times 3 \times 3$$
$$...$$

Continue the pattern for another six rows.

8 Calculating with and without a calculator

Using a calculator

Using a calculator can save you time, and help you with your working, as long as you know how to use it correctly.

Your calculator will only give the correct answer if you enter the correct calculation.

What type of calculator do you have?

A non-scientific calculator has the four functions +, −, × and ÷ and perhaps a square root key.

If you have this sort of calculator, you can use it for the exercises in this book.

A scientific calculator has a very large number of functions.

You will need a scientific calculator for your study of mathematics.

Try this sequence of keys.

If you get the answer 18, you have a non-scientific calculator. It worked through the calculation in the sequence that you keyed it in.

$$5 + 4 = 9$$
$$9 \times 2 = 18$$

If you get the answer 13, you have a scientific calculator.

A scientific calculator, as its name implies, is used by scientists and mathematicians. If there is a mixture of the operations +, −, ×, ÷, then it is correct practice to do any multiplication and division before addition or subtraction.

For the sequence of keys above the scientific calculator will work out:

$$4 \times 2 = 8$$
$$5 + 8 = 13$$

Using brackets

If you have a scientific calculator, and you are entering a calculation in which you need to add before multiplying, you must put in brackets.

$(5 + 4) \times 2 = 18$

If there are brackets in a calculation, you do the calculation in the brackets first, and so will your calculator.

Order of operations

BIDMAS is a **mnemonic** to help you remember this order of operations.

Brackets

Index numbers

Divide

Multiply

Add

Subtract

Examples

(i) Work out $(4 + 3) \times 7$

$(4 + 3) \times 7 = 7 \times 7$

$= 49$

(ii) Work out $4 + 3 \times 7$

$4 + 3 \times 7 = 4 + 21$

$= 25$

(iii) Work out $5^2 + 3$

$5^2 + 3 = 25 + 3$

$= 28$

Exercise 8.1

Complete these calculations. Remember to follow the BIDMAS rule. Look at how the calculations in the examples are set out, with the = signs in a column. Write your answers in the same way.

1 $3 \times 2 + 7$

2 $3 + 2 \times 7$

3 $3 \times (2 + 7)$

4 $9 + 6 \div 3$

5 $(9 + 6) \div 3$

6 $2 + 5 \times 6$

7 $(2 + 5) \times 6$

8 $2 + (5 \times 6)$

9 $(3 \times 2) + 7$

10 $(8 \div 4) - 2$

11 $\frac{1}{5}$ of 25

12 $\frac{1}{4}$ of 12

13 $\frac{1}{4}$ of $(16 + 4)$

14 $\frac{1}{4}$ of $16 + 4$

15 $28 \div 4 - 2$

16 $28 \div (4 - 2)$

17 $28 \div 4 - 35 \div 7$

18 $72 - 12 \div 6 - 4$

19 $(72 - 12) \div (6 - 4)$

20 $(24 \div 4 \times 3) - (24 \div (4 \times 3))$

Now use your calculator to check your answers.

Index numbers and the calculator

If you have a non-scientific calculator you will have to work out powers of numbers by repeated multiplication.

$$2^7 = 2 \times 2 \times 2 \times 2 \times 2 \times 2 \times 2$$

If you have a scientific calculator you can use the index number key:

x^y or $x^\square$

You would enter **2** **7** to get the answer 128

Exercise 8.2

Calculate the value of each expression:

(a) without a calculator

(b) with a calculator. If you did not get the same answer both times check the explanation above and try again. You may need to check your calculator manual.

1 3^4

2 4^3

3 $2^3 + 3^2$

4 $3^3 \div (5 - 2)$

5 $2^3 \div 4 - 2$

6 $(4 - 2)^2$

7 $2^3 \div (4 - 2)$

8 $(3^2 - 2^3)^2$

9 $4^2 + 3 \times 5$

10 $(6^2 \div 3^2)^2$

Exercise 8.3

For these problems you must write a suitable calculation, and then find the correct answer.

Example

A man was going to St Ives with seven wives.

Each wife had seven cats. How many were going to St Ives?

Number going $= (7 \times 7) + 7 + 1$ (7 lots of 7 cats + 7 wives + 1 man)

$= 49 + 7 + 1$

$= 57$

> Note that the calculation has been written in this order to follow the BIDMAS rule.

1 A man has four dogs. How many legs do the man and his dogs have altogether?

2 My grandmother has eight children, four sons and four daughters. Each son married and had two children. Each daughter married and had three children. How many were there in the family?

3 I have four discs of computer games. Three discs have four games on and one has seven. How many games do I have?

4 I have nine toffees. I eat five of them and then share the rest between my two best friends. How many does each friend get?

5 I am given £5 for Christmas, my brother is given £4 and my sister is given £3. My father says we must add the money together and then split the total equally. How much do we each get now?

6 My three friends and I had saved up a total of £15 between us. We each put in another £3. How much do we now have?

7 I am 11, my mother is three times as old as I am and my grandmother is twice as old as my mother. If my uncle is half as old as the sum of all our ages, how old is my uncle?

8 There are five days left until my birthday and I have to spend eight hours a day asleep. How many hours will I be awake before I wake up on my birthday?

Estimating

It is often useful to work out an **estimate** or approximate answer before trying to do an exact calculation to solve a problem. This gives you an idea of the size of answer you are expecting. Always be careful, though, when rounding, that you do not round to such a degree that you lose accuracy.

When you are approximating or estimating you can use the symbol ≈, which means **is approximately equal to**.

> ### Examples
>
> (i) I need £19 per week for travel and to pay for my music lesson. The term is 11 weeks long. How much money will I need?
>
> I am going to need £19 × 11. This is roughly 20 × 10 or £200
>
> Note that one number was rounded up a little and the other down a little, so it was a fair approximation.
>
> (ii) Find an estimate for 33 × 42
>
> 33 × 42 ≈ 30 × 40
>
> 30 × 40 = 1200
>
> In this case, both numbers are rounded down, so the estimate is too low. The actual answer is 1386

Exercise 8.4

Estimate an answer for each calculation. Say whether you think your estimate is fair, too high or too low.

1	32 × 59	6	310 × 49
2	29 × 99	7	612 × 72
3	102 × 52	8	590 × 620
4	7 × 503	9	4012 × 62
5	52 × 38	10	4200 × 3800

Now use your calculator to check all your answers, to see how accurate you were.

Think about division: does the same rule apply?

$$42 \div 38 \approx 40 \div 40$$
$$40 \div 40 = 1$$

Is this a fair approximation, as one number has been rounded up and the other has been rounded down?

Exercise 8.5

Estimate an answer for each calculation. Say whether you think your estimate is fair, too high or too low.

1 $123 \div 59$

2 $99 \div 19$

3 $315 \div 46$

4 $732 \div 23$

5 $786 \div 42$

6 $310 \div 49$

7 $612 \div 58$

8 $590 \div 610$

9 $4012 \div 789$

10 $4200 \div 3800$

Now use your calculator to check all your answers, to see how accurate you were.

Give your answers correct to 2 decimal places.

11 Try to write a rule for estimating with division.

Rules to follow when using a calculator

If you use a calculator incorrectly it can give you the wrong answer. This is almost certainly not because the calculator is faulty, but because you have entered the calculation incorrectly.

Follow these simple rules when using a calculator, to avoid mistakes.

1 Estimate the answer first.

2 Write down the calculation you are going to do before you press any buttons.

3 Do the calculation twice and make sure you get the same answer both times.

4 Check your answer. Does it look sensible?

Example

Max has 48p. Minnie has four times as much and I have half as much as Max. How much do we have altogether?

Estimate: $50 + (4 \times 50) + 25 = 275$

Max's money (rounded up) + Minnie's (4 times as much as Max's) + my money (half as much as Max's)

Now, following the BIDMAS rule, arrange the calculation correctly.

Total amount $= (48 \div 2) + (48 \times 4) + 48$

                $= 24 + 192 + 48$

                $= 264$

Note it is important when writing the answer to use the correct 'units'.

So altogether we have £2.64

Exercise 8.6

Follow the rules listed above as you complete this exercise.

1 Adam picked 56 apples, Belinda picked five times as many and I picked half as many as Adam. How many apples did we pick altogether?

2 456 people visit the village fête. One quarter of them each buy a cup of tea, which costs 57p and one third of them buy a slice of cake, which costs 72p. How much did the tea and cake stall make?

3 Which calculation gives the greater answer and by how much?

   (a) Add 15 squared to 16 squared

   (b) Add 15 and 16 and then square the answer

4 I buy 16 Sherbet Fountains at 23p each and 12 Jupiter Bars at 32p each. How much change do I have from a £20 note?

5 The whole school of 235 pupils went on a trip to a museum. One-fifth were picked up from the museum, and a quarter of the rest went home by themselves. The remainder were collected from school. How many were collected from school?

6 We have to drive for 5 hours. My sister says she is going to count every second. How many seconds will she have to count?

7 On our car journey we are playing 'Pub Cricket'. You score one run for each leg you can see on the pub sign. My brother sees *The King and Queen* so he scores four, since the King has two legs and so does the Queen. I see *The Coach and Horses*. This sign shows six horses, two coachmen, a guard and eight passengers. How many runs do I score?

8 It is 472 m from my house to Amy's house, and twice as far from Amy's to Bertie's. From Bertie's to Charlie's is half as far as the other two distances added together. If I walk from my house to Charlie's, picking up Amy and Bertie on the way, how far do I have to walk?

9 On my computer game you score 40 points for shooting a blue alien, 25 for a red one and 10 for the little yellow ones. If a green meanie gets you, then you lose 120 points. I shot 15 yellow, 7 red and 4 blue aliens before the green meanie got me. What was my score?

10 There were 29 748 supporters at this week's home game. One-sixth of them had club scarves, one-quarter of them had team shirts and one-half of them wore trainers. How many scarves, team shirts and trainers were there?

You have been learning about numbers and how to multiply and divide them. You have also learnt some rules to help you get the correct answers to questions. You know that it is important always to check your answers. In the next exercise, you have the opportunity to check other people's answers.

Exercise 8.7

Here are some calculations that have gone wrong. Can you find out why?

Rewrite either the question (on the left) or the answer (on the right) so that each statement is correct.

For the first five problems, rewrite the question on the left to make the answer on the right correct.

1   $13 - 2 \times 5 = 55$

2   $13 \times 16 = 2093$

3   $(3 + 5) \times (2 + 3) = 3 + 10 + 3$

   $\qquad\qquad\qquad = 16$

4   $2 + 5 \times 6 - 4 \div 2 = 36$

5   $30\,000 \div 60 = 5000$

For the next five problems, write the correct answer on the left and say where the original calculation went wrong.

6   $20\,000 = 2 \times 104$ (do not change any digits)

7   $50 \times 20 = 100$

8   MCMXIV is 1995

9   $52 \times 48 \approx 2000$

10   $122 \div 28 \approx 60$

In these problems, the calculation that has been done is wrong. Work out what the wrong calculation was and then write the correct one.

11   If it takes 5 minutes to boil one egg, it will take 60 minutes to boil 12 eggs.

12   If one bus takes 46 passengers, it will take 4232 buses to take 92 passengers.

13   In ten years there are 3650 days.

14   It takes 5 men 20 days to build a house and so it takes one man 4 days.

15   I have $2\frac{1}{2}$ litres of milk and I need to fill as many beakers as I can with $\frac{1}{5}$ litre.

   I can fill $\frac{1}{2}$ a beaker.

These questions are like those in Exercise 8.3 but you may need to go through more stages of working to find the answers. It is very important that you remember the BIDMAS rule and the rules you should follow when using a calculator. Write down every calculation that you make. Remember to check your answer to see if it makes sense.

1 Peter Piper picked a peck of pickled peppers. A peck is 2 gallons and there are 8 pints in a gallon. James picked four times as many peppers as Peter and I picked twice as many as Peter and James together. How many pints of pickled peppers did we have altogether?

2 Jack and Jill walk 750 metres up the hill. After Jack breaks his crown, Jill runs down the hill and then runs another 650 metres to the house to collect vinegar and brown paper. She then runs all the way back up the hill to find Jack, before taking him home again. How far has Jill travelled altogether, since meeting Jack at the bottom of the hill?

3 The Grand Old Duke of York had ten thousand men. He marched them up to the top of the hill, where a quarter of them decided to stay. He marched the rest down again. One-third of the remainder refused to go on, but he marched the rest up another hill, and this time only half came down with him. How many men did he have with him at the end of the march?

4 Humpty Dumpty sat on a wall that was 120 cm tall and 3 m wide. The bricks in the wall were 5 cm tall and 15 cm wide. How many bricks were there in the wall?

5 Mary Mary Quite Contrary had an interesting garden. There were three rows of silver bells with 15 bells in a row, five rows of cockle shells with 45 shells in a row and finally four rows of pretty maids with 5 maids in a row. How many bells, shells and maids were there in Mary's garden?

6 The Knave of Hearts offered the King of Hearts a choice of two interesting deals. On the first deal the King would be paid £1 this year, £2 next year, £3 the following year, and so on, going up each year by £1. On the second deal he would be paid 1p this year, 2p next year, 4p the following year and so on, doubling each year.

(a) Which deal will pay more at the end of five years?

(b) Which deal will pay more at the end of ten years?

(c) Which deal will pay more at the end of fifteen years?

7 The King was in the counting house, counting out his money. He had saved 150 guineas, and had then won another 40 from the Knave of Hearts.

(a) A guinea is worth 21 shillings. How much did he have in shillings?

(b) Unfortunately, he owed the cook four florins for each of four and twenty blackbirds, plus 16 florins for all the queen's honey. A florin is worth two shillings. The king also owed the maid 45 guineas in compensation for having lost her nose. How many shillings did he have left?

Summary Exercise 8.9

1 Write down the answer to each calculation. Use your calculator to check your answers.

(a) $(3 + 5) \times 4$

(d) $12 \div 4 + 2$

(b) $3 + 5 \times 4$

(e) $24 \div (8 - 2)$

(c) $12 \div (4 + 2)$

(f) $24 \div 8 - 2$

Now use a calculator to solve these problems. Remember the rules.

2 The cartridge for my printer will print 1000 A4 pages. I print 3 dozen pages per day. How many days will my printer cartridge last?

3 How many seconds are there in a week?

4 A long-distance lorry driver drives 450 miles every day. If he drives 24 days in total each month, how many miles does he drive in a year?

5 This half-term 35 children are going to France for a week. The cost of transporting them all is £520. Two excursions are planned: one costs a total of £215 and the other £340. Work out the total cost of the trip and then calculate how much the school will need to charge each child.

6 In a charity fund-raising event, we are sponsored £4.00 to clean a window, £4.50 to clean a pair of shoes and £7.50 to clean a teacher's car. In the week my class cleaned 56 windows, 35 pairs of shoes and 12 teachers' cars. How much money did we raise?

7 Jack was going to the fair to sell his mother's cow. He was given £70 for the cow but spent half the money on four beans, half the rest on a cask of ale and half the remainder on lunch. Luckily, one bean grew a tall enough beanstalk for him to climb up and collect 5 golden eggs, and he sold each for £7.99. How much money did he bring home to his mother?

Activity: Think of a number

1 **An amazing puzzle**

(a) Pick a number from 1 to 10 (including 1 or 10)

(b) Multiply your number by 9

(c) Add the digits of the number you created in step (b)

(d) Subtract 5 from the number created in step (c)

(e) Find the letter in the alphabet that corresponds to the number created in step (d), for example, 1 = A, 2 = B, 3 = C,...

(f) Pick a country in Europe that starts with the letter you found in step (e)

(g) Choose an animal that starts with the last letter of your country.

(h) Choose a colour that starts with the last letter of your animal.

(i) Let me guess what you chose.

An orange kangaroo in Denmark?

The chances are that you did! Try some different starting numbers and see if you get the same result. Try it on a friend and see if they get the same. Try to work out why it works.

2 A number trick

This is a really good trick to play on people who will not tell you their age. They may need a calculator.

(a) Ask them to pick a number from 1 to 9 (including 1 or 9)

(b) Then ask them to multiply that number by 2

(c) Next add 40 to the number they created in step (b)

(d) Multiply the number created in step (c) by 50

(e) If they've had their birthday already this year, get them to add the last two digits of this year (that would be 15 for 2015, for example) to the number created in step (d). If they haven't had their birthday yet this year, get them to do the same thing but then take away one.

(f) Then ask them to subtract the year they were born (for example, 1993) from the number created in step (e) and tell you the answer.

(g) Then amaze them by telling them that the first digit of their final number is the number they started with ... and the remaining number is their age!

Why does this work? Can you work it out?

3 Write a number puzzle of your own and try it out on your friends!

9 Decimals

In Chapter 1 you reviewed the difference between the Roman symbol-based system and the Arabian system, which is based on number place. Wherever he was in the world, primitive man started off counting on his ten fingers. It is interesting to see how different counting systems developed in different areas, and what different parts of the mathematical jigsaw are still in common use today.

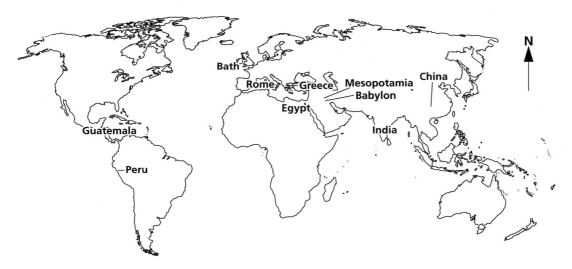

The Romans were by no means the only people to use symbols to represent numbers. The Greeks, the Egyptians and the Mesopotamians were others. The numerical system based on the numerals 0, 1, 2, 3, ..., 9, was developed in India and the Arabs based their system on it. The Incas in Peru also used a decimal system, as did the Maya in Guatemala and Mexico (although theirs was based on 20, not 10). The Babylonians based their system on 60

The Maya have had less influence on European history and literature than the Greeks and the Romans, yet they were responsible for two great achievements in mathematics. One was the calendar and the other was the symbol 0 (nought or zero). Without the symbol 0 it is impossible to show that there is a number missing in one of the columns when writing down a number, and thus the arithmetic that you do by writing numbers in columns becomes a hugely difficult task when counting forwards and backwards. It was almost impossible to do without an abacus.

It is not quite clear when the introduction of decimal places began. The Romans and Greeks used complex fractions. The Hindus used fractions but also used up to six places of decimals, with a space after the units. The decimal point itself was first introduced by Pelazzi of Nice in 1492 (but this was also frequently written as a comma and still is in continental Europe).

⃝ Decimals and place value

In Chapter 1 you considered the equivalence of fractions and decimal fractions (decimals) on the number line.

Converting decimals to fractions and fractions to decimals

The value of a digit is given by its place in the number. The decimal point separates the whole numbers from the fraction.

Hundreds   Tens   Units   ·   tenths   hundredths   thousandths

In your exercise book, you can write decimal numbers in columns, like this.

	Th	H	T	U	.	t	h	th
Nine tenths				0	.	9		
Four hundredths				0	.	0	4	
Two thousandths				0	.	0	0	2
Twenty-five thousandths				0	.	0	2	5
One thousand and five	1	0	0	5				
Four and 3 hundredths				4	.	0	3	
Five hundred and four and 7 thousandths		5	0	4	.	0	0	7

Decimals to fractions

When you convert decimals to fractions, first write the decimal as tenths, hundredths, thousandths and then cancel it by common factors until it is in its lowest terms.

Examples

(i) Write 0.8 as a fraction.

$$0.8 = \frac{8}{10} = \frac{4}{5}$$ 8 and 10 have a common factor, 2

(ii) Write 0.12 as a fraction.

$$0.12 = \frac{12}{100} = \frac{3}{25}$$ 12 and 100 have a common factor, 4

(iii) Write 1.025 as a mixed number.

$$1.025 = 1\frac{25}{1000} = 1\frac{1}{40}$$ 25 and 1000 have a common factor, 25

Exercise 9.1

Write these decimals as fractions or mixed numbers. Remember to simplify your answers to their lowest terms.

1	0.4	6	0.15
2	0.8	7	0.9
3	0.5	8	0.06
4	0.04	9	0.104
5	0.13	10	0.92

11	3.19	16	3.504
12	3.025	17	2.07
13	1.05	18	21.005
14	2.95	19	4.08
15	0.32	20	6.56

Fractions to decimals

There are various ways to convert fractions to decimals.

If the denominator is a factor of 10, 100 or 1000, write the equivalent fraction and then convert to a decimal.

Examples

(i) Write $\frac{2}{5}$ as a decimal.

$$\frac{2}{5} = \frac{4}{10}$$
$$= 0.4$$

(ii) Write $\frac{7}{25}$ as a decimal.

$$\frac{7}{25} = \frac{28}{100}$$
$$= 0.28$$

As a fraction is a way of writing a division, you can divide the numerator by the denominator.

Example

Write $\frac{3}{8}$ as a decimal.

$\frac{3}{8} = 3 \div 8$

$= 0.375$

Exercise 9.2

Write each of these fractions as a decimal.

1 $\frac{7}{10}$

2 $\frac{29}{100}$

3 $\frac{117}{1000}$

4 $\frac{1}{8}$

5 $\frac{9}{10}$

6 $\frac{3}{5}$

7 $\frac{1}{2}$

8 $\frac{7}{20}$

9 $\frac{3}{40}$

10 $\frac{99}{1000}$

11 $\frac{7}{8}$

12 $\frac{27}{50}$

13 $\frac{3}{4}$

14 $\frac{7}{40}$

15 $\frac{9}{25}$

16 $\frac{7}{200}$

17 $\frac{127}{500}$

18 $\frac{103}{250}$

19 $\frac{9}{50}$

20 $\frac{1}{125}$

Fraction families

The final way to convert fractions to decimals is to learn the common decimal and fraction equivalents. You can think of them as families.

Exercise 9.3

You could use your calculator to do the division calculations. Remember, when you use a calculator, you must write down the calculation that you are doing. This is a requirement in all examinations and so it is a good idea to get into the habit now.

Write each of these fractions as a decimal.

1 (a) $\frac{1}{4}$ (b) $\frac{1}{2}$ (c) $\frac{3}{4}$ (d) $\frac{4}{4}$

2 (a) $\frac{1}{8}$ (b) $\frac{3}{8}$ (c) $\frac{5}{8}$ (d) $\frac{7}{8}$

3 (a) $\frac{1}{5}$ (b) $\frac{2}{5}$ (c) $\frac{3}{5}$ (d) $\frac{4}{5}$

4 (a) $\frac{1}{10}$ (b) $\frac{3}{10}$ (c) $\frac{5}{10}$ (d) $\frac{7}{10}$

5 (a) $\frac{1}{16}$ (b) $\frac{3}{16}$ (c) $\frac{5}{16}$ (d) $\frac{7}{16}$

You should see that each fraction family has a related decimal family.

Make sure you learn the families really well. For example, once you know that:

$$\frac{1}{8} = 0.125$$

then you can work out $\frac{3}{8}$, $\frac{5}{8}$ and $\frac{7}{8}$

Recurring decimals

All of the fractions in the families above can be converted to decimals with fixed numbers of decimal places. There are called **terminating decimals.**

Sometimes you will find that a fraction does not convert to a terminating decimal.

Exercise 9.4

1 Use your calculator to investigate these families of fractions as decimals.

(a) thirds

(d) elevenths

(b) sixths

(e) sevenths

(c) ninths

2 (a) What can you say about the denominators of those fractions that do not recur?

(b) What can you say about the denominators of those fractions that do recur?

◯ Calculating with decimals

In Chapter 4, you added, subtracted, multiplied and divided decimal fractions (the four operations).

You saw that numbers with decimals behave in the same way as whole numbers, except that you must keep the decimal points lined up correctly.

Exercise 9.5

Here are some mixed questions to remind you of the basics.

1 How much change do I receive from a £10 note when I buy two boxes of biscuits costing £2.95 each?

2 If 4 packets of Brekkiewheat cost £5.12, what is the cost of one packet?

3 (a) I have £5 to buy a lettuce at 95p, 1 kg of tomatoes at £1.75 per kilogram and a cucumber at 80p. How much change should I have?

   (b) On the way home I buy a packet of crisps. I finally have 95p. How much did the packet of crisps cost?

4 I am saving up to buy a new game for the computer. It costs £29. I have already saved up £15.23. How much more do I need?

5 What is the total cost of two bunches of bananas at £1.72 each and three punnets of nectarines at £2.15 each?

6 I get £7 per week pocket money. Out of this I buy a travel card at £1.75 and every school day I buy a drink on the way home, which costs 35p. How much does that leave me?

7 I had saved up £15 but I broke a window and had to pay £5.25 towards having it mended. How much did I have left?

8 Is it better value to buy six single apples at 19p each or a bag of half a dozen at £1.10?

9 Copy and complete this shopping list.

   ... pencils at 20p each   = £1.20

   .... erasers at 35p each   = £1.75

   3 sharpeners at 65p each   = £ ...

   2 geometry sets at ... each = £3.98

   Total   = £ ...

10 Copy and complete this shopping list.

   2.5 kg of flour at £0.84 per kilogram = £ ...

   1.5 kg of sugar at £ ... per kilogram   = £1.44

   18 eggs at £1.45 per half dozen   = £ ...

   800 g of raisins at ... per 100 g   = £3.36

   Total   = £ ...

◯ Multiplying decimals by a decimal

In all the multiplication and division calculations that you have done so far, you have multiplied and divided by a whole number. What happens when you multiply and divide by a decimal?

Look at this rectangle with sides of lengths 0.3 metres and 0.5 metres.

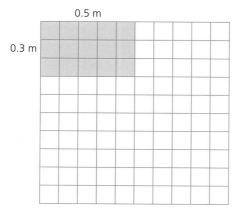

What is its **area**?

The area is $\dfrac{15}{100}$ of a square metre or 0.15 m^2

The calculation is:

$$\text{area} = 0.3 \times 0.5 \text{ m}^2$$
$$= 0.15 \text{ m}^2$$

The answer is interesting because it is smaller than the numbers that were multiplied together. This makes more sense if you think of the problem in terms of fractions.

$$0.3 = \frac{3}{10} \text{ and } 0.5 = \frac{5}{10}$$

$$\frac{3}{10} \times \frac{5}{10} = \frac{3 \times 5}{10 \times 10}$$

$$= \frac{15}{100}$$

$$= 0.15$$

If you multiply a positive number by a number less than one, you get a smaller answer.

● If you multiply tenths by tenths, you get hundredths.

● If you multiply tenths by hundredths, you get thousandths, ...

Another way of thinking about this is to look at the digits after the decimal point. In the example:

$$\text{area} = 0.3\,\text{m} \times 0.5\,\text{m}$$
$$= 0.15\ \text{m}^2$$

There are two digits in total after the decimal points, so you should have two digits after the decimal point in the answer.

> **Examples**
>
> (i) Multiply: 0.25×5
>
> $0.25 \times 5 = 1.25$ There are two digits after the decimal point.
>
> (ii) Multiply: 0.35×0.3
>
> $0.35 \times 0.3 = 0.105$ There are three digits after the decimal point.
>
> (iii) Multiply: 1.5×1.2
>
> $1.5 \times 1.2 = 1.80$ There are two numbers after the decimal point...
>
> $= 1.8$ ...but you do not need the 0 at the end.

Exercise 9.6

Multiply.

1 0.3×0.6

2 0.3×0.06

3 0.03×0.006

4 0.06×3

5 0.7×0.2

6 0.3×5

7 0.1×0.12

8 1.02×0.07

9 0.002×0.4

10 0.12×0.4

11 0.12×0.3

12 0.24×3

13 0.11×5

14 1.2×0.4

15 4.1×0.7

16 10.2×0.5

17 0.2×3.4

18 1.2×0.6

19 1.1×1.2

20 3.2×0.4

21 4.5×2

22 0.5×0.4

23 1.5×6

24 0.3×0.33

25 12.5×0.08

26 4.5×1.2

27 0.36×0.025

28 0.6×0.025

29 0.045×0.2

30 0.4×0.14

◯ Dividing by a decimal

You know that division is the inverse of multiplication.

It therefore follows that as $0.3 \times 0.5 = 0.15$

then $0.15 \div 0.3 = 0.5$

and $0.15 \div 0.5 = 0.3$

However, there is an easier way to look at it.

Write the division as a fraction.

Examples

(i) Divide: $0.15 \div 0.3$

$$0.15 \div 0.3 = \frac{0.15}{0.3}$$

$$= \frac{0.15 \times 10}{0.3 \times 10}$$ Multiply the numerator **and** the denominator by 10 to remove the decimal on the bottom.

$$= \frac{1.5}{3}$$

$$= 0.5$$

$0.15 \div 0.3 = 0.5$ Check: $0.3 \times 0.5 = 0.15$

(ii) Divide: $24 \div 0.008$

$$24 \div 0.008 = \frac{24}{0.008}$$

$$= \frac{24 \times 1000}{0.008 \times 1000}$$ Multiply the numerator and denominator by 1000 to remove the decimal on the bottom.

$$= \frac{24\,000}{8}$$

$$= 3000$$

$24 \div 0.008 = 3000$ Check: $0.008 \times 1000 \times 3 = 24$

Exercise 9.7

Calculate the answers to these divisions. Remember to check your answers.

1 $6 \div 0.3$	6 $40 \div 0.5$
2 $4 \div 0.4$	7 $8 \div 0.05$
3 $5 \div 0.05$	8 $1.6 \div 0.2$
4 $8 \div 0.02$	9 $2.4 \div 0.008$
5 $12 \div 0.3$	10 $3.6 \div 0.009$

11 $0.12 \div 0.3$	16 $0.6 \div 0.5$
12 $0.24 \div 0.3$	17 $0.36 \div 1.2$
13 $0.1 \div 0.5$	18 $0.54 \div 0.6$
14 $1.2 \div 0.4$	19 $1.44 \div 1.2$
15 $0.28 \div 0.7$	20 $0.048 \div 0.4$

If there are any remainders, write them as decimals.

21 $2.81 \div 0.2$	26 $4.56 \div 0.12$
22 $1.75 \div 0.4$	27 $0.738 \div 0.09$
23 $0.147 \div 0.03$	28 $0.48 \div 0.05$
24 $0.306 \div 0.006$	29 $0.045 \div 0.2$
25 $12.65 \div 0.005$	30 $0.14 \div 0.4$

Exercise 9.8

Solve these problems. Write your working clearly and check your answers.

1 What is the area of a square with sides of 0.4 m?

2 What is the area of a rectangle with sides of 0.4 m and 0.6 m?

3 A rectangle has an area of 2.4 m². The length of the rectangle is 0.8 cm. What is its width?

4 A square has an area of 0.81 cm². What are the lengths of its sides?

5 What is the cost of 0.3 kg of grapes at £4 per kilogram?

6 What is the cost of 0.7 kg of apples at £2.10 per kilogram?

7 How many pencils costing £0.12 can I buy with £5.40?

8 How many oranges costing £0.30 can I buy with a £2 coin? How much change will I receive?

9 What is the total cost of 20 pencil cases costing £0.70 each?

10 How many pens costing £0.15 can I buy with £5? How much change will I receive?

Recurring decimals investigation

You will need to use a calculator for these investigations. Remember to write down all your experiments, even if they do not work. If you work logically, you are more likely to see a pattern that will help you to find your answer faster.

This investigation explores whether you can find any fractions that have three-digit repeats, such as 0.123123123...

1 A recurring decimal is produced by a recurring pattern of remainders in the division calculation. Remember that 7ths, 9ths and 11ths give recurring decimals. Try dividing 1 by various multiples of these numbers. Record all your answers.

2 From your experiments in question 1 you should start to see a pattern in the fractions.

List all the fraction families that give two-digit repeats.

List all the fraction families that give three-digit repeats.

Write down any general rules that you have observed.

Summary Exercise 9.10

1 Write each decimal as a fraction.
  (a) 0.6   (b) 0.24   (c) 1.125

2 Write each fraction as a decimal.
  (a) $\frac{1}{25}$ (b) $\frac{7}{20}$ (c) $\frac{5}{8}$

3 Write each fraction as a recurring decimal.
  (a) $\frac{2}{3}$ (b) $\frac{4}{9}$ (c) $\frac{1}{6}$

4 I leave home with £2. My bus fare costs 80p and I buy myself a packet of crisps at 37p and a carton of juice at 48p. How much change do I have?

5 Calculate:
  (a) 0.6×0.3 (c) 5×0.002
  (b) 0.02×2.4 (d) 0.009×12

6 Calculate:
  (a) $0.6 \div 0.3$ (c) $5 \div 0.02$
  (b) $3.6 \div 0.09$ (d) $1.2 \div 0.05$

7 What is the area of a rectangle with sides of lengths 0.5 m and 0.4 m?

8 A rectangle has an area of 0.54 m². The length of the rectangle is 0.9 cm. What is its width?

9 What is the cost of 0.4 kg of potatoes at £1.80 per kilogram?

10 How many limes costing £0.25 can I buy for £2?

 # Negative numbers

Numbers below zero are called **negative numbers**. You have seen how they fit on the number line.

In this chapter you will learn how to calculate with negative numbers as well as positive numbers.

Credit and debit

First, think how negative numbers apply in everyday life. One obvious application is related to money.

If I have ten pounds then I am ten pounds **in credit**, but if I borrow ten pounds then I owe ten pounds so I am ten pounds **in debit**. Similarly if I have five pounds but then spend ten pounds, I am five pounds in debit, because I have spent five pounds that I did not have.

Exercise 10.1

1 I have £10 and I am given £6. How much am I in credit now?

2 I have £10 pounds and spend £6. How much am I in debit or credit now?

3 I have borrowed £5 but then my uncle gives me £10. How much am I in debit or credit now?

4 I have borrowed £10 from my mother and then £5 pounds from my sister. How much am I in debit or credit now?

5 I have £10 and I spend £15. How much am I in debit or credit now?

6 My best friend owes me £10, then he borrows another £2 from me. How much am I in debit or credit now?

7 I have saved £35 and I then borrow £15 from my mother and spend all £50 on some new clothes. How much am I in credit or debit now?

8 My mother has lent me £15 and has lent my sister £10. How much in credit or debit is my mother?

9 I have borrowed £500 from the bank.

   (a) How much in credit or debit am I?

   (b) I pay back £40 per month. How much in credit or debit am I by the end of twelve months?

10 My friend has borrowed £600 from the bank and pays back £60 per month. How much in credit or debit is he by the end of twelve months?

Calculating with negative numbers

When you started adding and subtracting you used the number line. You can use the number line to calculate with negative numbers, as well as with positive numbers.

You just need to extend the line backwards, so that it extends beyond 0 to include negative numbers.

Note the appearance of the negative sign.

⁻5   this is the **number** 5 below 0, you say 'negative 5'

−5   this is the **operation** of taking 5 away, you say it as 'minus 5' or 'less five' or 'subtract 5'

Addition and subtraction

To use the number line to add numbers, start with the first number, move forward the number of spaces to represent the second number and see where you end up.

Examples

(i)   Add: ⁻5 + 8

   ⁻5 + 8 = 3

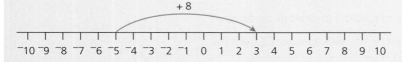

(ii)   Add: ⁻8 + 5

   ⁻8 + 5 = ⁻3

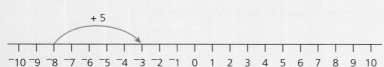

10 Negative numbers

To use the number line to subtract numbers, you start with the first number, move backwards the number of spaces to represent the second number and see where you end up.

Examples

(i) Subtract: 4 – 11

$4 - 11 = {}^-7$

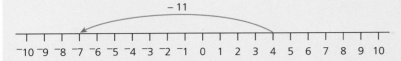

(ii) Subtract: $^-1 - 5$

$^-1 - 5 = {}^-6$

Exercise 10.2

Calculate the answers to these questions. First draw a number line across your page and use it to answer the first few questions. Then complete the calculations without using the number line.

1 3 + 4

2 $^-3 - 4$

3 $^-5 + 8$

4 2 – 8

5 $^-12 + 5$

6 $^-3 + 9$

7 3 – 7

8 $^-6 + 9$

9 $^-2 - 6$

10 $^-13 + 6$

11 $^-10 + 6$

12 $^-14 - 4$

13 $^-15 + 18$

14 2 – 18

15 $^-12 + 15$

16 $^-18 + 16$

17 $^-7 - 6$

18 $^-6 + 11$

19 $^-7 - 13$

20 $^-22 + 16$

◯ Brackets

In the previous exercise you started with a number, which may or may not have been a negative number, and you added or subtracted a positive number. Your answer may or may not have been a negative number.

Sometimes you will be working with two negative numbers.

If I have ten pounds and I am given five pounds then I could write this as a sum:

10 + 5 = 15

But if I owe ten pounds, and I borrow five more pounds my sum would be:

$^-$10 + ($^-$5) = $^-$15

I owe fifteen pounds in total.

Note the use of brackets in this sum. If you write + $^-$5 or − $^-$5 it is very easy to lose the negative sign that is attached to the negative number, so always use brackets to avoid confusion.

If I am ten pounds in credit and I spend five pounds, I could write:

$^+$10 − ($^+$5) = $^+$5 or 5

Normally you would not bother with the $^+$ but just write:

10 − 5 = 5

but the positive sign ($^+$) does help if you are confused about positives and negatives.

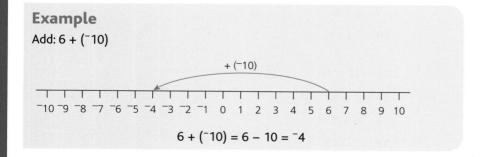

Example
Add: 6 + ($^-$10)

$$6 + (^-10) = 6 - 10 = {}^-4$$

Exercise 10.3

Use a number line to complete these calculations, if you find it helpful. Write out the question, the working and then the answer, as in the examples on the previous page.

1 $5 + (^-4)$

2 $4 + (^-2)$

3 $3 + (^-1)$

4 $^-3 + (^-4)$

5 $^-5 + (^-6)$

6 $4 - (^+4)$

7 $5 + (^-9)$

8 $3 + (^-4)$

9 $7 + (^-9)$

10 $^-6 - (^+4)$

11 $^-11 + (^-15)$

12 $^-13 + (^-7)$

13 $^-21 - (^+16)$

14 $^-13 + (^-19)$

15 $^-3 + (^-12)$

16 $^-4 + (^-17)$

17 $^-15 + (^-13)$

18 $28 + (^-16)$

19 $19 + (^-23)$

20 $^-15 + (^-31)$

Double negatives

On the number line $+ (^-5)$ is the same as subtracting 5, and so $- (^-5)$ must be the same as adding 5

It might sound strange, but if you are told: 'Don't not tidy your room today!' you know that you had better tidy it. The double negative makes a positive.

Think about what is happening on the number line.

Imagine you are standing on the number line. You face right (in a positive direction) and move forward when you are adding positive numbers. You face left and move forward when you are subtracting positive numbers.

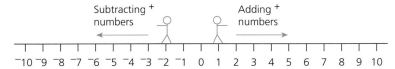

To add a negative number you must face right and move backwards; Therefore adding a negative number is the same as subtracting the equivalent positive number.

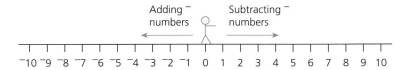

To subtract a positive number, you must face left and walk forwards.
Therefore subtracting a negative number is the same as adding.

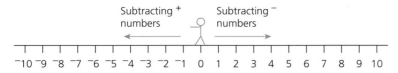

Example

Subtract: 7 – (⁻9)

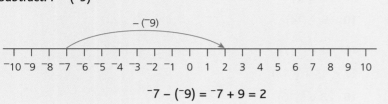

$$^-7 - (^-9) = ^-7 + 9 = 2$$

Exercise 10.4

Use a number line to complete these calculations, if you find it helpful. Write out
the question, the working and then the answer, as in the examples above.

1 5 – (⁻1)   6 9 – (⁻4)

2 7 – (⁻2)   7 4 – (⁻3)

3 ⁻3 – (⁻3)   8 ⁻5 – (⁻2)

4 ⁻4 – (⁻2)   9 3 – (⁻7)

5 ⁻6 – (⁻3)   10 5 – (⁻1)

11 ⁻6 – (⁻4)   16 23 – (⁺15)

12 1 – (⁺8)   17 ⁻32 – (⁻26)

13 ⁻3 – (⁻6)   18 20 – (⁺16)

14 9 – (⁺3)   19 ⁻14 – (⁺10)

15 12 – (⁻6)   20 ⁻30 – (⁻15)

Exercise 10.5

Now try some mixed examples without using a number line.

Use these examples to help you to remember the method.

$$3 + 5 = 8 \qquad\qquad 3 - 5 = {}^-2$$
$$3 + ({}^-5) = 3 - 5 = {}^-2 \qquad 3 - ({}^-5) = 3 + 5 = 8$$
$$ {}^-3 + 5 = 2 \qquad\qquad {}^-3 - 5 = {}^-8$$
$$ {}^-3 + ({}^-5) = {}^-3 - 5 = {}^-8 \qquad {}^-3 - ({}^-5) = {}^-3 + 5 = 2$$

1 $^-4 - 4$

2 $6 - 7$

3 $^-4 - (^+6)$

4 $^-1 + (^-3)$

5 $^-5 - (^-4)$

6 $4 + (^-2)$

7 $^-3 - (^+2)$

8 $1 + (^-6)$

9 $^-5 - (^-3)$

10 $3 + 5$

11 $^-14 - 26$

12 $13 - 35$

13 $^-16 + (^-5)$

14 $^-25 - (^-14)$

15 $3 - (^-19)$

16 $^-25 + (^-114)$

17 $^-17 - (^+23)$

18 $^-34 + 19$

19 $^-27 - 35$

20 $^-23 - (^-42)$

Multiplying with negative numbers

If 4×4 is the same as $2 + 2 + 2 + 2 = 8$, then:

$$4 \times (^-2) \text{ is the same as } (^-2) + (^-2) + (^-2) + (^-2) = {}^-8$$

What about $(^-4) \times (^-2)$?

$$(^-4) \times (^-2) = {}^+8$$

As $4 \times 2 = 8$ then $\qquad (^+4) \times (^+2) = 8 \text{ (or } {}^+8) \qquad 4 \times (^-2) = {}^-8$

$$(^-4) \times 2 = {}^-8 \qquad (^-4) \times (^-2) = 8 \text{ (or } {}^+8)$$

Using a calculator

On your calculator you should find a button like this $\boxed{\pm}$ which is the positive/negative button.

To check the above four multiplications you need to follow these four key sequences.

- $(^+4) \times (^+2) \rightarrow$ $\boxed{4}$ $\boxed{\times}$ $\boxed{2}$ $\boxed{=}$
- $(^-4) \times 2 \rightarrow$ $\boxed{4}$ $\boxed{\pm}$ $\boxed{\times}$ $\boxed{2}$ $\boxed{=}$

> Check the instructions for your calculator. Some have a [-] button which is pressed before the number to make it negative.

● $4 \times (^-2) \rightarrow$ [4] [X] [2] [±] [=]

● $(^-4) \times (^-2) \rightarrow$ [4] [±] [X] [2] [±] [=]

Exercise 10.6

Complete these multiplications. Use a calculator to check your answers.

1 $^-4 \times 5$

2 $4 \times (^-5)$

3 $^-4 \times (^-8)$

4 $5 \times (^-6)$

5 $(^-3) \times (^-5)$

6 $(^-2) \times (^-9)$

7 $^-3 \times 8$

8 $^-4 \times (^+8)$

9 $(^+4) \times (^-5)$

10 $^-2 \times (^-6)$

11 $(^-6) \times (^-9)$

12 $^-4 \times (^+4)$

13 $6 \times (^+4)$

14 $(^+6) \times (^-6)$

15 $(^-4) \times (^+9)$

16 $5 \times (^-5)$

17 $(^-7) \times 3$

18 $^-8 \times 2$

19 $(^+5) \times (^-8)$

20 $^-7 \times (^+8)$

Dividing with negative numbers

You know that whenever you write down a multiplication of two numbers there are two division facts that are associated with it.

If $2 \times 4 = 8$

then $8 \div 4 = 2$ and $8 \div 2 = 4$

In the previous section you saw that $4 \times (^-2) = ^-8$

From this you have $4 = ^-8 \div (^-2)$ and $^-2 = ^-8 \div 4$

You can see that:

● a negative number divided by a negative number gives a positive result.

● a negative number divided by a positive number or a positive number divided by a negative number gives a negative result.

Thus $8 \div 2 = 4$ and $(^+8) \div (^+2) = 4$ (or $^+4$) $8 \div (^-2) = ^-4$

$(^-8) \div 2 = ^-4$ $(^-8) \div (^-2) = 4$ (or $^+4$)

Exercise 10.7

Complete these divisions. Use a calculator to check your answers.

1 16 ÷ 8
2 (⁻24) ÷ 8
3 36 ÷ (⁻9)
4 ⁺25 ÷ (⁻5)
5 12 ÷ (⁻3)

6 ⁻18 ÷ (⁻6)
7 ⁻24 ÷ (⁻6)
8 ⁻18 ÷ 2
9 ⁻72 ÷ 9
10 35 ÷ (⁻7)

11 (⁻64) ÷ 8
12 (⁺45) ÷ 9
13 32 ÷ (⁻8)
14 ⁻28 ÷ 7
15 36 ÷ (⁻4)

16 ⁻12 ÷ (⁻1)
17 (⁻15) ÷ 3
18 20 ÷ (⁻4)
19 ⁻24 ÷ (⁻12)
20 ⁻100 ÷ (⁻10)

Exercise 10.8

Now try some mixed examples. You may need to follow the BIDMAS rule but remember that some brackets are there to avoid confusion between the symbols. The brackets do not always indicate that there is an operation to be done first.

Examples

(i) Calculate: 18 ÷ 2 × (⁻3)

| 18 ÷ 2 × (⁻3) = 9 × (⁻3) | Divide |
| = ⁻27 | Multiply |

(ii) Calculate: (⁻12) × (⁻3) − (⁻2)

(⁻12) × (⁻3) − (⁻2) = (⁻12) × (⁻3) + 2	Brackets
= 36 + 2	Multiply
= 38	Add

1 8 × (⁻2)
2 ⁻4 + 7
3 ⁻3 − 6
4 14 ÷ (⁻2)
5 (⁻3) − (⁻4)

6 35 ÷ (⁻5)
7 ⁻4 − (⁻7)
8 ⁻3 + 9
9 (⁻3) × (⁻6)
10 5 + (⁻10)

11 (⁻6) × 12

12 24 ÷ 8

13 ⁻6 + (⁻4)

14 (⁻4) × (⁻6)

15 ⁻7 – 3

16 (⁻4) × (⁻9)

17 (⁻36) ÷ (⁻9)

18 ⁻16 – 8

19 (⁻3) × (⁻12)

20 20 – (⁻4)

21 (⁻24) + 8 – (⁻3)

22 36 ÷ (⁻9) × (⁻3)

23 (⁺5) – (⁻5) + (⁻10)

24 12 × (⁻3) ÷ 4

25 (⁻12) ÷ (⁻6) × (⁻3)

26 (⁻8) ÷ (⁻4) × (⁻2)

27 (⁺2) × 9 ÷ (⁻6)

28 (⁻9) ÷ 3 × (⁻4)

29 (⁻24) – (⁻12) × (⁻3)

30 36 ÷ (⁻4) – (⁻3)

◯ Negative co-ordinates

When you plot **co-ordinates** on a grid, you usually start the numbers on each **axis** from 0. However, sometimes the values you are plotting may take negative values, so you can extend the axes of a **co-ordinate grid** below zero in both directions.

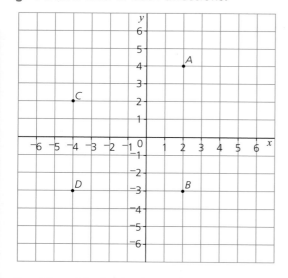

On this grid, the horizontal axis is the *x*-axis and the vertical axis is the *y*-axis.

The (*x*, *y*) co-ordinates are:

   A(2, 4)   B(2, –3)   C(⁻4, 2)   D(⁻4, ⁻3)

Remember, you always state the horizontal co-ordinate first.

Drawing axes

When you are drawing axes, remember these rules.

1 Always use a ruler.

2 Label the origin as 0. The origin is the point (0, 0)

3 Label the axes, usually, but not always, they are x and y.

4 Number the axes with the horizontal scale numbers under the axis and the vertical scale numbers to the left of the axis.

Exercise 10.9

1 Write down the co-ordinates of the points A to K on this pair of axes.

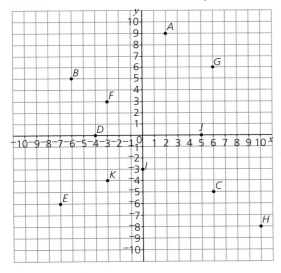

2 Draw a pair of co-ordinate axes, like those above, labelling each axis from $^-10$ to 10

Plot each set of points A, B, C and D. For each set, join the points in order, A to B, B to C, C to D and D to A. Write down the name of the shape $ABCD$.

(a) $A(^-4, 4); B(4, 4); C(4, ^-2); D(^-4, ^-2)$

(b) $A(1, 5); B(4, 1); C(1, ^-3); D(^-2, 1)$

(c) $A(2, 2); B(4, ^-2); C(^-2, ^-2); D(^-4, 2)$

(d) $A(4, 1); B(4, ^-4); C(^-1, ^-4); D(^-1, 1)$

(e) $A(4, 1); B(^-2, ^-2); C(^-4, 1); D(^-2, 4)$

(f) $A(1, 1); B(5, ^-3); C(^-3, ^-5); D(^-3, 0)$

3 Draw a pair of co-ordinate axes, with values of x and y from $^-6$ to 6

Plot and label these points.

$A(1, 4); B(3, 4); C(5, 2); D(5, 0); E(3, ^-2); F(1, ^-2); G(^-1, 0); H(^-1, 2)$

Join the points in alphabetical order, and then join A to H.

4 Draw a pair of co-ordinate axes, with values of x and y from $^-6$ to 6

Plot and label these points.

$A(^-2, 4); B(^-1, 2); C(1, 2); D(0, 0); E(1, ^-2); F(^-1, ^-2); G(^-2, ^-4); H(^-3, ^-2); I(^-5, ^-2);$
$J(^-4, 0); K(^-5, 2); L(^-3, 2)$

Join up the points in alphabetical order, and then join A to L.

5 Draw a pair of co-ordinate axes, with values of x and y from $^-6$ to 6

Plot and label these points.

$A(0, 4); B(2, 4); C(2, 2); D(4, 2); E(4, 0); F(2, 0); G(2, ^-2); H(0, ^-2); I(0, 0); J(^-2, 0);$
$K(^-2, 2); L(0, 2)$

Join up the points in alphabetical order, and then join A to L.

6 Draw a pair of co-ordinate axes, with values of x and y numbered from $^-10$ to 10

(a) Plot and label these points.

$A(7, 6); B(7, ^-6); C(5, ^-6); D(5, ^-2); E(3, ^-1); F(1, ^-2); G(1, ^-6); H(^-7, ^-6); I(^-7, 4); J(^-5, 4);$
$K(^-5, 3); L(^-3, 3); M(^-3, 4); N(^-1, 4); P(^-1, 3); Q(1, 3); R(1, 6); S(3, 6); T(3, 5); U(5, 5); V(5, 6)$

Join up the points in alphabetical order and then join A to V.

(b) The building you have drawn needs windows. Design a window for your building and give instructions, using co-ordinates, so that the windows can be drawn on the picture.

7 Draw a pair of co-ordinate axes, with values of x and y numbered from $^-10$ to 10

(a) Plot and label these points.

$A(5, 6); B(7, 3); C(7, ^-5); D(^-7, ^-5); E(^-7, 3); F(^-5, 6); G(^-3, 6); H(^-3, 7); I(^-2, 7); J(^-2, 6)$

Join up the points in alphabetical order and join A to J, and B to E.

(b) This building needs a door and two windows. Draw these on the grid. Under your drawing, write down the co-ordinates of each point you have used.

Extension Exercise 10.10

There are all sorts of patterns in co-ordinates. Here are a few for you to look at.

1

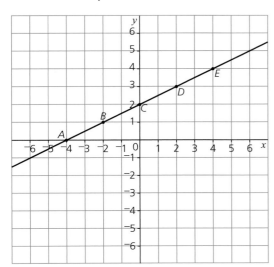

(a) This is a section of a straight line drawn on a graph. Write down the co-ordinates of points A, B, C, D and E.

(b) Look carefully at the co-ordinates you have written. You should see that the x-co-ordinates make a number series and the y-co-ordinates make a different number series. Describe these two series.

(c) If you take point A to be the first point on the line, B to be the second, what will be the co-ordinates of:
   (i) the sixth point   (ii) the 20th point?

(d) What will be the co-ordinates of the 10th point?

(e) Will these points lie on the line?

   (i) $(38, 22)$ (ii) $(100, 52)$ (iii) $(^-10, 3)$

(f) These are the co-ordinates of points that do lie on the line. Complete each pair of co-ordinates.

   (i) $(40, ?)$ (ii) $(?, ^-3)$ (iii) $(^-18, ?)$

2 Draw a pair of co-ordinate axes, with values of x and y numbered from $^-5$ to 5

On your graph, plot these points: $R(3, ^-5)$; $S(1, ^-2)$; $T(^-1, 1)$; $U(^-3, 4)$

Join the points $RSTU$ to make a straight line. Imagine the line is extended in both directions.

(a) Which of these pairs of co-ordinates lie on the line?

   (i) $(^-9, 13)$ (ii) $(^-13, 21)$ (iii) $(15, ^-23)$

(b) These are the co-ordinates of points that do lie on the line. Complete each pair of co-ordinates.

(i) (?, ⁻17) **(ii)** (201, ?) **(iii)** (?, ⁻20)

3 Suppose this pattern of hearts, diamonds, spades and clubs is continued in all directions.

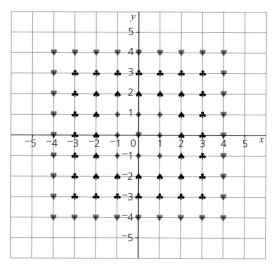

State which suit will be at each of these points.

(a) (5, 5) **(e)** (⁻7, ⁻6)

(b) (⁻10, ⁻8) **(f)** (⁻15, 10)

(c) (6, ⁻5) **(g)** (⁻7, ⁻7)

(d) (12, 14) **(h)** (11, ⁻13)

4 Copy this grid, and continue the spiral of numbers as far as you can.

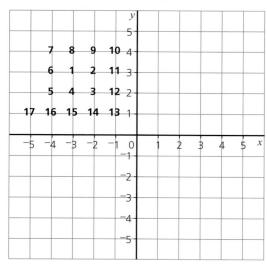

Give the co-ordinates of each of these numbered points.

(a) 35

(b) 80

(c) 95

(d) 100

(e) 120

(f) 144

(g) 165

(h) 200

Summary Exercise 10.11

Complete these calculations.

1 $^-7 + (^-3)$

2 $^-3 - 7$

3 $5 - (^-6)$

4 $9 - 10$

5 $^-6 - (^+7)$

6 $(^-4) \times 7$

7 $(^-6) \div (^-2)$

8 $16 \div (^-4)$

9 $^-25 + (^-15)$

10 $13 + (^-11)$

11 $(^-9) \div (^-3)$

12 $(^-3) \times 5$

13 $^-3 + 12$

14 $(^-5) \times (^-4)$

15 $10 - 8$

16 $^-6 + (^-2) \times (3)$

17 $(^-3) \times (^-6)$

18 $7 \times (^-2)$

19 $5 - 9$

20 $4 - (^-8)$

21 Using a scale of one centimetre for one unit, draw a pair of co-ordinate axes, with values of x and y numbered from $^-5$ to 5. Plot these points.

$A(0, 5); B(3,3); C(3, 0); D(0, ^-2); E(^-3, 0); F(^-3, 3)$

Join the points up in alphabetical order, then join A to F.

What is the name of the shape you have drawn?

22 Three corners of a **parallelogram** have the co-ordinates $(1, 3)$, $(1, ^-2)$ and $(^-3, 1)$. What are the co-ordinates of the fourth corner?

23 Two corners of a square have the co-ordinates $(1, 3)$ and $(1, ^-2)$

What are the co-ordinates of two other possible corners?

24. These are the co-ordinates of five points that lie on a straight line.

$(1, 3), (^-2, 0), (3, 5), (0, 2), (^-4, ^-2)$

Which of these points lie on the same line?

(a) $(^-3, ^-5)$

(b) $(1, ^-1)$

(c) $(^-8, 6))$

(d) $(^-5, ^-3)$

(e) $(^-1, ^-3)$

(f) $(^-9, 11)$

(g) $(^-17, ^-13)$

(h) $(^-100, ^-102)$

Activity: The balloon game

Have you ever wondered what keeps a hot-air balloon flying?

It's a very basic principle: hot air rises and cold air sinks. So the hot air in a hot-air balloon pushes upwards, keeping the balloon floating. A hot-air balloon has three major parts: the envelope, the burner and the basket. The basket is where passengers ride.

The burner is positioned above the passengers' heads and produces a huge flame to heat the air inside the envelope. The envelope is the colourful fabric bag that holds the hot air. When the air inside the envelope is heated, the balloon rises.

Balloons rise due to hot gases. Giving a burst of hot air will make the balloon rise and letting out hot air will make the balloon fall.

Balloons are also controlled by the use of sand bags. Sand bags make the balloon heavier, so releasing a sand bag will make it rise.

You can think of this in terms of positive and negative numbers.

Hot air is positive.	Add 1 burst of hot air:	$+ (^+1) = {}^+1$
	Release two bursts of hot air:	$- (^+2) = {}^-2$
Sandbags are negative.	Add one sand bag:	$+ (^-1) = {}^-1$
	Release two sandbags:	$- (^-2) = {}^+2$

The game

You will need two dice, one numbered $^+1$, $^-1$, $^+2$, $^-2$, $^+3$, $^-3$ and the other with three pluses (+) and three minuses (–). These are the operations. Trace the game board on the opposite page.

In the game, there are two balloons, one on each side of a wide chasm. Each player rolls the dice and then moves forward one square and then up or down the number of squares shown by the combination of the two dice. For the purposes of the game, you must assume it is possible to add sandbags to the balloon during its flight.

Players should use different-coloured pencils to record their tracks. The winner is the one who lands their balloon as close to level 0 as possible, and has not gone too high (over $^+10$) or too low (under $^-10$) on the way there!

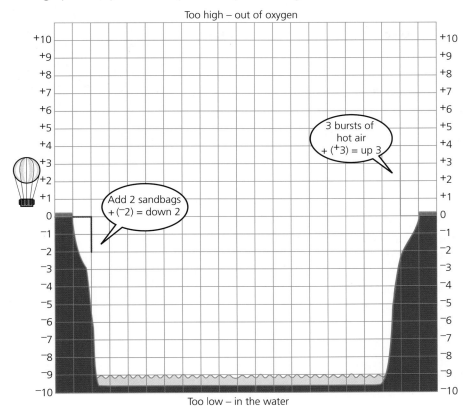

11 Algebra

In this chapter you will find many problems that you could solve in your head with no working out. However, that is not the point of these exercises. You are going to learn a new skill that you can use to solve much more complicated problems later on.

◯ Solving word puzzles

There are various ways of solving puzzles. Some are very simple and you can just do them without really thinking about them. Others are more difficult and need careful thought. It becomes easier to solve harder puzzles if you can look at the simple puzzles and work out some rules. One way of solving a puzzle is to write it as an expression with unknown numbers shown as boxes.

Example

After she had been given £50, Charlotte spent some of the money and then had £24 left. How much did she spend?

You can write this puzzle as: $50 - \square = 24$

Now you know that to find the missing number you can take 24 from 50

$\square = 50 - 24$

$\quad = 26$

So she spent £26. Check the answer: £50 − £26 = £24

Some puzzles, like those at the end of Chapter 2, use symbols while others, such as the puzzle at the of Chapter 6, use letters. As you solve this set of puzzles, once you have found the answer write down the calculation that you did in your head.

Examples

(i) $\square \div 4 = 7$

$\quad\quad \square = 28 \quad (7 \times 4 = 28)$

(ii) $n + 7 = 15$

$\quad\quad n = 8 \quad (15 - 7 = 8)$

Exercise 11.1

Work out the missing numbers. When you have solved each puzzle, write down the answer and the calculation that you did in your head.

1 $8 + \triangle = 11$

2 $\bullet - 5 = 10$

3 $7 + \blacklozenge = 13$

4 $\square + 8 = 20$

5 $15 - \spadesuit = 9$

6 $12 - \clubsuit = 3$

7 $3 + \blacktriangledown = 4$

8 $\heartsuit + 6 = 25$

9 $\square - 14 = 6$

10 $12 + \bullet = 18$

11 $2 \times \blacktriangledown = 14$

12 $18 \div \bigcirc = 3$

13 $\square \times 5 = 30$

14 $\blacklozenge \div 4 = 6$

15 $\heartsuit \times 7 = 21$

16 $\blacksquare \div 3 = 9$

17 $36 \div \dagger = 6$

18 $\blacklozenge \times 8 = 56$

19 $3 \times \square = 30$

20 $72 \div \triangle = 9$

Look again at the answers to the puzzles above. Do you see that you had to rearrange the numbers in the puzzle to get the answer? It is easy to do this with simple puzzles but you will need some rules if you are going to solve more complicated problems.

To find the rules, you need to think about what the puzzle means.

You know that = means 'is exactly equal to'.

If you think about an old-fashioned balance, then putting the equals sign between the amounts on the two sides means that one side balances the other.

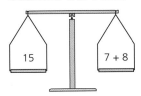

To maintain the balance, if you want to take something from one side you must take the same amount from the other, otherwise the amounts on the two sides will no longer be equal.

Try this with some more puzzles.

Example

♥ + 3 = 9

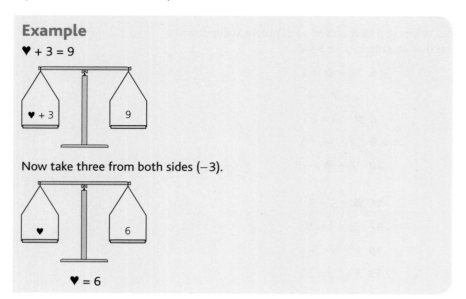

Now take three from both sides (−3).

♥ = 6

Similarly, what you add to one side you must add to the other:

Example

♦ − 5 = 4

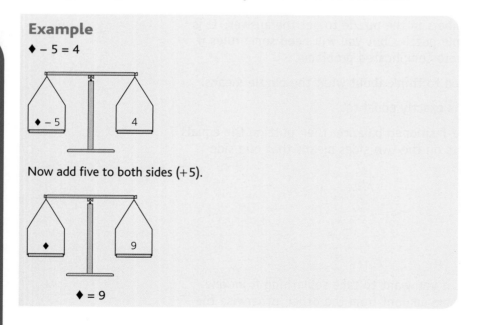

Now add five to both sides (+5).

♦ = 9

Equations

Puzzles like these, in which you have an unknown quantity (or quantities) in a calculation that is written with an equals sign, are called **equations**. It is very important that, as you solve the equation, step by step, you always used the equals sign correctly.

11 Algebra

Therefore, just as for the balance, the rule is:

Whatever you do to one side, you must do the same to the other.

To write the equations for the puzzles more simply, you can leave out the balance pans.

Using letters

Instead of drawing a symbol, you can use the letter x to represent the unknown number.

Note that this is an italic letter x, not the × that means 'multiply'.

From now on, you should write what you are doing to both sides of the equation before you write the answer. For each step of the solution, keep the equals signs aligned in a column. As always, it is a good idea to check your answer.

Examples

(i)

$$x + 12 = 7$$

(-12) $\qquad$ (-12) $\qquad$ Subtract 12 from both sides.

$$x = {}^-5$$ $\qquad$ Check: ${}^-5 + 12 = 7$

(ii)

$$9 = x - 14$$

$(+14)$ $\qquad$ $(+14)$ $\qquad$ Add 14 to both sides.

$$23 = x$$ $\qquad$ Check: $23 - 14 = 9$

So $x = 23$

Exercise 11.2

Follow the steps in the examples above to calculate the value of x.

1 $x + 3 = 10$

2 $x + 5 = 9$

3 $x + 9 = 4$

4 $x - 4 = 9$

5 $x + 5 = 11$

6 $x - 7 = 12$

7 $x + 3 = 9$

8 $x - 9 = 12$

9 $x + 8 = 7$

10 $6 = x - 4$

11 $7 = 4 + x$

12 $3 = x - 5$

13 $9 = x + 4$

14 $15 = 6 + x$

15 $12 = 7 + x$

16 $x - 19 = 45$

17 $25 = 16 + x$

18 $12 + x = 17$

19 $17 = x - 12$

20 $x + 16 = 11$

More than one

Some puzzles involve more than one of an unknown quantity.

Harry had eighty pence, then he bought four apples and had twelve pence left. How much did each apple cost?

Let x represent the price of one apple.

Then the puzzle becomes: $80 = 12 + x + x + x + x$

You do not want to keep writing x again and again.

You could write $4 \times x$ but that is confusing.

The rule is that you write it as $4x$

The puzzle has turned into an equation: $80 = 12 + 4x$

Before you try to solve this puzzle, look more closely at how to write groups of xs.

$$x + x = 2x$$
$$x + x + x = 3x$$
$$x + x + x + x = 4x$$

and as $2x + 3x = (x + x) + (x + x + x)$, then $2x + 3x = 5x$

So you count up how many xs there are, and write the number in front.

Of course you do not always have to use x for the unknown number. You could choose to use y, a, b, c, d or any letter you like.

Using letters in place of unknown numbers is called **algebra**.

Note that when you are using algebra, you do not use the $\times$ sign or the $\div$ sign.

$$3 \times x = 3x \qquad \text{and} \qquad a \div 4 = \frac{a}{4}$$

Expressions

A group of numbers, symbols and operators (such as + and ×) grouped together that show the value of something is called an **expression**. Before you do anything else with the expression it is good practice to make it as simple and concise as possible. This is called **simplifying** the expression.

Each part of an expression is called a **term**. As you simplify an expression, you will add, subtract, multiply or divide the terms.

When an expression has terms in exactly the same variable, and you can combine them by adding and subtracting, you are **collecting like terms**.

Examples

(i) Simplify: $c + c + c$

$c + c + c = 3c$

(ii) Simplify: $4 \times b$

$4 \times b = 4b$

(iii) Simplify: $(3 \times y) + y + y + y$

$(3 \times y) + y + y + y = 3y + 3y$

$\qquad\qquad\qquad\qquad = 6y$

(iv) Simplify: $(a + a + a) \div (a + a)$

$(a + a + a) \div (a + a) = 3a \div 2a$

$\qquad\qquad\qquad\qquad = \dfrac{3a}{2a}$

$\qquad\qquad\qquad\qquad = \dfrac{3}{2} = 1\dfrac{1}{2}$

Exercise 11.3

Simplify these expressions.

1 $a + a + a + a$

2 $3 \times b$

3 $x + x + x + x + x + x$

4 $5 \times x$

5 $a \div b$

6 $y + y + y - y - y$

7 $a + a + a + a - a + a$

8 $b + b - b - b - b - b$

9 $3 \times y$

10 $y + y + y - y - y$

11 $(3 \times x) \div 4$

12 $(4 \times x) - x - x$

13 $a + a + a + (3 \times a)$

14 $(6 \times b) - b - b - b - b$

15 $c + c + c - c - c$

16 $y + y + y + y + y - (2 \times y)$

17 $(5 \times x) - x - x - x - x$

18 $(2 \times b) + b + b + b$

19 $(3 \times y) - y$

20 $(2 \times a) \div (3 \times a)$

21 $(4 \times x) + (2 \times x)$

22 $(5 \times y) - (3 \times y)$

23 $(6 \times a) - (3 \times a)$

24 $(7 \times b) + (4 \times b)$

25 $(5 \times x) \div (3 \times x)$

26 $(6 \times a) + (3 \times a) + (2 \times a)$

27 $(4 \times b) + (2 \times b) - (8 \times b)$

28 $(5 \times a) \times (7 \times a)$

29 $(8 \times y) \div (2 \times y)$

30 $(3 \times x) \div (6 \times x)$

Two missing numbers

You could use any letter to represent an unknown number. If you have a puzzle with two unknown numbers, then you will need two letters.

For example, if a stands for a number of apples and b stands for a number of bricks, clearly you cannot combine a and b into a single term. Apples must be kept separate from bricks.

Examples

(i) Simplify: $x + x + x + x + y + y + y$

$$x + x + x + x + y + y + y = 4x + 3y$$

(ii) Simplify: $4x + 5y - 3x + 2y$

$$4x + 5y - 3x + 2y = x + 7y$$

(iii) Simplify: $a + a + a + b - a - a - b - b$

$$a + a + a + b - a - a - b - b = 3a + b - 2a - 2b$$
$$= a - b$$

(iv) Simplify: $(a + a + a + a) \div (b + b)$

$$(a + a + a + a) \div (b + b) = 4a \div 2b$$
$$= \frac{4a}{2b}$$
$$= \frac{2a}{b}$$

Exercise 11.4

Simplify each of these expressions.

1 $2 \times a - 4 \times b$

2 $x + x + y - x - x - x - y$

3 $a + a + a + b - b$

4 $2a + b + b + a$

5 $12a - 4b - 3a + b$

6 $4c + 2b - c - b$

7 $5a - 3c + 2a + 3c$

8 $2a + 2b + 4a + 3b$

9 $2x - x - x$

10 $x - x - x + y$

11 $3a - b - b - b$

12 $4x + 3y - x - 2y$

13 $3x + x + x - y$

14 $4x + 3y - x - y$

15 $4b + 3a - 2b - 4a$

16 $6x - 7y - 2y + x$

17 $4a - 2c + 3a + 4c$

18 $3a - 3x + 2x - 3a$

19 $4b + 2c + 2b - 2c$

20 $5a - 2b - b + 2a$

21 $a \div b$

22 $(3 \times x) \div y$

23 $a + a + a + (3 \times b)$

24 $(5 \times x) - (3 \times y)$

25 $(7 \times b) + (4 \times a)$

26 $5 \times a \times b$

27 $3 \times a \times b + 2 \times a \times b$

28 $(5 \times a) \div (7 \times b)$

29 $(8 \times y) \div (2 \times y)$

30 $(6 \times a) \div (3 \times b)$

Numbers and letters don't mix!

You know that you can't combine different letters into a single term.

Suppose you have the expression $3c + 7$. If c stands for the price of a carrot, what does the number 7 stand for? It depends on the puzzle, but you cannot add the 3 from $3c$ to the 7

$3c + 7$ is very different from $10c$. You must be very careful to keep the numbers that are standing on their own separate from the numbers that tell you how many of the unknown value (x, y, z, ...) you have.

> **Example**
>
> Simplify: $3a + 6 - 2a + 3$
>
> $3a + 6 - 2a + 3 = a + 9$

Exercise 11.5

Write each expression in its simplest form.

1 $2a + 4 + a$

2 $2x - 4 + x + 2$

3 $x - 1 + x + 4$

4 $3b + 2 - b - 5$

5 $3c + 4c + 3$

6 $5a - 2 + a + 4$

7 $5 + 2b - 6 + 2b$

8 $5 + 2b - 6 - 2b$

9 $6 - 3x - 4 + 3x - 2$

10 $5y + 3 - 6y - 4 + y + 1$

Writing algebra

Here is a summary of what you have learnt so far about the rules for writing number sentences that include letters for unknowns.

● An **expression** is group of numbers, symbols and operators.

● You cannot **solve** an expression, but you may be able to **simplify** it.

● An **equation** contains an equals sign.

● You can **solve** equations.

Remember that expressions and equations written in algebraic form do not include multiplication signs or division signs.

$$3 \times x = 3x \qquad x \div 3 = \frac{x}{3}$$

$3 \times x$ means $3x$ and $1 \times x$ means x. When you only have one x you write it as x, not as $1x$ and you would never write $0x$

You always write $3 \times x$ as $3x$, never as $x3$

Note, too, that when you are multiplying or collecting like terms with, for example, letters a, b and c, it is good practice to write the letters in the product or expression in alphabetical order, as a, b, c rather than b, c, a. Although it is not an absolute rule, it is a mathematical convention.

$a \times c \times b$ is written as abc

Finally, remember that equals signs should always go neatly underneath each other.

Exercise 11.6

Look at each of these expressions. Either they have not followed the 'good practice' convention or they are not in their simplest form. Write each one appropriately.

1 $8 \times a$

2 $1x$

3 $c \div 3$

4 $3x \div 2$

5 $0x$

6 $3c + 2a - b$

7 $x5$

8 $a \times 4$

9 $b4 \div 5$

10 $3b - 1c$

11 $4a \div 2a$

12 $3 \times b \div 2$

13 $\frac{4c}{2}$

14 $3 \times 2x$

15 $2 \times a + 4 \times a$

16 $2ba$

17 $4b + 2a$

18 $\frac{6a}{3b}$

19 $3a - 2a - a$

20 $8ab \div 2a$

Back to the apples

Think back to the apples. The equation was:

$80 = 12 + 4x$

Taking the 12 from both sides:

$68 = 4x$

If 4 'somethings' make 68, you must divide both sides by 4

$17 = x$

$x = 17$

Notice that you should turn the answer round, if necessary, to put the unknown on the left-hand side. Therefore each apple costs Harry 17 pence.

Now look at the examples below. They can be answered in just one stage, as in Exercise 11.1

There is no reason why the answer cannot be a negative number or a fraction. If the answer is a fraction, leave it as a fraction. Do not use decimals.

Remember to check your answer.

Examples

Solve these equations.   (i) $6a = 3$ (ii) $7 + x = 4$

(i) $\qquad 6a = 3$

$\quad (\div 6) \qquad\qquad (\div 6)$

$$a = \frac{3}{6}$$

$$a = \frac{1}{2}$$ Check: $6 \times \dfrac{1}{2} = 3$

(ii) $\qquad 7 + x = 4$

$\quad (-7) \qquad\qquad (-7)$

$$x = {}^-3$$ Check: $7 - 3 = 4$

Exercise 11.7

Solve these equations.

1 $4a = 20$

2 $3b = 9$

3 $x + 12 = 30$

4 $\dfrac{c}{4} = 3$

5 $\dfrac{a}{2} = 5$

6 $y - 8 = 4$

7 $a + 9 = 6$

8 $c - 2 = {}^-5$

9 $\dfrac{b}{6} = 5$

10 $\dfrac{x}{2} = 3$

11 $2a = 6$

12 $x + 7 = 2$

13 $4b = 7$

14 $3y = {}^-2$

15 $\dfrac{x}{4} = {}^-1$

16 $4 = d - 2$

17 $2 = 5b$

18 $24 + d = 6$

19 $1 = 3a$

20 $\dfrac{c}{3} = {}^-2$

You were able to solve the last set of equations with just one stage of working.

This next set needs two or three stages of working.

Note that you always take away or add terms first and then do the multiplication or division last.

Examples

Solve these equations.   (i) $3x + 4 = 8$ (ii) $7 + 3a = 4$

(i) $3x + 4 = 8$

   (-4) (-4)

           $3x = 4$

   $(\div 3)$ $(\div 3)$

             $x = \dfrac{4}{3}$

             $x = 1\dfrac{1}{3}$ Check: $3 \times \dfrac{4}{3} + 4 = 8$

(ii) $7 + 3a = 4$

   (-7) (-7)

           $3a = {}^-3$

   $(\div 3)$ $(\div 3)$

           $a = {}^-1$ Check: $7 + 3 \times {}^-1 = 4$

Exercise 11.8

Solve these equations.

1   $2x + 3 = 5$

2   $3a + 2 = 8$

3   $4b + 1 = 9$

4   $3c - 8 = 4$

5   $4x - 1 = 7$

6   $2x - 3 = 9$

7   $4a - 2 = 7$

8   $4b - 1 = 11$

9   $3c - 7 = 5$

10   $4x - 1 = 6$

11   $3 + 5y = 18$

12   $3 = 7 + 2a$

13   $9 = 3 + 2b$

14   $3 = 1 + 4c$

15   $4 + 2x = 10$

16   $3y + 18 = 3$

17   $3 = 5a - 7$

18   $5 = 2b + 3$

19   $3 = 1 + 4c$

20   $4 + 2x = 8$

Now solve the puzzles

Now you can solve equations, you can work on puzzles.

For each puzzle below, you will need to write a simple equation and then solve it.

Remember: You must start by saying what your letter represents, for example, 'Let x be the width,' or whatever is required.

When you finish, you must answer the question.

As a general rule, if the question involves only numbers, you may answer with a number. If the question is a sentence or story, answer with a short phrase or sentence.

Example

Jemima had 5 house points. She has just won some more and now she has a total of 14

How many house points has she just won?

Let the number of house points she has just won be x

Then $\qquad 5 + x = 14$

$\qquad (-5) \qquad\qquad (-5)$

$\qquad\qquad x = 9$

Answer: She has just won 9 house points.

Exercise 11.9

Answer each question by forming an equation and solving it.

1 I think of a number, add 5 and the answer is 8. What was the number?

2 I had 6 games for my computer. I receive some more for my birthday and now I have 9 games. How many games was I given for my birthday?

3 My average mark last term was bad, so I worked hard and my average rose by 18%. This term it was 72%. What was it last term?

4 Monty had five roses in bloom but overnight more came into bloom and today he has 22. How many bloomed overnight?

5 I had a box of chocolates. After everyone in the class (22 of them!) had each had one, there were only five left. How many did I have to start with?

6 Lorraine had some eggs in the refrigerator but she used seven to make pancakes and then had two for breakfast. After that there were only two left. How many were there to start with?

7 I had 15 tennis balls last month, but I have lost a few over the weeks and this month I have only eight left. How many did I lose?

8 My father is on a diet. This month he weighs 80 kg after losing 8 kg in two months. What did he weigh before the diet?

So far the problems have involved adding or subtracting to find the value of x. Sometimes you will also need to multiply or divide.

9 I have a bag of sweets that I share among my five friends and myself. We each have six sweets. How many were in the bag?

10 My father is four times as old as I am, and he is 44. How old am I?

Practice with two-stage equations

Example

If you treble my age and add 4 you have my mother's age of 40

How old am I?

Let my age be x years.

Then
$$3x + 4 = 40$$
$$(-4) \qquad\qquad (-4)$$
$$3x = 36$$
$$(\div 3) \qquad\qquad (\div 3)$$
$$x = 12$$

I am 12 years old.

Exercise 11.10

1 Flying saucers cost 4p each. I bought several and had 28p change from a £1 coin. How many did I buy?

2 My garden is 20 m long. The length is (three times the width) plus 2 m. What is the width of my garden?

3 In our sponsored swim I swam three times as many lengths as my best friend, plus five extra lengths. If I swam 83 lengths, how many did my best friend swim?

4 It takes me 8 minutes to complete our fitness circuit. In one hour I did several circuits and had 12 minutes left. How many circuits did I complete?

5 I have saved up £30. I reckon that during the holidays I can go to the cinema six times and I will then have £3 left over. How much does one trip to the cinema cost?

6 If I halve my father's age and then add 10, I get my mother's age. My mother is 36. How old is my father?

7 My brother is twice as old as my sister and I am 11. The sum of all three of our ages is 32. How old is my brother?

8 My best friend's mother is the same age as my mother. If you add their ages together and then add 2 you have the age of my grandfather. If my grandfather is 86, how old is my mother?

◯ Formulae

You have looked at expressions and at equations but you also use algebra to write a rule, or **formula**.

Consider this:

You have a line of length L cm that is divided into two. The length of one part is x cm and the length of the other is y cm.

You could say that the total length of the line is x cm plus y cm but it is simpler to write a formula:

$$L = x + y$$

You can use the formula to find the total length L for different values of x and y.

> Formula is a Latin word and means 'rule'. The plural of formula is formulae and not formulas.

> Note in the original statement that L, x and y all have the same units – centimetres.

> **Example**
>
> If $L = x + y$ find the value of L when $x = 4$ and $y = 6$
>
> $L = x + y$
>
> $\quad = 4 + 6$
>
> $\quad = 10$ So the length of the line is 10 cm.

When you use formulae you follow some simple rules. These may seem unnecessary when you are doing simple calculations but, as with equations, the rules are important to stop us making mistakes when formulae become more complicated.

1 First write the formula.

2 Substitute numbers for the letters.

3 Calculate.

4 Write the answer with the correct units (if there are any).

> You know that when you are writing expressions you do not write the multiplication sign ×. Sometimes × is left in a formula.

Here are some more examples with different formulae:

Examples

(i) If $A = a \times b$ find the value of A when $a = 6$ and $b = 7$

$$A = a \times b \qquad \text{Formula}$$

$$= 6 \times 7 \qquad \text{Substitute}$$

$$= 42 \qquad \text{Calculate and answer}$$

(ii) If $X = \dfrac{a + b}{c}$, find the value of X when $a = 3$, $b = 9$ and $c = 4$

$$X = \dfrac{a + b}{c} \qquad \text{Formula}$$

$$= \dfrac{3 + 9}{4} \qquad \text{Substitute}$$

$$= \dfrac{12}{4} \qquad \text{Calculate}$$

$$= 3 \qquad \text{Answer}$$

You can substitute a negative number into a formula. When you do so it is a good idea always to write the negative number in brackets and then work out what to do with the signs.

> Take extra care with negative numbers.

Example

If $M = a - b$, find the value of M when $a = 5$ and $b = {}^-6$

$$M = a - b \qquad \text{Formula}$$

$$= 5 - ({}^-6) \qquad \text{Substitute}$$

$$= 5 + 6 \qquad \text{Calculate}$$

$$= 11 \qquad \text{Answer}$$

Exercise 11.11

1 If $L = x + y$ find the value of L when:

(a) $x = 3$ and $y = 5$

(b) $x = 8$ and $y = 7$

(c) $x = 12$ and $y = 23$

(d) $x = 10$ and $y = 7$

2 If $A = a \times b$ find the value of A when:

(a) $a = 6$ and $b = 8$

(b) $a = 8$ and $b = 9$

(c) $a = 6$ and $b = {}^-3$

(d) $a = {}^-3$ and $b = {}^-8$

3 If $X = \dfrac{a + b}{2}$, find the value of X when:

   (a) $a = 4$ and $b = 6$ **(c)** $a = 13$ and $b = {}^-3$

   (b) $a = 8$ and $b = 12$ **(d)** $a = 6$ and $b = {}^-9$

4 If $P = s - t$, find the value of P when:

   (a) $s = 6$ and $t = 2$ **(c)** $s = 10$ and $t = {}^-8$

   (b) $s = 3$ and $t = 7$ **(d)** $s = {}^-5$ and $t = {}^-10$

5 If $A = 2x - y$ find the value of A when:

   (a) $x = 5$ and $y = 3$ **(c)** $x = 8$ and $y = {}^-5$

   (b) $x = 5$ and $y = 8$ **(d)** $x = {}^-10$ and $y = {}^-4$

6 If $Y = 2ab$ find the value of Y when:

   (a) $a = 3$ and $b = 5$ **(c)** $a = 8$ and $b = {}^-2$

   (b) $a = 7$ and $b = 4$ **(d)** $a = {}^-5$ and $b = {}^-8$

7 If $V = 3s - 2t$, find the value of V when:

   (a) $s = 2$ and $t = 1$ **(c)** $s = 8$ and $t = {}^-4$

   (b) $s = 3$ and $t = 5$ **(d)** $s = {}^-2$ and $t = {}^-5$

8 If $Q = \dfrac{a + 2b}{c}$, find the value of Q when:

   (a) $a = 3$, $b = 4$ and $c = 2$ **(c)** $a = 12$, $b = {}^-5$ and $c = 2$

   (b) $a = 5$, $b = 8$ and $c = 3$ **(d)** $a = 3$, $b = {}^-12$ and $c = {}^-3$

9 If $X = \dfrac{2ab}{3}$ find the value of X when:

   (a) $a = 3$ and $b = 5$ **(c)** $a = 9$ and $b = {}^-2$

   (b) $a = 6$ and $b = 5$ **(d)** $a = {}^-4$ and $b = {}^-5$

10 If $Y = 2ab - c$ find the value of Y when:

   (a) $a = 4$, $b = 5$ and $c = 12$ **(c)** $a = 6$, $b = 3$ and $c = {}^-5$

   (b) $a = 4$, $b = 7$ and $c = 15$ **(d)** $a = 2$, $b = {}^-3$ and $c = {}^-12$

> You will meet more formulae in Chapter 19

You have been solving problems by letting letters stand for unknowns and then writing equations.

In more complicated problems, you will sometimes find that you have more than one equation.

1   A school has 340 pupils. There are 280 pupils in Year 7 and below, and 160 in Year 7 and above. Find how many pupils there are in Year 7 in the school.

If you let the number of pupils in Year 7 be x, you could show this in a diagram like this.

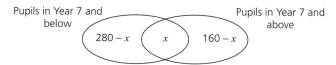

Pupils in Year 7 and below   Pupils in Year 7 and above

$280 - x$ x $160 - x$

(a) Use the three values in the diagram to write an expression for the total number of pupils.

(b) Form an equation for the total number of pupils and solve it.

(c) How many pupils are there in Year 7?

Solve the rest of these problems by forming and solving equations. Use similar diagrams to the one above if it helps.

2   When we took my baby brother to the clinic, he would not keep still and caused the scales to wobble. So my father held the baby and the scales read 75 kg, then my mother held the baby and the scales read 72 kg, and finally my father held my mother while she held the baby and the scales read 140 kg.

(a) What did the baby weigh?

(b) What did my mother weigh?

3   At the café, sausage and chips costs £2.40 and egg and double chips costs £1.80. If egg and sausage costs £3.00, how much is a single portion of chips?

4   A man was trying to weigh his dog. He had some old-fashioned balance scales but no weights. He only had a cabbage weighing one kilogram, a bag of sugar weighing four kilograms and a pumpkin weighing ten kilograms. The man weighed the dog and thought that it weighed 7 kg.

(a) Draw a picture to show how he weighed the dog, using the weights available. Show the weights clearly.

(b) However, he did not notice that the dog had made a hole in the bag and half of the sugar had spilled out. Find the true mass of the dog.

Summary exercise 11.13

1 Solve these equations.

   (a) $a + 4 = 6$

   (b) $b - 2 = 7$

   (c) $c + 3 = 8$

   (d) $d - 7 = 3$

2 Simplify these expressions:

   (a) $3 \times x$

   (b) $a + a + a + a + a$

   (c) $b + b + b + b + b - (2 \times b)$

3 Simplify these expressions.

   (a) $3x + 2y + 2x + 6y$

   (b) $2x - 4 + 3x + 6$

   (c) $3a - 4b + 2a + 5b$

   (d) $4a + 4 - 2a - 4$

   (e) $4c - 5x + 2c - 2x$

   (f) $2b - 4 + 3b - b$

4 Solve these equations.

   (a) $2x = 8$

   (b) $3a = 7$

   (c) $\dfrac{b}{2} = 7$

   (d) $\dfrac{c}{5} = {}^-3$

5 Solve these equations.

   (a) $2x + 3 = 5$

   (b) $7 + 3a = {}^-5$

   (c) $3a - 5 = 7$

   (d) $\dfrac{b}{3} + 2 = 4$

   (e) $5 + 2b = 2$

   (f) $4 - 2x = 3$

   (g) $4 - 2y = 2$

   (h) $3 - \dfrac{a}{4} = 5$

For each of the next five questions, write an equation and then solve it to find the answer.

6 I had twelve coloured pencils but I lost some and now I have five left. How many pencils did I lose?

7 If I treble my age and add seven, I have my father's age. My father is 46. How old am I?

8 I think of a number, double it and subtract 5. The answer is 17. What was my number?

9 I divide my mother's age by three and subtract three. The answer is my brother's age. If my brother is 11, how old is my mother?

10 There are 140 children in the school. Everyone either takes extra music lessons or extra swimming or both. If 85 have extra music and 66 do swimming, how many do both?

11 If $A = x - 2y$ find the value of A when:

    (a) $x = 8$ and $y = 2$

    (b) $x = 3$ and $y = {}^-5$

12 If $Z = \dfrac{2x - y}{3}$ find the value of Z when:

    (a) $x = 8$ and $y = 10$

    (b) $x = 7$ and $y = {}^-4$

Activity: The shopkeeper's dilemma

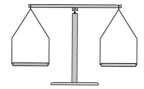

One day a shopkeeper had all his weights stolen! Luckily his good friend the grocer is going to lend him some.

But how many weights should the shopkeeper ask for? He needs to be able to weigh all weights from 1 oz to 40 oz. Which weights should he ask for to allow him to do this? (The weights can only be whole numbers.)

This is quite a tricky problem, so try to make it simpler. If the shopkeeper could only choose two weights, which two weights should he choose so that he could weigh 1 oz, 2 oz, 3 oz, and 4 oz?

Now if he can add a third weight to the first two, which would allow him to weigh the most extra weights?

Now add a fourth weight.

How many weights does he need in total, to be able to weigh every weight between 1 oz and 40 oz?

 # Shapes and symmetry

What do you recall about the properties of shapes? In this chapter, you will look at some more shapes and consider their properties.

One very important property of shapes is **symmetry**.

Symmetry

There are two types of symmetry, **line symmetry** and **rotational symmetry**. A pattern or shape may have one, neither or both. Symmetry is all around you; you will see it in nature, art, architecture and engineering. Just look at this building and this snowflake!

Line symmetry

A shape has line symmetry if it can be folded exactly in half, so that one half lies over the other and both halves match. One half is a **reflection** of the other.

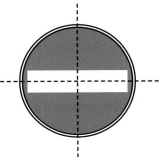

When you take a shape with line symmetry and fold it into two **congruent** halves, the fold line is a **line of symmetry**. Some shapes have more than one line of symmetry. For example, you could fold this 'no entry' sign along either the vertical line or the horizontal line.

Either way, each half of the shape is a **mirror image** of the other half. In fact, lines of symmetry can be vertical, horizontal or diagonal, as you can see if you look back at the snowflake above.

To check this, hold a mirror along each of the lines of symmetry drawn above. You will see that the reflection in the mirror is identical to the pattern that it is hiding.

You can use a mirror to help you to solve line symmetry problems.

Another useful tool when you are studying symmetry, and other topics in geometry, is tracing paper. Use some to trace over the house and the snowflake above. Fold the tracing paper over so that one half of the picture lies exactly over the other. The crease is a line of symmetry. Use your tracing paper to find all the lines of symmetry in the snowflake.

Rotational symmetry

A figure has rotational symmetry if you can move it through a fraction of a turn and it looks the same in its new position as it did at first. For some shapes, you can do this more than once, so that each time you rotate it through the same fraction of a turn it looks exactly as it did at first.

The **order of rotational symmetry** is the number of times that you can rotate the shape by the same fraction of a turn, and it will still look the same, before it is back in its original position.

You cannot have rotational symmetry of order one, because that shape would have no rotational symmetry.

To visualise the idea of rotational symmetry, think about a small child's shape-matching puzzle.

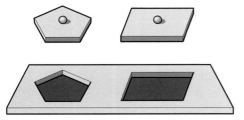

Every time you move the pentagon through one-fifth of a turn, it looks like the original object. It has **rotational symmetry of order 5**

What can you say about the parallelogram? Every time you move it through half a turn, it looks the same as the original object. It has **rotational symmetry of order 2**

The order of rotational symmetry is the number of positions in which the shape looks the same as it did originally, when you turn it around its mid point.

Exercise 12.1

1 These are some road signs that are in common use.

(a) Copy any that have line symmetry. Draw on them all their lines of symmetry.

(b) Copy any that have rotational symmetry. Write the order of rotational symmetry under the sign you have drawn.

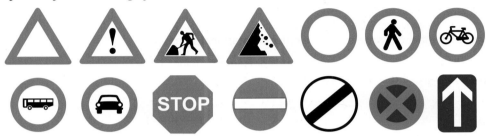

2 These patterns are only half finished. Copy each pattern and shade squares, so that it is symmetrical about the line of symmetry shown.

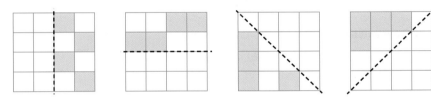

3 Copy these partly finished patterns. Shade squares, so that each pattern is symmetrical about its line of symmetry. This time, you will need to shade squares on both sides of the line.

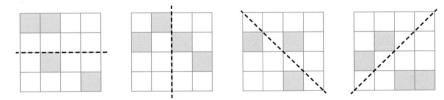

4 (a) These patterns all have two or more lines of symmetry, as did the 'no entry' sign at the start of the chapter. Copy the patterns and use a mirror to find all the lines of symmetry.

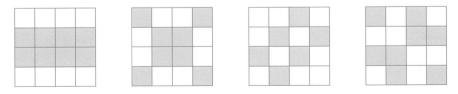

(b) Under each drawing, write down the order of rotational symmetry.

5 (a) These patterns all have two or more lines of symmetry but the patterns are incomplete. Copy them and shade squares, so that each pattern is symmetrical about the given lines of symmetry.

 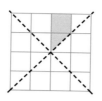 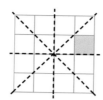

(b) Under each drawing, write down the order of rotational symmetry.

6 (a) These shapes are drawn on triangular grids or isometric paper. Copy them and draw all the lines of symmetry.

(b) Under each drawing, write down the order of rotational symmetry.

(c) Is there a relationship between the number of lines of symmetry and the order of rotational symmetry?

7 These patterns are partly completed. Copy them and shade triangles, so that each pattern is symmetrical about the lines of symmetry shown. You will need to shade triangles on both sides of the lines, so you may need to move your mirror around to help you find all of them.

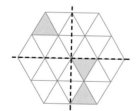 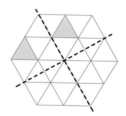 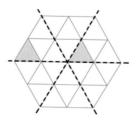

8 Make six copies of this hexagon.

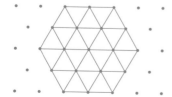

Colour the triangles in a different way to the patterns above so that the resulting pattern has:

(a) rotational symmetry of order three and no line symmetry

(b) one line of symmetry and no rotational symmetry

(c) no lines of symmetry and rotational symmetry of order 2

(d) two lines of symmetry and rotational symmetry of order 2

(e) three lines of symmetry and rotational symmetry of order 3

(f) six lines of symmetry and rotational symmetry of order 6

◯ Quadrilaterals

A **quadrilateral** is a closed four-sided plane shape.

Quadrilateral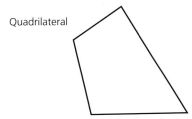

Some quadrilaterals have special properties, such as **equal sides** or **equal angles**.

You already know how to mark equal sides with small dashes and parallel lines with single arrows.

If two pairs of lines on the same figure are parallel, as are the opposite sides of a square or rectangle, you mark the second pair with double arrows.

Here is a summary of special quadrilaterals.

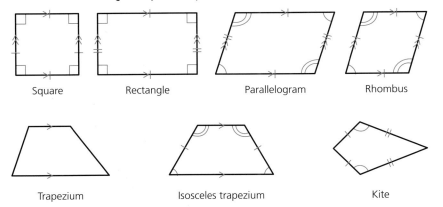

Square   Rectangle   Parallelogram   Rhombus

Trapezium   Isosceles trapezium   Kite

Another special quadrilateral is the **isosceles arrowhead**. An isosceles arrowhead has two pairs of equal sides and one pair of equal angles.

The plural of trapezium is trapezia.

 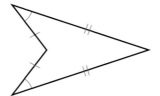

Exercise 12.2

Use the information in the diagrams above to answer these questions.

1   Look at each of the quadrilaterals, below, in turn. Follow these steps, for each one.

   (a) Trace the quadrilateral.

   (b) Fold your tracing in half, or use a mirror, and find all the lines of symmetry.

   (c) Hold your tracing down by placing the tip of your pencil on its centre. Gently rotate the tracing until it has made a full turn, to work out its order of rotational symmetry, if it has any.

   (d) Stick your tracing in your exercise book.

   (e) Under your tracing, copy and complete these sentences. If it has no rotational symmetry, write that down.

   This is a ... . It has ... lines of symmetry and rotational symmetry of order ... .

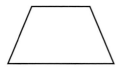  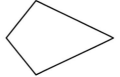 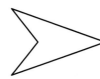

2 Look again at the quadrilaterals in question 1, in turn. Follow these steps, for each one.

   (a) Trace the quadrilateral and label it *ABCD*.

   (b) Mark any equal or parallel sides.

   (c) Draw in the diagonals *AC* and *BD*.

   (d) Stick your tracing into your exercise book.

   (e) Measure the diagonals and, if necessary, the angles between them. Below your tracing of the quadrilateral, write any of these properties that are true.

   - The diagonals are equal.

   - The diagonals are perpendicular.

   - The diagonals bisect each other.

   - The diagonals bisect each other at right angles.

   - One diagonal only is bisected by the other.

3 Which two special quadrilaterals have two pairs of parallel sides and two pairs of equal sides?

4 Which special quadrilateral has two pairs of equal sides but no parallel sides?

5 Which special quadrilateral has all four sides equal but no right angles?

6 Which special quadrilateral has only one pair of parallel sides but another pair of equal sides?

7 Which special quadrilateral has two pairs of equal sides and four right angles?

8 Which special quadrilateral has just one pair of parallel sides?

9 Which special quadrilateral could have only two right angles? Sketch it and mark the right angles.

10 Copy and complete these sentences.

   - A kite has two pairs of adjacent sides that are ... .

   - A kite has only one pair of angles that are ... .

Polygons

Polygons are many-sided plane shapes. The name comes from the Greek *polus*, meaning **many**, and *gonia*, meaning **angle**. You frequently meet the prefix *poly* in words such as:

- polyglot – a person who speaks many languages
- polychrome – having several colours

Polygons may be **regular** or **irregular**. In regular polygons, all the sides are the same length and all the **interior angles** are equal.

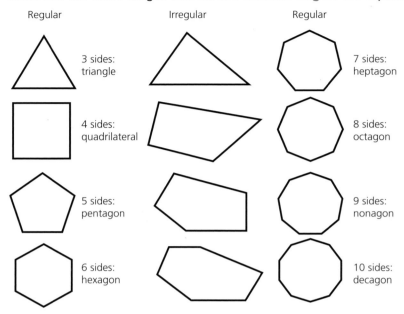

Regular
3 sides: triangle

Irregular

Regular
7 sides: heptagon

4 sides: quadrilateral

8 sides: octagon

5 sides: pentagon

9 sides: nonagon

6 sides: hexagon

10 sides: decagon

Exercise 12.3

You will need square and triangular spotted paper for this exercise.

1 On triangular spotted paper, draw a regular polygon with three sides. Name it.

2 On square spotted paper, draw a regular quadrilateral. Name it. Write down the number of right angles in this quadrilateral.

3 On square spotted paper, draw a pentagon with two right angles.

4 On square spotted paper, draw a pentagon with three right angles.

5 On triangular spotted paper, draw a regular hexagon. Write down the size of each angle.

6 On triangular spotted paper, draw a non-regular hexagon with three pairs of parallel sides.

7 On triangular spotted paper, draw two lines like this.

Use these two lines as the basis for drawing:

(a) a non-regular hexagon

(b) an octagon

(c) a heptagon

(d) a rectangle

(e) a pentagon with two right angles

(f) as many more different hexagons as you can

(g) as many more different octagons as you can.

8 Look at these regular polygons.

Trace each one and then follow these steps.

(a) Fold your tracing in half, or use a mirror, and find all the lines of symmetry.

(c) Hold your tracing down by placing the tip of your pencil in its centre. Gently rotate the tracing until it has made a full turn, to work out its order of rotational symmetry, if it has any.

(d) Stick your tracing in your exercise book.

(e) Under your tracing, copy and complete these sentences.

This is a ... It has ... lines of symmetry and rotational symmetry of order ...

If it has no rotational symmetry, write that down.

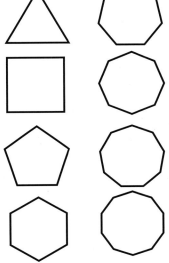

Angles in a polygon

When you construct a polygon you often start with a circle.
You draw a radius, then you calculate the angle you will need at the centre, between this radius and the next. The value of this angle is:

$$\frac{360°}{\text{number of sides}}$$

The other angles that you need to know are the **interior angle** and the **exterior angle**.

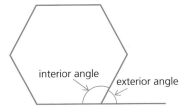

As the interior and exterior angles meet on a straight line they must add up to 180°

Angle sum of a polygon

You already know that a triangle has an angle sum of 180°
You can use this fact to find the angle sum of other polygons.

Example

Find the angle sum of a pentagon.

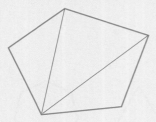

A pentagon can be divided into three triangles.

Angle sum of a pentagon = 3 × 180° = 540°

Exercise 12.4

1 Draw a quadrilateral. Divide it into triangles. Find the angle sum of a quadrilateral.

2 Draw a hexagon and divide it into triangles. Find the angle sum of a hexagon.

3 Draw a heptagon and divide it into triangles. Find the angle sum of a heptagon.

4 Draw an octagon and divide it into triangles. Find the angle sum of an octagon.

5 Copy and complete this table.

Name	Number of sides	Number of triangles	Angle sum
Triangle	3	1	180°
Quadrilateral	4		
Pentagon	5	3	540°
Hexagon	6		
Heptagon	7		
Octagon	8		
Nonagon	9		
Decagon	10		
Dodecagon	12		
Icosagon	20		

6 Hence, write a formula for A, the angle sum of a polygon with n sides.

7   Now consider the regular polygons. All of the angles in a regular polygon are equal. Divide the angle sum (found in question 5) by the number of angles, to find the interior angle of a regular:

(a) quadrilateral   (e) octagon

(b) pentagon   (f) nonagon

(c) hexagon   (g) decagon.

(d) heptagon

8   (a) Calculate the interior angle of a regular 15-sided polygon.

(b) Calculate the interior angle of a regular 20-sided polygon.

Extension Exercise 12.5

1   In the diagram, a square shares a side with a regular hexagon. Find the sizes of the angles marked x, y and z. Give reasons for your answers.

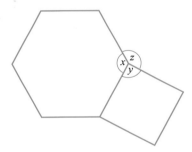

2   In the diagram, a regular hexagon shares a side with a regular octagon. Find the sizes of the angles marked x and y. You may need to find some other angles first. Show each step of your calculations clearly and give reasons for your answers.

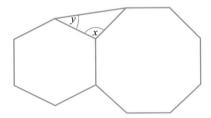

3   In the diagram, a regular hexagon shares a side with a regular pentagon. Find the sizes of the angles marked x and y. You may need to find some other angles first. Show each step of your calculations clearly and give reasons for your answers.

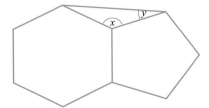

1 Copy the four six-by-six squares below.

(a) On these two, shade squares so that the patterns are symmetrical about the lines of symmetry shown.

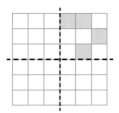 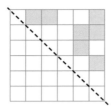

(b) On these two, shade the minimum possible number of squares so that there are two lines of symmetry. Mark the lines of symmetry.

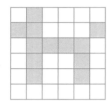 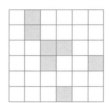

2 Copy and colour these squares, so that the patterns match the descriptions.

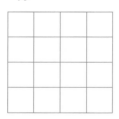 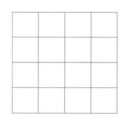 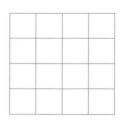 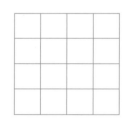

1 line of symmetry
no rotational symmetry

2 lines of symmetry
rotational symmetry of order 2

0 lines of symmetry
rotational symmetry of order 2

4 lines of symmetry
rotational symmetry of order 4

3 Some special quadrilaterals have the same number of lines of symmetry as their order of rotational symmetry. Which are they?

4 Name a special quadrilateral that has no right angles but its diagonals bisect each other.

5 One quadrilateral has no right angles. Its diagonals are equal but do not cross at right angles. Draw it and name it.

6 On square spotted paper, draw an octagon.

(a) Mark any equal sides and equal angles.

(b) Make another copy of your octagon and this time colour it so that it has two lines of symmetry and rotational symmetry of order 2

7   On square spotted paper, draw a pentagon.

(a) Mark any equal sides and equal angles.

(b) Make another copy of your pentagon and this time colour it so that it has one line of symmetry and no rotational symmetry.

8 (a) What is the angle sum of a dodecagon (12 sides)?

(b) What is the size of an interior angle of a regular dodecagon?

Activity: Mirror on the square

For this investigation you will need a mirror, a pair of scissors and centimetre-squared paper.

You are going to investigate the shapes you can make by cutting a square into two parts, and then adding each part to its own reflection.

Draw a square of side 3 cm, in the middle of your page.

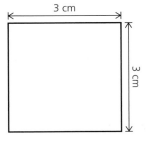

A square has four lines of symmetry, and so there are only four ways you can cut your square so that a reflection in the mirror will make the square whole again.

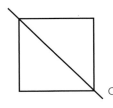

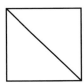

If you cut the square along a line that is not a line of symmetry you will make different shapes.

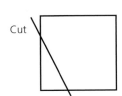

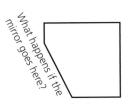

Try to make as many different shapes as you can. Remember the mirror must go on the cut edge.

Can you find:

(a) a square, a rectangle, a kite, a rhombus, a parallelogram, a trapezium

(b) an irregular quadrilateral

(c) a pentagon, a hexagon, a heptagon, an octagon

(d) any other shape?

Can you find any rules about the shapes you can find, as opposed to the shapes you cannot?

13 Transformations

In Chapter 10 you drew some two-dimensional shapes on a co-ordinate grid. In this chapter, you will find out what happens to these shapes when you make simple changes to them.

What are transformations?

First, a reminder of some vocabulary.

Exercise 13.1

You will need tracing paper for this exercise.

When you transform a shape, by translating, reflecting or rotating it, always check that the resulting shape is congruent to the original. This means that the shapes are exactly the same shape and the same size.

The original shape, before the transformation, is the object and the final shape, after the transformation, is the image.

1 These shapes are all congruent.

Check, by tracing the first one and then finding out if your shape exactly matches the other three images. You may have to turn your tracing round, or flip it over.

A translation is a movement of a shape, up or down, forward or back, or diagonally. The resulting image is exactly congruent to the original shape. The object has been translated to form the image.

2   These red shapes are all look like translations of the original blue shape but one of them is not, because it is not congruent to the others.

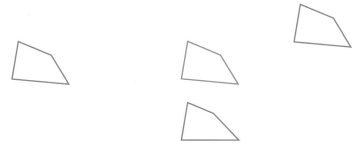

Use tracing paper to find out which one is not congruent to the others. For the true translations, work out how many centimetres left or right and how many centimetres up or down they have moved.

A **reflection** is the result of reflecting an object to form an image. The image is exactly the same distance away from a straight line (the **line of reflection**) as the object. The image is congruent to the object but has been flipped over. It looks as if the object has been reflected in a mirror placed along the line of reflection. Lines drawn from corresponding points in the object and image are at right angles to the line of reflection.

3   The red shape is a reflection of the blue shape, in the dotted line.

Check that the shapes are congruent by tracing over both shapes and the line, then folding your tracing. Your crease should be on the dotted line. Open out your tracing and join up corresponding points. What do you notice? The dotted line is the mirror line.

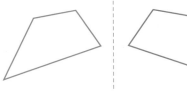

A **rotation** is a turn. The image shows the position of the object after it has been rotated through a number of degrees, either **clockwise** or **anticlockwise**, about a **centre of rotation**.

The resulting image is congruent to the original object, but is at a different angle to the vertical and horizontal and therefore may look different. It is important to check that the object and image after a rotation are still congruent. Tracing paper is useful.

4   The red shape is a rotation of the blue shape about the point marked X. Use tracing paper to check that the shapes are congruent.

Trace over the shape and then put your pencil at the point X. Carefully rotate the shape, around the point X, until it fits exactly over the red shape. Through how many degrees has your object been rotated? In which direction?

You will see transformations used in many designs, on fabric, on paper or in buildings.

● X

5 Look at this image of a tile. What transformations you can identify?

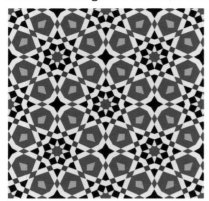

Straight lines

When you describe some transformations, you sometimes need to refer to a straight line.

To describe a straight line, you look at the x-co-ordinates and the y-co-ordinates of points on the line.

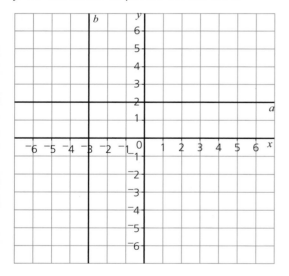

On this grid, line a runs through the points (⁻5, 2), (⁻3, 2), (1, 2), (4, 2)

All the y-co-ordinates are 2. The line is called $y = 2$

Line b runs through the points (⁻3, ⁻5), (⁻3, ⁻3), (⁻3, 1), (⁻3, 4)

All the x-co-ordinates are ⁻3. The line is called $x = ⁻3$

Exercise 13.2

1 Look at this co-ordinate grid, then write down the equations of the lines a–g.

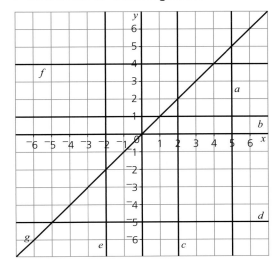

2 Draw a pair of co-ordinate axes, with values of x and y from ⁻6 to 6. Add these lines to your grid.

(a) $x = 4$

(b) $y = 3$

(c) $x = ⁻5$

(d) $y = ⁻4$

(e) $x = ⁻y$

3 Find the lines $x = 0$ and $y = 0$. What other names describe them?

Translations

In rotations and reflections, the image is in a different place from the object, and is a different way round (rotation) or flipped over (reflection). Sometimes you just want an image to be in a new place, but stay the same way round. To do this, you need to slide the object across the page. As you saw in Exercise 13.1, when an image is in a different place from the object, but is the same way round, you have a translation.

This diagram shows a translation of '3 units right and 1 unit up'.

Notice that the translation is described in the same order as a pair of co-ordinates: the horizontal (x) direction first, then the vertical (y) direction.

Now look at this grid.

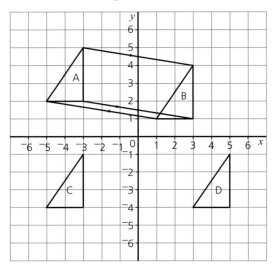

- The translation from A to B is 6 units right, 1 unit down.

- The translation from A to C is 0 units right, 6 units down.

- The translation from C to D is 8 units right, 0 units down.

- The translation from D to B is 2 units left, 5 units up.

Exercise 13.3

1 Describe the translation that maps:

(a) A to B

(b) C to B

(c) C to D

(d) B to D

(e) D to A

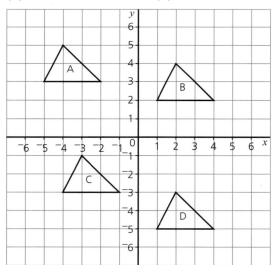

2 Describe the translation that maps:

(a) A to B   (c) D to B   (e) D to E

(b) B to C   (d) A to D   (f) E to A

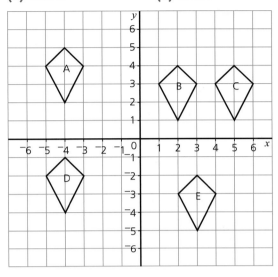

3 Draw a pair of co-ordinate axes, with values of x and y numbered from ⁻6 to 6
  On your grid, draw a triangle A with vertices at (5, 5), (5, 3) and (2, 4)

> A **vertex** is a corner, so the vertices of a triangle are the three corners.

(a) Draw triangle B, the image of A after a translation of 7 left and 3 down.

(b) Write down the co-ordinates of the vertices of triangle B.

(c) Draw triangle C, the image of B after a translation of 3 right and 2 up.

(d) Write down the co-ordinates of the vertices of triangle C.

(e) Describe the translation that will map triangle A to triangle C.

4 Draw a pair of co-ordinate axes, with values of x and y numbered from ⁻6 to 6
  On your grid, draw a shape P with vertices at (⁻2, 2), (⁻2, 4), (⁻4, 5) and (⁻4, 1)

(a) What is the name of shape P?

(b) Draw the shape Q, the image of P after a translation of 3 right and 3 down.

(c) Write down the co-ordinates of the vertices of shape Q.

(d) Draw shape R, the image of Q after a translation of 2 right and 4 down.

(e) Write down the co-ordinates of the vertices of shape R.

(f) Describe the translation that will map shape R to shape P.

5 Draw a pair of co-ordinate axes, with values of x and y numbered from ‾6 to 6
On your grid, draw a shape K with vertices at (‾4, ‾4), (‾3, ‾5), (‾2, ‾4) and (‾3, ‾2)

  (a) What is the name of shape K?

  (b) Draw the shape L, the image of K after a translation of 4 right and 5 up.

  (c) Write down the co-ordinates of the vertices of shape L.

  (d) Draw shape M, the image of L after a translation of 2 left and 3 down.

  (e) Write down the co-ordinates of the vertices of shape M.

  (f) Describe the translation that will map shape M to shape K.

6 Look at your answers to question 4. Copy and complete these sentences.

The vertices of the original object P were (‾2, 2), (‾2, 4), (‾4, 5) and (‾4, ‾2)
The combined two translations resulted in the image moving ... units right
and ... units down. The vertices of the final image R were ... .

7 Look at your answers to question 5. Copy and complete these sentences.

The vertices of the original object K were (‾4, ‾4), (‾3, ‾5), (‾2, ‾4) and (‾3, ‾2)
The combined two translations resulted in the image moving ... units right / left
and ... units up / down. The vertices of the final image M were ... .

8 (a) A point $P(4, 2)$ is translated to a point Q by a translation of 4 units right
and 2 units up, followed by a translation of 5 units left and 3 units down.
What are the co-ordinates of Q?

  (b) A point $R(‾2, ‾5)$ is translated to a point S by a translation of 3 units left
and 2 units down followed by a translation of 1 unit right and 3 units
down. What are the co-ordinates of S?

  (c) A point $W(‾3, 1)$ is translated to a point X by a translation of 5 units right
and 4 units up, followed by a translation of 1 unit right and 6 units down.
What are the co-ordinates of X?

◯ Reflections

Mathematically, a **reflection** is the image of an
object in a line of symmetry.

On this grid, triangle X is a reflection of triangle
A in the x-axis and triangle Y is a reflection of
triangle A in the y-axis.

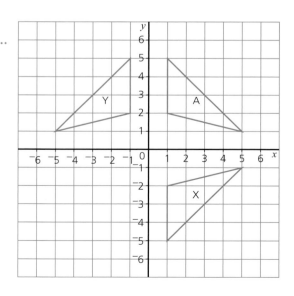

Exercise 13.4

You may wish to use a mirror or tracing paper to check your answers to this exercise.

1 (a) Copy this grid and triangle A into your exercise book.

(b) Draw a reflection of triangle A in the x-axis. Label this new shape B.

(c) Draw a reflection of triangle A in the y-axis. Label this new shape C.

(d) Draw a reflection of triangle B in the y-axis. Label this new shape D.

(e) Is the new shape D a reflection of any other shape? If so, in which line?

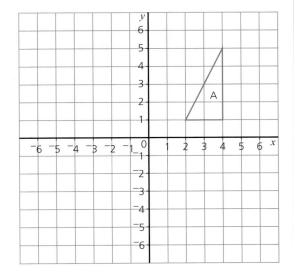

2 (a) Draw a pair of co-ordinate axes, with values of x and y numbered from ⁻6 to 6. On your grid, copy shape E, below.

(b) Draw a reflection of shape E in the x-axis and label it F.

(c) Draw a reflection of shape E in the y-axis and label it G.

(d) Draw a reflection of shape G in the x-axis and label it H.

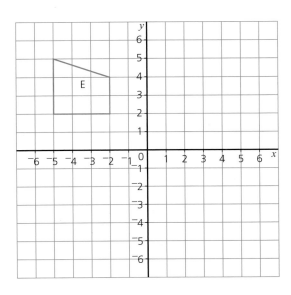

3 (a) Draw a pair of co-ordinate axes, with values of x and y numbered from
⁻6 to 6. On your grid, draw the mirror line $y = 2$. Copy shape P.

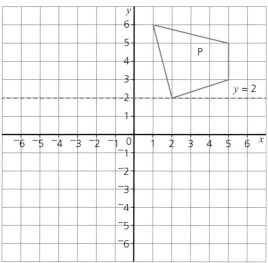

(b) Draw a reflection of shape P in the line $y = 2$ and label it Q.

(c) Draw a reflection of shape P in the y-axis and label it R.

(d) Draw a reflection of shape R in the line $y = 2$ and label it S.

4 (a) Draw a pair of co-ordinate axes, with values of x and y numbered from
⁻6 to 6. On your grid, draw the mirror line $x = 1$

(b) Draw triangle A with vertices at (1, 4), (5, 3) and (2, 2)

(c) Draw a reflection of shape A in the line $x = 1$ and label it B.

(d) Draw a reflection of shape A in the x-axis and label it C.

(e) Draw a reflection of shape C in the line $x = 1$ and label it D.

5 (a) Draw a pair of co-ordinate axes, with values of x and y numbered from
⁻6 to 6. Use a scale of one centimetre to represent one unit. On your grid,
draw the mirror line $y = x$

(b) Draw shape W with vertices at (1, 1), (1, 4), (3, 4), and (3, 1)

(c) Draw a reflection of shape W in the line $y = x$ and label it X.

(d) Draw a reflection of shape W in the x-axis and label it Y.

(e) Draw a reflection of shape Y in the line $y = x$ and label it Z.

> This is the line
> through all the points
> where the y-value is
> equal to the x-value.

6 (a) Draw a pair of co-ordinate axes, with values of x and y numbered from
⁻6 to 6. On your grid, draw the mirror line $x = ⁻1$.

(b) Draw triangle A with vertices at (⁻1, 5), (⁻5, 4) and (⁻3, 1)

(c) Draw a reflection of shape A in the line $x = ⁻1$ and label it B.

(d) Draw a reflection of shape A in the x-axis and label it C.

(e) Draw a reflection of shape C in the line $x = ⁻1$ and label it D.

◯ Rotations

Unlike a translation, a rotation changes the **orientation** of the shape, or the way it looks on the page.

To be able to draw a shape after a rotation you need to know:

● the centre of rotation

● the angle of rotation

● the direction of rotation – clockwise or anticlockwise.

Look carefully at the shapes in this co-ordinate grid.

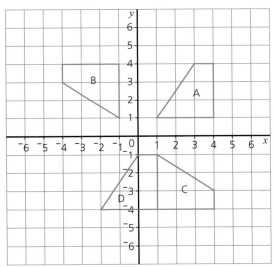

Use tracing paper to check these statements.

● B is the image of A after a rotation of 90° anticlockwise about the origin.

● C is the image of A after a rotation of 90° clockwise about the origin.

● D is the image of C after a rotation of 90° anticlockwise about (1, ⁻4)

Note that for a rotation of 180° it does not matter if the direction is clockwise or anticlockwise. Here A is rotated 180° about the point *P* to the image E.

Exercise 13.5

You may wish to use tracing paper to check your rotations.

1 Look at the images on this grid.

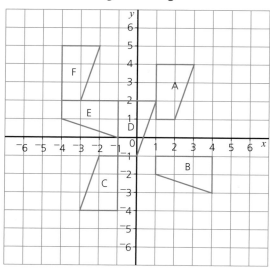

Write, in full, the rotation that maps:

(a) shape A to shape B

(b) shape A to shape C

(c) shape C to shape D

(d) shape D to shape E

(e) shape E to shape F

(f) shape C to shape B.

2 (a) Draw a pair of co-ordinate axes, with values of x and y numbered from $^-6$ to 6. Use a scale of one centimetre to represent one unit.
On your grid, copy shape S and point $P(3, 1)$.

(b) Draw the image of shape S after a rotation of 180° about the point P. Label it T.

(c) Draw the image of shape S after a rotation of 90° anticlockwise about the point P. Label it V.

(d) Describe the rotation that maps shape T to shape V.

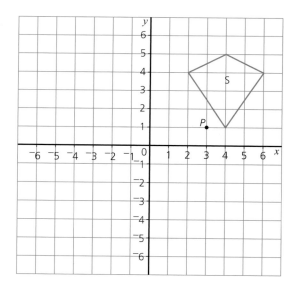

3 (a) Draw a pair of co-ordinate axes, with values of x and y numbered from
‾6 to 6. On your grid, draw triangle A with vertices at (4, 1), (1, 1) and (3, 4)

(b) Draw the image of A after a rotation of 90° clockwise about the origin.
Label it B.

(c) Draw the image of A after a rotation of 90° anticlockwise about the
origin. Label it C.

(d) Draw the image of B after a rotation of 180° about the point (1, ‾3) and
label it D.

4 (a) On a pair of axes with values of x and y from ‾6 to 6, draw shape P with
vertices at (1, ‾3), (3, ‾2), (5, ‾3) and (3, ‾4)

(b) What type of shape is P?

(c) Draw the image of P after a rotation of 90° anticlockwise about the
origin. Label it Q.

(d) Draw the image of P after a rotation of 180° about the point (0, ‾3)
Label it R.

(e) Describe the rotation that maps shape Q to shape R.

5 (a) Draw a pair of co-ordinate axes, with values of x and y numbered from
‾6 to 6. On your grid, draw shape W with vertices at (‾5, 2), (‾4, 4), (‾3, 4)
and (‾1, 2)

(b) What type of shape is W?

(c) Draw the image of W after a rotation of 180° about the origin. Label it X.

(d) Draw the image of X after a rotation of 180° about the point (0, ‾2)
Label it Y.

(d) Draw the image of X after a rotation of 90° anticlockwise about the
origin. Label it Z.

(e) Describe the rotation that maps shape Y to shape Z.

6 (a) Draw a pair of co-ordinate axes, with values of x and y numbered from
‾6 to 6. On your grid, draw shape A with vertices at (‾5, ‾3), (‾3, ‾1),
(‾2, ‾2) and (‾4, ‾4)

(b) What type of shape is A?

(c) Draw the image of A after a rotation of 90° anticlockwise about the
origin. Label it B.

(d) Draw the image of B after a rotation of 180° about the point (2, ‾2)
Label it C.

(e) Describe the rotation that maps shape A to shape C.

You have been using the transformations: translation, rotation and reflection. Sometimes an image may be produced by more than one of these transformations.

B could be the image of A after:

- a translation of 4 units right
- a reflection in the line $x = 3$
- a rotation of 180° about the point (3, 3)
- a rotation of 90° clockwise about the point (3, 1)
- a rotation of 90° anticlockwise about the point (3, 4)

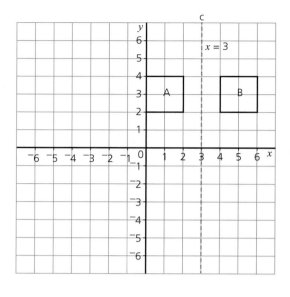

1 Look carefully at this grid.

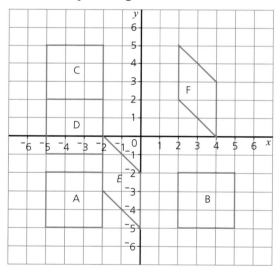

(a) Is B a reflection of A in the x-axis or the y-axis?

(b) Is C a rotation of A 90° clockwise or 90° anticlockwise about the origin?

(c) Describe a transformation that maps C to B.

2 Looking at the grid in question 1, write down all the possible transformations that could map:

(a) A to B

(b) A to C

(c) C to D

(d) B to C

(e) E to F

Summary Exercise 13.7

1

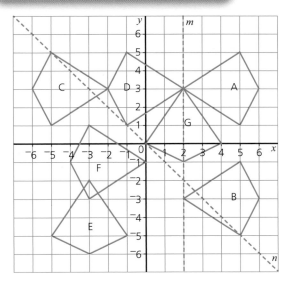

(a) Write down the equation of line *m*.

(b) Write down the equation of line *n*.

(c) Describe the transformation (and there may be more than one possibility) that maps:

    (i)   kite A to kite B   (v)   kite B to kite F

    (ii) kite A to kite C   (vi) kite C to kite F

    (iii) kite A to kite D   (vii) kite G to kite E

    (iv) kite A to kite E

2 (a) Draw a pair of co-ordinate axes, with values of x and y numbered from $^-6$ to 6. On your grid, draw triangle A with vertices at $(^-2, 2)$, $(^-2, 4)$ and $(^-5, 2)$

  (b) Draw the reflection of triangle A in the y-axis. Label it B.

  (c) Draw the rotation of triangle A 90° clockwise about the origin. Label it C.

  (d) Draw the image of triangle A after a translation of 6 units right and 3 units down. Label it D.

  (e) Write down the co-ordinates of D.

3 (a) Draw a pair of co-ordinate axes, with values of x and y numbered from $^-6$ to 6. On your grid, draw shape A with vertices at $(3, 0)$, $(2, 2)$, $(3, 4)$ and $(4, 2)$

  (b) What kind of quadrilateral is A?

  (c) Draw the reflection of A in the y-axis and label it B.

  (d) Draw the rotation of B 90° anticlockwise about the origin and label it C.

(e) Draw the image of C after a translation of 6 units right and 2 units up and label it D.

(f) Write down the co-ordinates of D.

4 (a) Draw a pair of co-ordinate axes, with values of x and y numbered from ⁻6 to 6. On your grid, draw triangle A with vertices at (2, 2), (3, 5), (5, 2)

(b) Draw the reflection of A in the x-axis. Label it B.

(c) Draw the rotation of A of 180° about the origin. Label it C.

(d) Draw the image of A after a translation of left 2 and down 4 and label it D.

(e) Describe the transformation that maps B to C.

Activity: Maths from stars – design a tile

You considered this tile in the first exercise in this chapter.

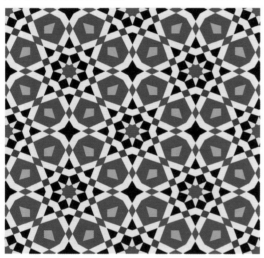

Can you see how the pattern starts with an eight-pointed star?

Use some graphics software to design a tile of your own. Start with a star, extend the sides and see where that leads you. You may wish to research some other tiling patterns first.

14 Measurement

◯ Time

The Egyptians divided the clock into 12 hours of daytime and 12 hours of night-time. This is known because various sundials from the period have been found to be marked with hours. Egyptian, and then Greek, astronomers found 60 to be very useful for working with fractions, as it has so many **factors**.

You know that there are:

- 60 seconds in a minute
- 60 minutes in an hour
- 24 hours in a day
- 7 days in a week.

But how many weeks are there in a month?

The number of days – and thus weeks – in a month varies. The calendar currently in use is the **Gregorian calendar**, introduced in 1582 by Pope Gregory XIII. In this calendar, February has either 28 or 29 days, while the other months have either 30 or 31 days. A useful way to remember them is by the nursery rhyme:

> *Thirty days have September,*
>
> *April, June and November.*
>
> *All the rest have thirty-one,*
>
> *Except for February alone,*
>
> *And that has twenty-eight days clear*
>
> *And twenty-nine in each leap year.*

The history behind the different number of days is not clear. A **lunar month** is approximately 30 days. Many civilisations have worked on a year of 12 months of 30 days, plus 5 extra feast days, to make 365 days in a solar year. The word month comes from the word moon. As the Earth orbits the Sun, the number of hours of daylight changes.

This is because the axis of the Earth is tilted at about 23° from the perpendicular to the plane of its orbit. This diagram shows how the longest and shortest days – the **solstices** – occur and the days when the length of the day equals the length of the night – the equinoxes. These were all celebrated by ancient civilisations and often still are, in modern times too.

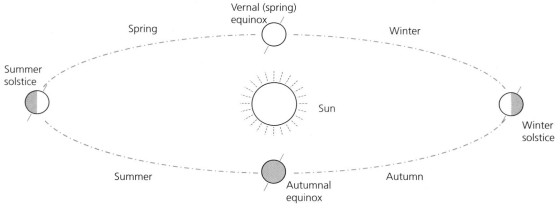

To be more precise, there are very nearly $365\frac{1}{4}$ days in a year. This is why every fourth year is a **leap year** with 366 days. If you want to be even more accurate, a year is 365.2422 days long and so only every fourth 'end of a century year' counts as a leap year – which is why the year 2000 was a leap year but the year 1900 was not.

British Summer time

In the UK the clocks are set forward in the spring to give longer summer evenings. They are set back again in the autumn to give more daylight in the morning. In the UK, clocks are set to **Greenwich Mean Time** (GMT) from October to March and to **British Summer Time** (BST) from March to October. Many other countries do the same.

In the USA, summer time is called 'daylight saving time'. There, autumn is known as fall. A useful way to remember which way to put your clocks is: 'Spring forward, fall back'.

Time zones

As the Earth spins on its axis, different parts of the world are in daylight. When the UK is in daylight, countries on the other side of the globe, such as China, will be in darkness. To allow for this, the Earth is divided into strips, with each strip being a different **time zone**. You will study this in more detail in geography.

The 24-hour clock

It is usual to talk about a day as being in two sections, each of 12 hours. You can differentiate between morning and afternoon by using a.m. (*ante meridiem* = before midday) and p.m. (*post meridiem* = after midday). Increasingly, there is a need to avoid confusion, particularly when giving the time of an event, or on schedules such as train timetables, and so the 24-hour clock is used.

Compare the three ways of describing time.

Using past or to	12-hour clock	24-hour clock
Ten o'clock	10.00 a.m.	10:00
Quarter past two (afternoon)	2.15 p.m.	14:15
Five to midnight	11.55 p.m.	23:55
Midnight	00.00	00:00
Noon	12.00 noon	12:00

These times may also be written without a colon between the hours and the minutes, for example, 0700, 2315

Exercise 14.1

Use the facts above about years, months and the 24-hour clock to answer these questions.

1 Which of these years are leap years?

 (a) 2014   (b) 2020   (c) 2000   (d) 2100   (e) 2016

2 How many days is it from:

 (a) the beginning of January to the end of March in a non-leap year

 (b) the beginning of October to the end of December

 (c) the beginning of April to the end of June?

3 (a) Which is the shortest period of three consecutive months?

 (b) Which is the longest period of three consecutive months?

4 Our school term runs from 2 September to 19 December. How many days is this?

5 August Bank Holiday is always the last Monday in August. If 1 August is a Wednesday, what will be the date of the August Bank Holiday?

6 My birthday, 11 August 2014, fell on a Monday. On what day will it fall in:

 (a) 2016

 (b) 2017?

7 This is a calendar for the month of July 2016. To answer this question, you should begin by finding out whether 2016 is a leap year.

JULY 2016						
M	T	W	T	F	S	S
				1	2	3
4	5	6	7	8	9	10
11	12	13	14	15	16	17
18	19	20	21	22	23	24
25	26	27	28	29	30	31

In 2016 what day of the week are these dates?

(a) 30 June   (c) 3 August   (e) Christmas Day

(b) 31 May   (d) 31 January   (f) your birthday

8 Write these times in the 24-hour clock system.

(a) 7.15 a.m.   (c) 12.50 p.m.   (e) 6.45 p.m.

(b) 20 past midnight   (d) 4.25 p.m.   (f) 12.45 a.m.

9 Write these times in the 12-hour clock system, followed by a.m. or p.m.

(a) 11:15   (c) 07:45   (e) 00:15

(b) 13:20   (d) 20:20   (f) 12:23

10 My school day starts at 08:25 and finishes at 15:55. How long do I stay I at school? Give your answer to the exact number of hours and minutes.

11 (a) On the 27 March, the clocks go forward. I go to bed at 10 p.m. My alarm is set for 7 a.m. Will I have an hour more to sleep or an hour less?

(b) On 30 October, the clocks go back. I go to bed at 10:30 p.m. My alarm is set for 9 a.m. Will I have an hour more to sleep or an hour less?

12 Around the world, there are different time zones.

Going east, the time is ahead: Paris is UK time + 1 hour, Turkey is UK time + 2 hours, Perth (Australia) is UK time + 8 hours, Sydney (Australia) is UK + 11 hours.

Going west, the time is behind: New York (USA) is 5 hours behind, Los Angeles (USA) is 8 hours behind.

(a) At noon UK time, what will the time be in:

(i) Paris   (iii) Sydney   (v) Los Angeles?

(ii) Turkey   (iv) New York   (vi) Perth

(b) What time will it be in the UK, when it is 8:00 a.m. in:

(i) Paris   (iii) Sydney   (v) Los Angeles?

(ii) Turkey   (iv) New York   (vi) Perth

Length, mass and capacity

Nowadays, apart from time, most measurements are recorded in **metric units**, based on 10, 100, 1000... This is because, as you have seen in previous chapters, it is very easy to multiply and divide by 10, 100, 1000... and thus convert between units and subunits. This is the **decimal system**.

In the UK, you will still meet some units such as miles (for distances) and pounds (for mass/weight). These are **imperial units** from the **imperial system**, which was largely replaced in the UK in the late twentieth century. There is more about imperial units at the end of this chapter.

The metric system

The idea of a system of measurement based on 10, 100 and 1000 was suggested at various times from the Middle Ages onwards but it was only in France, during the French Revolution at the end of the eighteenth century, and during the subsequent reforms made by Napoleon, that the opportunity for a complete change was taken.

In Britain the change to **decimalisation** began in the 1960s and, to a large extent, the metric measurements for volume, mass, temperature and length are now used uniformly with the rest of Europe. However, most people in the UK still measure distances in miles and many give their weight (or, strictly speaking, their mass) in stones and pounds, and their height in feet and inches.

Metric units

The metric system is based on one basic unit for each type of measurement. You measure:

● **length** in **metres** (m)

● **mass** in **grams** (g)

● **capacity** (**volume**) in **litres** (l)

> **Capacity** is the amount of space that is inside an empty container and is measured in litres. **Volume** is the measure of the amount of space occupied by a three-dimensional object and is measured in cubic units (see Chapter 20). However, if you are talking about the substance held inside the container, such as water, it is commonly referred to as its volume.

For larger units of measurements, you measure in one thousand times the basic unit:

● length in **kilometres** (km)

● mass in **kilograms** (kg)

For smaller units of measurement you measure in one thousandth of the basic unit:

- length in **millimetres** (mm)
- mass in **milligrams** (mg)
- capacity in **millilitres** (ml)

As well as these measurements based on units of 1000 (in Latin, *mille* = 1000), you will use subunits based on 100 (in Latin, *centum* = 100). Thus:

- 1 **centimetre** (1 cm) = $\dfrac{1}{100}$ of a metre

- 1 **centilitre** (1 cl) = $\dfrac{1}{100}$ of a litre.

From this it follows that:

$$10 \, mm = 1 \, cm$$

and $\quad 10 \, ml = 1 \, cl$

Finally there is one extra unit of mass: 1000 kg = 1 **tonne** (or **metric ton**).

You can use these facts to convert between units. Before you start, ask yourself: 'Is my answer going to be a smaller or larger number?' Write down the calculation that you are doing and check that the answer makes sense.

Examples

(i) Write these lengths in metres: (a) 50 cm (b) 3 km (c) 300 mm

   (a) 50 cm is 50 ÷ 100 = 0.5 m

   (b) 3 km is 3 × 1000 = 3000 m

   (c) 300 mm is 3 ÷ 1000 = 0.3 m

(ii) What is 450 kg in tonnes?

   450 kg is 450 × 1000 = 450 000 tonnes ✗

   Check: My answer does not make sense, it is too large!

   450 kg is 450 ÷ 1000 = 0.45 tonnes ✓

Exercise 14.2

1 Write these lengths in metres.

   (a) 200 cm

   (b) 0.4 km

   (c) 400 mm

   (d) 35 km

   (e) 5 km

   (f) 305 cm

   (g) 25 cm

   (h) 25 mm

2 Write these masses in grams.

(a) 20 kg   (b) 3000 mg   (c) 0.4 kg   (d) 350 mg

3 Write these capacities in litres.

(a) 200 ml   (b) 30 000 ml   (c) 25 cl   (d) 0.5 cl

4 Write these lengths in centimetres (cm).

(a) 200 mm   (b) 2 km   (c) 300 m   (d) 5 m

5 Write these masses in kilograms (kg).

(a) 3500 g   (b) 40 g   (c) 25 000 mg   (d) 75 000 g

6 Write these capacities in millilitres (ml).

(a) 10 litres   (b) 350 litres   (c) 0.5 litres   (d) 7 cl

7 Write these lengths in millimetres (mm).

(a) 32 cm   (b) 4.5 cm   (c) 0.63 m   (d) 4 km

8 Write these masses in milligrams (mg).

(a) 320 g   (b) 5500 g   (c) 1.5 g   (d) 0.5 kg

9 Write these lengths in kilometres (km).

(a) 35 600 m   (c) 32 000 cm

(b) 455 m   (d) 4 500 000 mm

10 Write these masses in tonnes.

(a) 4000 kg   (c) 600 000 g

(b) 450 kg   (d) 7 500 000 g

◯ Calculating with measurements

If you need to add or subtract measurements, you must first make sure that they are expressed in the same units. You may need to change some units.

Example

Add: 1.2 m + 23 cm + 15 mm

1.2 m + 23 cm + 15 mm = 120 cm + 23 cm + 1.5 cm

$$= 144.5 \text{ cm}$$

Exercise 14.3

1 I walk for 400 m, swim for 800 m and then run for 2.4 km. How far have I travelled? Answer in kilometres (km).

2 Our science teacher divides a 2 kg bag of salt equally among 20 of us for an experiment on dissolving. How many grams of salt do we each receive?

3 Milk from a 6-litre bottle can fill 48 small glasses. How many millilitres of milk is in each glass?

4 A 3 km race is divided into 12 stages so that each of my team of 12 runs one stage. What is the length of each stage?

5 I have four pieces of string. They are 3 m, 45 cm, 205 cm and 25 mm long. What total length, in centimetres, do I have?

6 If I pour 3 cups of concentrated orange juice, each of volume 350 ml, and 6 mugs of water, each of volume 550 ml, into a jug, how many litres of diluted juice will I have in the jug?

7 Jamie, the school chef is baking a batch of puddings. He mixes: 1.5 kg of flour, 700 g of sugar, 820 g of dried fruit and 40 mg of baking powder.

   What is the total mass, in grams, of these ingredients?

8 A door is 1.8 m high and 90 cm wide. What total length of wood, in metres, do I need to make the frame?

9 A window is 80 cm high and 1.2 m wide. What total length of wood do I need to make the frame?

10 The chemistry teacher is weighing out some ingredients. She has two beakers each containing 1.4 kg of chemical A, three test tubes each containing 360 g of chemical B, and four lab spoons each containing 650 mg of chemical C. What is the total mass, in grams, of all the chemicals?

11 My mother sent me shopping to buy 3 kg of potatoes at 67p per kilogram and a pineapple for £1.35. How much change did I have from a five-pound note?

12 I filled 8 glasses of volume 265 ml from a jug containing 3.5 litres of squash. How much was left in the jug?

13 A builder is making concrete with:

   70 × 40 kg bags of cement

   120 × 25 kg bags of sand

   4 × 1 tonne bags of pebbles.

   What is the total mass of his mixture, in tonnes?

14 My naughty little sister is trying to reach the biscuit tin. She starts with a chair of which the seat is 0.9 m above the ground. She puts a box that is 12 cm high on that, and then a book that is 25 mm thick on the box. She then stands on the book. My little sister is 1.1 m tall and can reach 30 cm above her own height. Can she reach the biscuit tin, if it is 2.5 m above the floor?

Imperial units

In the UK, distances are measured in **miles**. Older people may weigh themselves in stones and pounds, and measure their height in feet and inches. Many drinks are sold by the pint and buckets are measured in gallons. If you go shopping, you may find that some goods are sold by weight in pounds, and by lengths in feet or yards.

Imperial units are still in common usage in the USA although their actual measures may vary from those in the UK. It is therefore very useful to understand this system of measurement as well as the metric system.

Mass

16 **ounces** (oz) = 1 **pound** (lb)

14 pounds (lb) = 1 **stone** (st)

1 **ton** (t) = 2240 pounds (lb)

Length

12 **inches** (in) = 1 **foot** (ft)

3 **feet** (ft) = 1 **yard** (yd)

1760 yards (yd) = 1 **mile** (m)

Capacity

2 **pints** (pt) = 1 **quart** (qt)

8 pints (pt) = 1 **gallon** (gall)

Examples

(i)   What is 130 lb in stones and pounds?

130 lb = 130 ÷ 14 stones

= 9 r 4

= 9 stones 4 pounds

(ii)   What is 3.2 yards in feet?

1 yard = 3 feet

3.2 yards = 3 × 3.2 feet

= 9.6 feet

> When converting units, always take care to show your working.

Exercise 14.4

1   Write each of these measurements in the units shown.

(a)   4 yards in feet

(b)   5 feet 6 inches in inches

(c)   50 inches in feet and inches

(d)   5 miles in yards

2 Write each of these measurements in the units shown.

   (a) 4 lb in ounces

   (b) 120 ounces in pounds and ounces

   (c) 3.5 tons in pounds

   (d) 160 lb in stones and pounds

   (e) 9 stone 4 pounds in pounds

   (f) 5000 lb in tons and pounds

3 Write each of these measurements in the units shown.

   (a) 5 gallons in pints   (c) 30 quarts in gallons and pints

   (b) 100 pints in gallons and pints   (d) 20 pints in quarts

4 A barrel holds 36 gallons of beer. How many pints is that?

5 What fraction of a gallon is a quart?

6 Horse races are often measured in furlongs. A furlong is 220 yards.

   (a) How many feet are there in a furlong?

   (b) What fraction of a mile is a furlong?

7 Building materials used to be sold by the hundredweight (cwt).
  One hundredweight is 112 lb.

   (a) How many stones are there in a hundredweight?

   (b) What fraction of a ton is a hundredweight?

8 A square mile is 640 acres.

   (a) How many square yards are there in a square mile?

   (b) How many square yards are there in an acre?

Metric to imperial equivalents

Here are some useful conversions, giving **equivalent units** in the two systems.

Mass

1 lb ≈ 450 g

1 kg ≈ 2.2 lb   Add $\frac{1}{10}$ and multiply by 2

Length

1 metre ≈ 39 in or 3 feet and 3 in   Multiply by $3\frac{1}{4}$

1 kilometre ≈ $\frac{5}{8}$ mile   Multiply by 5 then divide by 8

1 foot ≈ 30 cm

5 miles ≈ 8 km

Capacity

1 pint ≈ 600 ml

1 gallon ≈ 4.5 litres

1 litre ≈ 1.7 pints

10 litres ≈ 2.2 gallons

Exercise 14.5

1 Write each of these measurements in the units shown.

   (a) 5 kg in pounds   (d) 4 oz in grams

   (b) 12 lb in kilograms   (e) 75 kg in stones and pounds

   (c) 0.25 kg in pounds   (f) 10 stones in kilograms

2 Write each of these measurements in the units shown.

   (a) 10 metres in feet and inches   (d) 150 miles in kilometres

   (b) 240 km in miles   (e) 6 yards in metres

   (c) 10 feet in metres   (f) 0.25 metres in inches

3 Write each of these measurements in the units shown.

   (a) 5 pints in litres   (c) 0.25 gallons in millilitres

   (b) 50 litres in gallons   (d) 500 ml in pints

4 Wine is served in a 125 ml glass. What fraction of a pint is this?

5 An old book tells me to take 3 yards of ribbon. What is this, in metres?

6 An athlete collapsed after drinking 4 gallons of water. How many litres is that?

7 Amy drives for 120 miles to get to Dover, then crosses the Channel and drives for 290 km to reach Paris.

How far is the total journey (not including the ferry crossing) in:

(a) miles   (b) kilometres?

8 My American cousin tells me that he weighs 95 lb. I weigh 42 kg.

(a) Who is the heavier?

(b) What is the difference in: (i) kilograms   (ii) pounds?

9 I am 155 cm tall. What is that in feet and inches?

10 My car will, on average, use 6.5 litres of fuel for every 100 km. My American cousin has a car that will, on average, travel 46 miles per gallon of fuel. Whose car has the more efficient fuel usage?

Extension Exercise 14.6

1 This is a story in imperial units. Rewrite it in metric units. You need to know that there were 20 shillings in one pound (£).

Emily was going shopping for her mother. She walked two miles into the village. She had a five-pound note in her pocket. Emily bought 2 lb potatoes for 5 shillings, 8 ounces of mushrooms for 10 shillings and half a dozen oranges for 13 shillings.

Emily walked 100 yards down the road to the haberdashery shop. Emily then bought 3 yards of blue ribbon and 5 feet of knicker elastic. That cost her 25 shillings.

Emily was tired and the shopping was heavy and so she stopped at the sweet shop and bought 4 ounces of bull's eyes for 2 shillings.

2 Rewrite this story in imperial units, given that there were 20 shillings in one pound (£) and 12 old pence (d) in one shilling.

Carlos went shopping for his mother. He bicycled 4 kilometres to the shops where he spent 60 pence on 3 kg potatoes, 80 pence on 400 grams of mushrooms and £1.20 on 6 oranges.

Carlos also went to the haberdashery shop where he bought 4 metres of pink ribbon and 50 cm of gold braid. That cost him £2.30

Carlos was hungry and so he bought 250 grams of peanut crunch for 60p.

3 Write some stories of your own and give them to a friend to rewrite.

Summary Exercise 14.7

1 Which of these years are leap years?

   (a) 1500   (b) 1968   (c) 2024

2 How many days are there from:

   (a) 1 May to 31 July   (b) 1 February to the end of June in 2016?

3 Write these times as 24-hour clock times.

   (a) quarter past eleven in the morning

   (b) twenty to eight in the evening

   (c) half-past midnight

4 An aeroplane leaves London at 1555 and reaches Shanghai 11 hours and 20 minutes later. What time will it arrive:

   (a) in UK time

   (b) in Shanghai time, which is 7 hours ahead of the UK?

5 Write 200 cm in:

   (a) metres   (b) millimetres   (c) kilometres.

6 Write 5 kg in:

   (a) grams   (b) milligrams   (c) tonnes.

7 Write 50 ml in:

   (a) litres   (b) centilitres.

8 Write each of these measurements in the units shown.

   (a) 5 yards in feet   (c) 40 inches in feet and inches

   (b) 2 lb in ounces   (d) 5 gallons in pints

9 Write each of these measurements in the units shown.

   (a) 320 km in miles   (c) 4 m in feet and inches

   (b) 2 kg in pounds   (d) 5 pints in litres

10 I travel 100 km, having left home at 8 a.m. on Monday, carrying 5 litres of water and 6 kg of food. By Tuesday I have reached my destination and have 300 ml of water left and 450 g of food.

   (a) How much water have I used?

   (b) How much food have I eaten?

   (c) How far have I travelled, in miles?

Activity: Make a sundial

As the Earth spins on its axis, different areas face towards the Sun. As the Sun seems to travel across the sky, shadows on the ground change direction. Humans discovered a long time ago that they could use this fact. The angle of the shadow, from a fixed line, could tell them the time of day. They discovered the **sundial**.

■ This photo shows a Roman sundial in Tarragona, Spain

You can make a very simple sundial yourself from a paper plate and a stick. Place the stick in the centre of the paper plate and position it in the light from the Sun. Every hour, mark the line on the plate where the shadow falls and write the hour by it.

At the end of the day you should have a complete sundial.

Try this on different days of the year. Does this method always tell the time accurately? What about the length of the shadows? Do these change with the seasons? How could you use your sundial to tell if you were nearing an equinox or solstice?

Percentages

Percentages are used a lot in everyday life. They are linked to **fractions** and **decimals**. For example, you will often find that the mark for a test or examination is given as a percentage. Why do teachers do this?

Why use percentages?

Look at some of Dave's marks. This might give you a clue.

- History: 60 out of 80
- English: 63 out of 90
- Maths: 52 out of 65

How do you know which was Dave's best subject?

A percentage is a mark out of a hundred, from the word Latin *centum*, meaning a hundred.

If you work out Dave's marks as percentages, then:

- History: $\dfrac{60}{80} = \dfrac{3}{4} = \dfrac{75}{100} = 75\%$

- Maths: $\dfrac{63}{90} = \dfrac{7}{10} = \dfrac{70}{100} = 70\%$

- English: $\dfrac{52}{65} = \dfrac{4}{5} = \dfrac{80}{100} = 80\%$

Even though his mark for English looked as if it was the lowest, it was actually Dave's best result!

Percentages are often used as a way of comparing values, for example:

- price increases – up 10%
- discounts – 25% off
- pay rises – 5% increase
- service charge – 10% service will be added to the bill.

They are also used to describe particular groups.

- 10% of the class come to school by bus.
- 45% are boys and therefore 55% are girls.

◯ Looking at percentages

The easiest way to think of a percentage is as a fraction.

$$1\% = \frac{1}{100}$$

Look at this square, which is divided into 100 small squares.

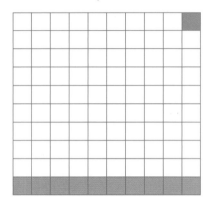

- 1 square (1%) is coloured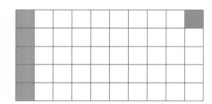
- 10 squares (10%) are coloured
- 89 squares (89%) are not coloured.

In this example each small square represents 1% of the whole.

Now look at this rectangle, which is divided into 50 squares.

- 1 square is coloured ▢ which is $\frac{1}{50}$ of the total.

$$\frac{1}{50} = \frac{2}{100} = 2\%$$

- 5 squares are coloured ▢ which is $\frac{5}{50}$ of the total.

$$\frac{5}{50} = \frac{10}{100} = 10\%$$

In this example each small square represents 2% of the whole.

Exercise 15.1

You will need squared paper and isometric paper for this exercise.

1 A square is divided into 100 small squares.

    (a) Colour 10% red.   (c) Colour 25% yellow.

    (b) Colour 3% blue.   (d) What percentage of the whole is not coloured?

2 A triangle is divided into 100 small triangles.

    (a) Colour 15% red.   (c) Colour 30% yellow.

    (b) Colour 5% blue.   (d) What percentage of the whole is not coloured?

3 A rectangle is divided into 100 small squares.

    (a) Colour 50% red.   (c) Colour 15% yellow.

    (b) Colour 35% blue.   (d) What percentage is not coloured?

4 A rectangle is divided into 50 small squares.

    (a) Colour 1% red.

    (b) Colour 10% blue.

    (c) Colour 20% yellow.

    (d) How many squares are not coloured? What percentage of the whole square is not coloured?

5 A triangle is divided into 25 small triangles.

    (a) Colour 1 triangle red. What percentage is that?

    (b) Colour 20% blue.

    (c) Colour 16% yellow.

    (d) What percentage of the whole is not coloured?

Percentages as fractions

You have seen that:

$$\frac{1}{50} = \frac{2}{100} = 2\%$$

To change a fraction into a percentage, you need to turn it into an equivalent fraction with a denominator of 100

There are some percentages that you need to know and should learn by heart.

Look at this square.

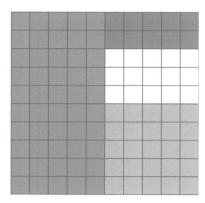

- 50% of it is shaded ■ $50\% = \dfrac{50}{100} = \dfrac{1}{2}$

- 25% of it is shaded ■ $25\% = \dfrac{25}{100} = \dfrac{1}{4}$

- 10% of it is shaded ■ $10\% = \dfrac{10}{100} = \dfrac{1}{10}$

Exercise 15.2

1 Copy and complete these statements.

   (a) $50\% = \dfrac{\square}{100} = \dfrac{1}{\square}$ (b) $25\% = \dfrac{25}{\square} = \dfrac{\square}{4}$ (c) $\square\% = \dfrac{10}{100} = \dfrac{1}{\square}$

2 Copy and complete these statements.

   (a) $20\% = \dfrac{\square}{100} = \dfrac{1}{\square}$ (b) $5\% = \dfrac{5}{\square} = \dfrac{\square}{20}$ (c) $\square\% = \dfrac{4}{100} = \dfrac{1}{\square}$

3 Copy and complete these statements.

   (a) $40\% = \dfrac{\square}{100} = \dfrac{4}{\square} = \dfrac{\square}{5}$ (b) $60\% = \dfrac{60}{\square} = \dfrac{\square}{10} = \dfrac{3}{\square}$ (c) $\square\% = \dfrac{80}{100} = \dfrac{8}{\square} = \dfrac{\square}{5}$

4 Copy and complete these statements.

   (a) $15\% = \dfrac{\square}{100} = \dfrac{3}{\square}$ (b) $90\% = \dfrac{90}{\square} = \dfrac{\square}{10}$ (c) $\square\% = \dfrac{65}{100} = \dfrac{13}{\square}$

5 Copy and complete these statements.

   (a) $35\% = \dfrac{\square}{100} = \dfrac{7}{\square}$ (b) $55\% = \dfrac{55}{\square} = \dfrac{\square}{20}$ (c) $\square\% = \dfrac{75}{100} = \dfrac{3}{\square}$

6 Copy and complete these statements.

(a) $8\% = \dfrac{\square}{100} = \dfrac{\square}{\square}$

(d) $\square\% = \dfrac{13}{100} = \dfrac{\square}{\square}$

(b) $72\% = \dfrac{72}{\square} = \dfrac{\square}{\square}$

(e) $\square\% = \dfrac{48}{100} = \dfrac{\square}{\square}$

(c) $24\% = \dfrac{24}{\square} = \dfrac{\square}{\square}$

(f) $\square\% = \dfrac{14}{100} = \dfrac{\square}{\square}$

Percentages of a whole

The first square you looked at was divided into 100 equal parts. You saw that if 11% was coloured, then 89% was not coloured, since 11 + 89 = 100

In a school, if 11% of the students are boys, then 89% must be girls.

Exercise 15.3

1 In our school, 35% of the teachers are male. What percentage are female?

2 In a bag of sweets, 10% are red, 20% are yellow and the rest are green. What percentage are green?

3 In a glass of orange squash, 15% is concentrate. What percentage is water?

4 I have read 30% of my new book. What percentage do I still have left to read?

5 At school, 60% of my day is spent in lessons, 15% in break time, 10% at registration. The rest of the day is spent having lunch. What percentage is spent having lunch?

6 In a box of muesli, 45% of the ingredients are oat flakes, 30% are wheat flakes, 15% are raisins and the rest are banana chips. What percentage are banana chips?

7 In a survey a teacher found that 15% of the class come to school by bus, 40% by car, 25% walk and the rest come by train. What percentage come by train?

8 In a mixed bag of potato crisps there are equal numbers of ready salted, cheese and onion, smoky bacon and salt and vinegar flavours. What percentages of each flavour are in the bag?

Finding a percentage of an amount

As 10% is the same as $\dfrac{1}{10}$, to find 10% of any value you can just divide by 10

Examples

(i) Find 10% of £250

$$10\% \text{ of } £250 = 250 \div 10$$
$$= £25$$

(ii) Find 10% of 6 kg

$$10\% \text{ of } 6\,kg = 6000\,g \div 10$$
$$= 600\,g$$

> In this example, it is best to turn kilograms into grams to make the division easier.

You can use a similar method to find other percentages.

Examples

(i) Find 20% of £250

$$10\% \text{ of } £250 = 250 \div 10 \qquad \text{First divide by 10}$$
$$= £25$$
$$\text{So } 20\% \text{ of } £250 = 25 \times 2 \qquad \text{Now multiply by 2 because } 20\% = 2 \times 10\%$$
$$= £50$$

(ii) Find 60% of £40

$$10\% \text{ of } £40 = 40 \div 10$$
$$= £4$$
$$\text{So } 60\% \text{ of } £40 = £4 \times 6 \qquad \text{Multiply by 6 because } 60\% = 6 \times 10\%$$
$$= £24$$

(iii) Find 35% of £40

$$10\% \text{ of } £40 = £4 \qquad \text{Begin by dividing } £40 \text{ by } 10 = £40 \div 10$$
$$30\% \text{ of } £40 = £12 \qquad \text{Making it up to } 30\% = £4 \times 3$$
$$5\% \text{ of } £40 = £2 \qquad \text{Calculate the } 5\% = £4 \div 2$$
$$\text{So } 35\% \text{ of } £40 = £14$$

> Use the fact that 5% is half of 10%. Keep the working in columns, then add to get the final solution.

Exercise 15.4

1 Find 10% of £50

2 Find 10% of £65

3 Find 10% of £2

4 Find 10% of 200 g

5 Find 10% of 3 km

6 Find 10% of 5 kg

7 Find 20% of £60

8 Find 20% of £25

9 Find 20% of £7

10 Find 20% of 800 g

In some of these questions, you might want to change the units, for example,
2 hours = 120 minutes.

11 Find 20% of 4 km

12 Find 20% of 8 kg

13 Find 30% of £80

14 Find 70% of £300

15 Find 40% of 500 g

16 Find 80% of 400 m

17 Find 90% of 8 kg

18 Find 60% of 5 km

19 Find 30% of 2 hours

20 Find 40% of 50 cm

21 Find 45% of £60

22 Find 15% of £200

23 Find 35% of 400 g

24 Find 85% of 600 m

25 Find 95% of 5 kg

26 Find 55% of 8 km

27 Find 65% of 480 g

28 Find 45% of 3 hours

29 Find 15% of 20 yards

30 Find 55% of 4 minutes

Working out percentages

Percentages as fractions

You have seen the importance of learning some of the percentages
and fractions that occur most often. Here are some very commonly
used percentages displayed as fractions.

$$50\% = \frac{1}{2} \quad 10\% = \frac{1}{10} \quad 25\% = \frac{1}{4} \quad 20\% = \frac{1}{5} \quad 75\% = \frac{3}{4}$$

It is also worth remembering:

- half of 25% is 12.5%

- half of $\frac{1}{4}$ is $\frac{1}{8}$

therefore $12.5\% = \frac{1}{8}$

Sometimes, when you need to use these percentages, it is quicker to
complete any calculations by treating them as fractions and then cancelling.

Example

Find 25% of £40

25% of £40 $= \frac{1}{4}$ of 40

$\qquad = \frac{1}{{}_1 4} \times 40^{10}$

$\qquad = £10$

Exercise 15.5

1 Find 10% of £75

2 Find 25% of £60

3 Find 50% of £2

4 Find 20% of £50

5 Find 75% of 1 kg

6 Find 12.5% of 400 m

7 Find 25% of 800 g

8 Find 20% of 1 hour

9 Find 12.5% of 19.6 kg

10 Find 20% of 15 m

11 Find 50% of 5 kg

12 Find 25% of 200 g

13 Find 20% of 300 m

14 Find 12.5% of 2 kg

15 Find 75% of 200 g

16 Find 25% of 3 km

17 Find 62.5% of 4 feet

18 Find 40% of 3 hours

19 Find 70% of 2 km

20 Find 37.5% of 24 hours

Percentages as decimals

It can often be useful to treat percentages as decimals.

Since $1\% = \dfrac{1}{100}$ you can write it as 0.01

Similarly, you can write $5\% = \dfrac{5}{100}$ as 0.05

And you can write $45\% = \dfrac{45}{100}$ as 0.45

Exercise 15.6

Write these percentages as decimals.

1 6%

2 13%

3 52%

4 65%

5 4%

6 72%

7 100%

8 200%

9 150%

10 75%

11 50%

12 20%

13 40%

14 89%

15 3%

◯ Comparing fractions, decimals and percentages

You should now see that percentages, fractions and decimals are all equivalent ways of writing the same numbers.

Suppose you are given a mixture of percentages, fractions and decimals. How could you find out which is the largest? The most efficient way is to write them all as decimals.

Example

Write these in order, smallest first.

33% $\dfrac{3}{10}$ 0.35

33% = 0.33 $\dfrac{3}{10}$ = 0.3   0.35   Write them all as decimals.

Now it is easy to put them in the correct order.

0.3   0.33   0.35

Now write them in their original form.

$\dfrac{3}{10}$ 33%   0.35

Exercise 15.7

Write these in order, smallest first.

1 55% $\dfrac{1}{2}$ 0.52

2 $\dfrac{1}{4}$ 27%   0.26

3 13%   0.12 $\dfrac{1}{8}$

4 $\dfrac{3}{4}$ 72%   0.77

5 22% $\dfrac{1}{5}$ 0.21

6 78% $\dfrac{4}{5}$ 0.79 $\dfrac{7}{10}$

7 0.909   95% $\dfrac{9}{10}$ 0.92

8 $\dfrac{13}{20}$ 65%   0.66 $\dfrac{3}{5}$

9 42% $\dfrac{2}{5}$ 0.414 $\dfrac{9}{20}$

10 $\dfrac{3}{8}$ 38%   0.308 $\dfrac{3}{10}$

Writing one amount as a percentage of another

You know that you can change between percentages, fractions and decimals.

You can use this fact to calculate one amount as a percentage of another amount.

Start by writing the first amount as a fraction of the second.
Then write that fraction as a percentage.

> **Example**
>
> There are 20 pupils in the class. Five of them wear glasses.
>
> What percentage of the pupils in the class wear glasses?
>
> $\frac{5}{20} = \frac{1}{4}$ Form a fraction.
>
> $\frac{1}{4} = 25\%$ Change to a percentage.
>
> Therefore 25% of the class wear glasses.

Exercise 15.8

For this exercise, it will help if you can remember the percentage and fraction families you learnt earlier.

1 In a bag of 12 sweets, 3 are green. What percentage are green?

2 In a group of 30 children, 15 are boys. What percentage are girls?

3 We have school lunch 5 days a week. Once a week we have chips. On what percentage of days do we have chips?

4 In a bunch of 16 flowers, 12 are yellow. What percentage are yellow?

5 In a group of 10 children, 2 have red bicycles. What percentage have red bicycles?

6 Mum gives me salad for supper 8 times in 20 days. What percentage of my suppers is that?

7 At the fair I have 5 attempts to win a goldfish. I succeed twice. What percentage of my attempts were a success?

8 I score 40 out of 50 for a science test. What percentage is that?

9 Bob scores 36 out of 60 for a science test. What percentage is that?

10 In a spelling test, I get 2 out of 16 wrong. What percentage do I get wrong?

11 In five hours of television, one and a half hours are devoted to news. What percentage is this?

12 There are 240 pages in my book and I have read 60 of them so far. What percentage is this?

13 On a journey of 200 km, we stop after 160 km. What percentage of the journey have we left to go?

14 I get 17 out of 20 for maths and 21 out of 25 for science. Which of these is the higher percentage?

Percentages and shopping

Shops may offer **discounts** during a special sale, or as a promotional offer. A discount is a **reduction** in price. Discounts are often expressed as percentages. Another name for a discount is **percentage decrease**.

To calculate a price after a discount, you need to work out the discount as a percentage of the **original price** of the item, then subtract the value of the discount from the original price.

Prices often go up, as well, and this may be quoted as a **percentage increase**.

To calculate a percentage increase, you need to work out the increase as a percentage of the original amount. Then you add the value of the calculated percentage increase to the original amount.

Exercise 15.9

1 The price of Chocolate Munchy bars has gone up 5%. They used to cost 60p. What is the new price?

2 Trainers are usually £35 but this week they are being sold with a 20% discount. What is the price this week?

3 There is a '25% off everything' sale at Horrid's today. In the sale what is the price of:

(a) a box of handkerchiefs, normally £12

(b) a television, normally £200

(c) a computer game, normally £37.50?

4 For every 250 g of sweets sold, the shop is giving away 10% extra free. I pay for 750 g. How many grams do I get altogether?

5 On Bank Holiday Monday the DIY shop gives 10% off everything. What is the cost of:

(a) a rake, normally costing £12.90

(b) a plant pot, normally costing £2.50

(c) a barbecue, normally costing £32?

6 We spend £60 on a meal and Dad leaves a 15% tip. How much does he leave?

7 The supermarket says that if you buy four bottles of cola, then you get an extra one free. Mum says that is one out of four free, so that is 25% but Dad says it is one out of five, so only 20%. Who is right?

8 A pencil is 12.5% more expensive when bought on its own instead of in a pack of 6. If a pack of six costs 96p, what is the cost of a single pencil?

Extension Exercise 15.10

Percentages and symmetry

Look at these two squares.

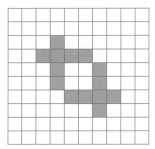 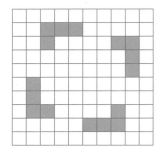

This one has two lines of symmetry and rotational symmetry of order 2 14% of it is coloured.

This has no lines of symmetry, it has rotational symmetry of order 4 16% of it is coloured.

You can make many attractive designs by using line and rotational symmetry.

1 Use a square like those above to draw a design with four lines of symmetry and rotational symmetry of order 4. It should be 25% blue and 40% yellow.

2 Use another square for a design with no lines of symmetry but with rotational symmetry of order 4. It should be 30% blue, 20% red and 40% yellow.

Summary Exercise 15.11

1 **(a)** Draw a ten by ten square and colour 12% of it red and 20% blue.

(b) What percentage of the square is not coloured?

2 If 34% of a group of children are boys, what percentage are girls?

3 Copy and complete these statements.

(a) $25\% = \dfrac{\square}{100} = \dfrac{1}{\square}$

(b) $\square\% = \dfrac{20}{100} = \dfrac{1}{\square}$

(c) $75\% = \dfrac{\square}{\square} = \dfrac{\square}{4}$

(d) $24\% = \dfrac{\square}{100} = \dfrac{\square}{\square}$

(e) $35\% = \dfrac{\square}{100} = \dfrac{\square}{\square}$

(f) $72\% = \dfrac{\square}{100} = \dfrac{\square}{\square}$

4 Work out these amounts.

(a) 10% of £40

(e) 12.5% of £40

(b) 30% of 500 g

(f) 25% of 2 kg

(c) 40% of 120 cm

(g) 20% of 300 m

(d) 45% of £200

(h) 75% of 1200 g

5 There are 240 pupils in the school and 25% of them walk to school. Calculate how many pupils walk to school.

6 I scored 15 out of 20 in my French test. What is that as a percentage?

7 Write these in order, smallest first.

41% $\frac{2}{5}$ 0.404

8 There is 20% off in the Sparks and Measures sale.

What is the sale price of:

(a) a jumper, normally costing £40

(b) a pair of trousers, normally costing £24

(c) a pair of socks, normally costing £3?

Ratio and proportion

Ratio

What do you understand when you hear the word **ratio**? It is often used in news items, for example, when they are comparing hospitals they may quote the 'nurse to patient ratio'. This because it is important to consider whether there are enough nurses to look after the patients.

■ One nurse to eight beds

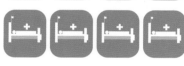

Ratio can also be used to describe patterns. Although there are lots of beads in this necklace, you can see there is a pattern: there is one red bead to every four black beads.

Note the use of the word 'to' in the above examples. When writing ratios mathematically you use the colon sign : to represent 'to'.

Ratio of nurses to beds is 1 : 8

Ratio of red beads to black beads is 1 : 4

You could write these the other way round, but then the numbers would change too.

Ratio of beds to nurses is 8 : 1

Ratio of black beads to red beads is 4 : 1

◯ Ratio in patterns

Look at this a pattern of black and white dots.

You can see that there are six black dots and four white dots.

Ratio of black dots to white dots is 6 : 4

However, like fractions, you should always write a ratio in its simplest form by dividing by any common factors.

So the ratio of black dots to white dots is 3 : 2

Make sure you have the ratio the correct way round, as you could also say:

The ratio of white dots to black dots is 2 : 3

Exercise 16.1

1 Write the ratio of black dots to white dots in each pattern.

(a)   (b)   (c)   (d)

2 Write down the ratio of white dots to black dots in these patterns.

(a)   (b) 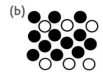 (c)   (d)

3 Draw patterns of black and white dots in your exercise book, with:

  (a) black dots to white dots in the ratio

   (i) 2 : 3 (ii) 1 to 5

  (b) white dots to black dots in the ratio

   (i) 2 : 3 (ii) 1 to 3

4 I have a pattern with 15 blue stars and 12 white stars.

  What is the ratio of:

  (a) blue stars to white stars

  (b) white stars to blue stars

  (c) white to the total number of stars?

5 In our school there are 360 pupils.

    (a) There are 40 teachers. What is the teacher-to-pupil ratio?

    (b) There are 135 girls. What is the ratio of boys to girls?

    (c) 90 pupils board and the rest are day pupils. What is the ratio of boarders to day pupils?

6 There are 120 plants in my garden. 90 have white flowers, the rest have coloured flowers.

    (a) What is the ratio of white flowers to coloured flowers?

    (b) Of the coloured flowers, 25 are pink. What is the ratio of white flowers to pink flowers?

    (c) What is the ratio of pink flowers to the whole number of flowers?

7 A builder mixes 5 kg of sand with 500 g of cement.

    (a) What is the ratio of cement to sand?

    (b) He adds the mix to 2 kg of water. What is the ratio of water to the sand–cement mix?

8 140 pupils go on a trip. 50 of them are boys. 80 of them are vegetarian. 8 teachers go with the trip.

    (a) What is the ratio of girls to boys?

    (b) What is the ratio of vegetarian to non-vegetarian pupils?

    (c) What is the teacher-to-pupil ratio (to the nearest whole number)?

◯ Working with ratio

Just as you can **cancel** ratios to put them in their lowest terms, you may need to multiply ratios to solve problems. At the beginning of the chapter you read about a nurse-to-bed ratio of 1 : 8. You can use that ratio to find out how many patients may be cared for by a total of six nurses.

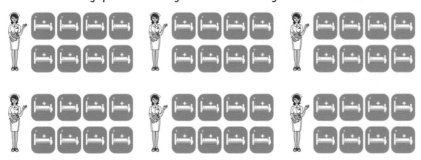

You can see that with six nurses, there will be 6 × 8 = 48 beds, so the six nurses could care for 48 patients.

You would write it down like this.

The ratio of nurses to beds (and therefore patients) is 1 : 8

     6 : 48   Multiply both sides by 6 (× 6)

Sometimes you may need to perform an additional calculation.

Just as with algebra, you can write down what you have done to both parts of the ratio.

Examples

(i) Chris is making a pattern with blue beads and red beads.

    The ratio of blue beads to red beads is 2 : 5

    If she has 65 red beads, how many blue beads does she need?

    The ratio of blue beads to red beads is 2 : 5

$$= ? : 65$$

    The find the number of blue beads, start by dividing 65 by 5. This gives 13

    If you multiply 5 by 13, you must multiply 2 by 13

    The ratio of blue beads to red beads is 2 × 13 : 5 × 13

$$= 26 : 65$$

    Chris needs 26 blue beads.

(ii) A line PR is marked with a point Q so that the ratio $PQ : QR$ is 2 : 3

    If the length of PQ is 8 cm, what is the length of QR?

    $PQ : QR = 2 : 3$

        $= 8 : ?$ As 8 ÷ 2 = 4, multiply 3 by 4

        $= 8 : 12$

    The length of QR is 12 cm

Exercise 16.2

1 Draw a line PQ 10 cm long and mark on it a point R so that $PR : RQ = 1 : 4$

2 Draw a line XY 8 cm long and mark on it a point Z so that $XZ : ZY = 3 : 5$

3 Draw a line AB 10 cm long and mark on it a point C so that $AC : CB = 2 : 3$

4 A line AC is marked with a point B.

  (a) AC = 9 cm and the ratio $AB : BC = 1 : 2$ What is the length of:

    (i) AB (ii) BC?

  (b) AB = 4 cm and the ratio $AB : BC = 1 : 5$ What is the length of:

    (i) BC (ii) AC?

  (c) BC = 15 cm and the ratio $AB : BC = 3 : 5$ What is the length of:

    (i) AB (ii) AC?

5 A line *XZ* is marked with a point *Y*.

   (a) *XY* = 2 m and the ratio *XY* : *YZ* = 1 : 4
   What is the length of:

   (i) *YZ*   (ii) *XZ*?

   (b) *YZ* = 3.5 m and the ratio *XY* : *YZ* = 3 : 7
   What is the length of:

   (i) *XY*   (ii) *XZ*?

   (c) YZ = 8.75 m and the ratio *XY* : *YZ* = 1 : 7
   What is the length of:

   (i) *XY*   (ii) *XZ*?

6 I am making a pattern of gold and silver dots. The ratio of gold dots to silver dots is 1 : 3. If I have 25 gold dots, how many silver dots do I need?

7 A florist is making bunches of flowers. The ratio of yellow roses to red roses is 2 : 5. If she has 100 red roses, how many yellow roses does she need?

8 In the dining room, the ratio of tables to chairs is 1 : 9. If there are 144 chairs, how many tables are there?

9 Bronze is an alloy of tin and copper in the ratio 2 : 11. If a mix uses 800 g of tin, how much copper will be needed?

10 To be safe, the ratio of the narrowest width of a scaffolding tower to its height should not be less than 3 : 7

   (a) What is the safe maximum height for a scaffolding tower of base 2 m by 3 m?

   (b) I want to reach a height of 14 m. What should the minimum width of my scaffolding tower be?

Using ratio

Look again at question 9, in which you considered making bronze. This is an alloy of tin and copper, mixed in the ratio 2 : 11

If you know how much bronze you want, you can work out the amounts of tin and copper.

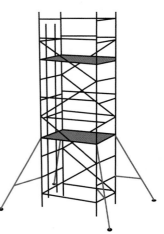

As the ratio is 2 : 11, you know that there are 13 parts altogether, to make up one batch. You could write this out like this.

The ratio of tin to copper to the total amount = 2 : 11 : 13

The next example shows you the method.

Example

White gold is made from an alloy of nickel and gold in the ratio $1 : 9$
How much nickel and gold will I need to make a 500 g ingot of white gold?

The ratio of nickel to gold to the total amount $= 1 : 9 : 10$

$$= \boxed{} : \boxed{} : 500$$

To find what you need to multiply by, calculate $500 \div 10 = 50$

Then $50 \times 1 = 50$ and $50 \times 9 = 450$

Then the ratio of nickel to gold to the total amount $= 50 : 450 : 500$

I need 50 g of nickel and 450 g of gold.

To solve this sort of problem, you need to follow these steps.

1 Find the total number of parts.

2 Work out the amount in one part (usually by dividing).

3 Work out the amounts in all the parts (by multiplying).

4 Answer the question.

It is good practice to work out the amounts in all the parts and then to answer the question, as this will mean you have to check that all your parts add up to the whole, and that you double check what the question is asking.

Examples

(i) Fruit cordial concentrate is mixed with water in the ratio $1 : 5$
How much cordial will I need to make 3 litres of juice?

3 litres = 3000 ml

The ratio of concentrate to water to total $= 1 : 5 : 6$

$$= 500 : 2500 : 3000$$

$3000 \div 6 = 500$
$500 \times 5 = 2500$

I will need 500 ml of cordial.

(ii) A line AC, 10 cm long is marked with a point B so that the ratio $AB : AC$ is $2 : 5$ What is the length of BC?

As AC is 5 parts, BC must be $5 - 2 = 3$ parts

$AB : BC : AC = 2 : 3 : 5$

$\qquad = 4 : 6 : 10$

$10 \div 5 = 2$
$2 \times 3 = 6$

$BC = 6$ cm

1 (a) Draw a line *PQ* 10 cm long and mark on it a point *R* so that *PR* : *PQ* = 1 : 4

   (b) Draw a line *XY* 10 cm long and mark on it a point *Z* so that *XZ* : *XY* = 1 : 5

   (c) Draw a line *AB* 8 cm long and mark on it a point *C* so that *AC* : *AB* = 3 : 5

2 A line *AC*, 12 cm long is marked with a point *B*.

   (a) The ratio *AB* : *AC* = 1 : 6. What are the lengths of *AB* and *BC*?

   (b) The ratio *AB* : *AC* = 1 : 8. What are the lengths of *AB* and *BC*?

   (c) The ratio *AB* : *AC* = 3 : 5. What are the lengths of *AB* and *BC*?

3 A line *XZ* is marked with a point *Y*.

   (a) The ratio *XY* : *YZ* is 2 : 7 and *XZ* = 27 cm. What are the lengths of *XY* and *YZ*?

   (b) The ratio *XY* : *XZ* is 1 : 7 and *YZ* = 24 cm. What are the lengths of *XY* and *XZ*?

4 Bronze is an alloy of copper and tin mixed in the ratio 11 : 2
   If I need to make 26 kg of bronze, how much copper and tin will I need?

5 Orange cordial concentrate has to be mixed with water in the ratio 1 : 4
   How much water and how much concentrate do I need to make 2 litres of orange drink?

6 The ratio of teachers to pupils going to the theatre is 1 : 11
   If the school bought 132 tickets, how many pupils went to the theatre?

7 In a school the ratio of boys to girls is 2 : 3. If there are 550 pupils in the school, what is the number of:

   (a) boys   (b) girls?

8 Fertiliser must be mixed with water in the ratio 1 : 6 before being sprinkled on the lawn. My bucket holds 4.2 litres and I am going to make the largest mix I can.

   (a) How much fertiliser will I need?

   (b) How much water should I add?

   (c) If 1 litre of mix will treat 50 m² of lawn, what is the largest area my bucketful be able to treat?

9 My mother's famous 'winter warmer' is a mix of tea and ginger cordial in the ratio 5 : 3

   (a) How much ginger cordial would I need to make 5 litres of 'winter warmer'?

   (b) Ginger cordial comes in 75 cl bottles. How many litres of 'winter warmer' could I make from one bottle of ginger cordial?

10 For the end-of-term party we have designed a fruit punch. We mixed 2 litres of orange juice with 350 ml of pineapple juice and 150 ml of cranberry juice.

   (a) What is the ratio of orange juice : pineapple juice : cranberry juice?

   (b) For the party, we need to make 50 litres of punch. How much of each ingredient will we need?

> Always start by identifying how many parts are in the whole.

Proportion

Sometimes you will not be given a ratio but you will be told the amount of one quantity that you need to compare or mix with another. Examples of this include:

● recipes, where you are given the quantity of the ingredients for a particular number of servings (or of biscuits) for example.

● equivalent quantities such as miles and kilometres.

Such quantities are in **direct proportion**. That means that if one changes, the other changes at the same rate. If you double the number of biscuits you make, you must double the quantities of all the ingredients in the recipe.

You know that 5 miles is approximately equal to 8 km.

Multiplying by 2, then 10 miles is approximately equal to 16 km.

Now divide by 10, to find that 1 mile is approximately 1.6 km.

You have reached this conclusion by multiplying and dividing the miles and the kilometres by the same numbers, in turn.

This is a very useful method and can be applied in many situations.

Example

This is Johnnie's recipe for 16 flapjacks.

　　150 g of syrup

　　200 g of butter

　　300 g of oats

(i) How many grams of oats will he need, if he wants to make 20 flapjacks?

For 16 flapjacks he needs 300 g oats

For 1 flapjack he needs 300 ÷ 16 g oats

For 20 flapjacks he needs 20 × 300 ÷ 16 g oats

$$= 6000 ÷ 16$$
$$= 375 \text{ g oats}$$

(ii) He has 1 kg of butter. How many flapjacks can he make?

With 200 g of butter he can make 16 flapjacks,

With 1 kg of butter he can make 16 × 5 flapjacks.

He can make 80 flapjacks.

You should see that if you follow a recipe you must keep the quantities of the ingredients in the same proportion.

1 You are told that a distance of 8 km is approximately equal to 5 miles.

   (a) Luc travelled 240 km. Approximately how many miles is that?

   (b) Jack travelled 100 miles. Approximately how many kilometres is that?

2 Vicky is travelling at 60 miles per hour.

   (a) How far will she travel in 3 hours?

   (b) How long with it take her to travel 20 miles?

3 You are given that there are 2240 lb in a ton.

   (a) How many pounds are there in a quarter of a ton?

   (b) How many tons are there in 11 200 lb?

4 When Leon went on holiday, €10 was worth £8

   (a) How many euros might he get in exchange for a £50 note?

   (b) What was the value, in pounds sterling, of €250 at that time?

5 My grandmother said that to make a perfect cake you needed equal amounts of flour, butter and sugar and 2 eggs to every 125 g of flour.

   (a) If am using 500 g of flour, how many eggs will I need?

   (b) If I only have one egg, what is the total amount of flour, sugar and butter that I will need?

6 To provide a platter of cheese and biscuits for five people, I need 15 biscuits and 200 g of cheese.

   (a) If I have four platters of cheese and biscuits, how many people can I feed?

   (b) I have bought 1 kg of cheese. How many biscuits do I need?

   (c) How many people can I then feed?

> If your answer is not exact, round it to the nearest whole number.

7 These are the ingredients in a recipe for 12 chocolate crispies.

   50 g butter

   100 g chocolate

   100 g cereal flakes

   (a) If I want to make 20 chocolate crispies, how much butter will I need?

   (b) If I have 250 g of chocolate, how many chocolate crispies can I make?

   (c) If I only have 80 g of cereal flakes, how many chocolate crispies can I make?

8 I have found this recipe for icing cup cakes.

   To ice 8 cup cakes:

   100 g icing sugar

   15 ml spoon of water

4 glace cherries

I want to ice 10 cup cakes.

How much icing sugar and water will I need?

9   This is a recipe for carrot soup for 6 people.

4 large carrots, peeled and roughly chopped

$\frac{1}{2}$ large onion, roughly chopped

900 ml vegetable stock

(a) How many carrots will I need, to make enough soup to feed 10 people?

(b) How much stock will I need, to make enough soup to feed 8 people?

(c) I only have three carrots. How many people can I serve with carrot soup, and how much stock will I need?

10 According to the manufacturer, my car does 50 miles to the gallon of fuel.

(a) How many miles will it go if I fill up with 12 gallons of fuel?

(b) If 10 litres is approximately 2.2 gallons, how many miles will my car go for each litre of petrol?

(c) I need to travel 33 miles. How many litres will this use?

(d) If petrol costs £1.60 a litre, what will it cost to drive a journey of 200 miles?

Ratio and scale

When you look at maps and plans you may not realise that you are using ratio. Maps and plans are drawn to **scale**, and the scale is a ratio. This can be expressed as 1 cm for every 10 m, 1 cm to 50 cm, or 1 : 100

This is an architect's scale drawing of a new house, with a model of the house in three dimensions. These help his clients to see what their new house will be like.

When you are working with scale drawings and models, make sure that the measurements of the scaled image and the actual image are the same way round as in the ratio.

Before you start on each problem, write the measurements of both the scaled image and the actual image in the same units.

Examples

(i) I have a model of a house, made to a scale of 1 : 50

If the model is 15 cm tall, how high is the actual house?

The ratio of the scale model to the real house is 1 : 50   Write the scale.

So 1 cm represents 50 cm   Put in the units (make sure they are the same)

and 15 cm represents 750 cm   Scale up.

So 15 cm represents 7.5 m   Convert the units.

The real house is 7.5 m high.

(ii) I have a map drawn to a scale of 1 : 25 000

If the distance between two villages is 4 km by road, what will it be on the map?

Scale : real = 1 : 25 000

So 1 cm represents 25 000 cm.

Which means that 1 cm represents 250 m   (÷ 100 to turn cm to m)

or 1 cm represents 0.25 km   (÷ 1000)

Then 16 cm represents 4 km   (× 16)

The distance on the map will be 16 cm.

Exercise 16.5

1 A model house is made to a scale of 1 : 10

   (a) What does 1 cm on the model house represent?

   (b) If the model is 50 cm high, how high is the actual house?

   (c) If the actual house has a width of 6 m, what is the width of the model?

2 A model yacht is made to a scale of 1 : 50

   (a) What does 1 cm on the model yacht represent?

   (b) If the model is 25 cm long how long is the actual boat?

   (c) If the mast on the actual yacht is 6 m high, how high is the mast on the model?

3 I am drawing a plan of the classroom to a scale of 1 : 40

   The classroom is 6 m by 8 m. What are the dimensions of my plan?

4 I have a model of a World War II aeroplane made to a scale of 1 : 48

   (a) The height of the model is three inches. What was the height of the original aeroplane?

The plane would have been built using feet and inches, which is why the scale is 1 : 48

Remind yourself of how many inches in a foot.

(b) The wingspan of the model is 13 inches. What was the wingspan of the original aeroplane?

(c) The length of the original aeroplane was 40 feet. What is the length of the model?

5 I have been given a construction kit to build a model of the Mary Rose.
The scale is 1 : 200

(a) The dimensions of the model are 16.4 cm length by 7 cm beam.
What were the length and beam of the original ship?

(b) The depth under the water line of the original ship was 4.6 m. What is the depth of the model?

(c) The original ship carried 80 guns. How many guns will there be on the model?

6 I am planning a walk and have a map with scale 1 : 25 000

(a) What distance on the map represents 1 km on the ground?

(b) My planned walk is 6 cm on the map. What is that in kilometres?

7 This is part of a map of an area near Sheffield, drawn to a scale of 1 : 50 000

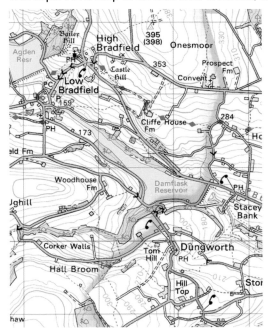

(a) Measure the distance by road from the phone box in High Bradfield to the phone box at Stacey Bank.

(b) Calculate the distance in kilometres.

(c) Measure the distance in a straight line from the church in High Bradfield to the church in Dungworth. Calculate the true distance in kilometres.

8 This is part of a map of the Peak District, drawn to a scale of $2\frac{1}{2}$ inches to a mile.

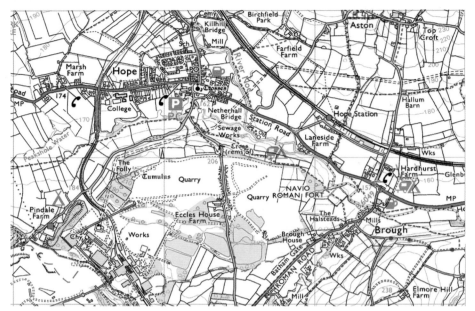

(a) Measure the distance, by road, from the phone box near Marsh Farm (west of Hope) to Hope Station (east of Hope).

(b) Calculate the distance in miles.

(c) Measure the distance in a straight line from the church with the spire in Hope to the nearest camp site. Calculate the true distance in miles.

Scale drawing

For these next exercises you will need to remember what you learned about bearings, in Chapter 3

Example

This diagram is drawn to a scale of 1 cm to 10 m

Find the bearing and distance of *B* from *A*

AB = 2.4 cm which represents 24 m

The bearing of *B* from *A* is 140°

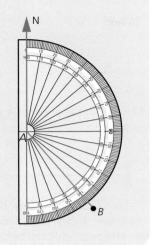

Exercise 16.6

These diagrams are all drawn to the scale marked.

Measure each drawing and thus find the bearing of *B* from *A* and the distance *AB*.

1 Scale 1 cm to 10 m

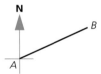

2 Scale 1 cm to 5 m

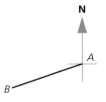

3 Scale 1 cm to 50 m

4 Scale 1 cm to 5 m

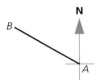

5 Scale 1 : 10 000 m

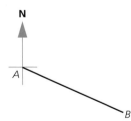

6 Scale 1 : 50 000 m

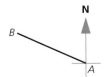

7 Scale 1 : 100 000 m

8 Scale 1 : 25 000 m

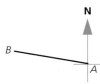

9 Now find the bearing of *A* from *B* in the previous eight questions. Measure the drawings to check your answers.

Exercise 16.7

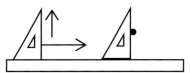

Now use what you have learnt about bearings to draw diagrams to answer the questions in this exercise. For each one, you should mark the points clearly with a cross and draw a north line from the point indicted before you measure or draw a bearing.

When you have one north line you can use a ruler and a set square to draw other north lines parallel to the first.

Line the set square up on the ruler against the north line, then slide the set square along the ruler.

1 The village Alpha lies 3.5 km from the village Pippa on a bearing of 114°. The village Beta lies 4 km from Alpha on a bearing of 216°. Draw a plan of the three villages to a scale of 1 cm to 0.5 km and measure the bearing of Alpha from Beta, and the distance from Pippa to Beta.

> You see it says from Beta. You should draw a north line from the point that marks the position of Beta.

2 A church lies 7 km from my house on a bearing of 072°. A water tower lies 6 km from my house on a bearing of 283°. Draw a plan of the three points, to a scale of 1 cm to 1 km. Measure the bearing and distance of the church from the water tower.

3 The town of Delta lies 15 km from the town Echo on a bearing of 212°. The town of Foxtrot lies 12 km from Echo on a bearing of 164°. Draw a plan of the three towns, to a scale of 1 cm to 2 km. Measure the bearing and distance of Foxtrot from Delta.

4 A soldier marches 8 km from base, on a bearing of 195°, then changes direction and marches 7 km, on a bearing of 312°. Draw a plan of his march and find his new bearing and distance from his base.

◯ Ratio and algebra

Draw a line AB 10 cm long and mark on it a point X so that
$AX : XB = 1 : 4$

From this, you can see that $AX = 2$ cm and $XB = 8$ cm

You can also see that $AX : AB = 1 : 5$

Now draw a line AB 10 cm long and mark on it a point X so that
$AX : XB = 1 : x$

This time you have an unknown x and so you cannot work out
AX and XY

If you have one other piece of information then you may be able to
form an equation and solve it.

Examples

(i) A line AB is 8 cm long. A point X lies on the line so that $AX : XB = 1 : x$

If $AX = 2$ cm, write an equation and solve it to find the value of x

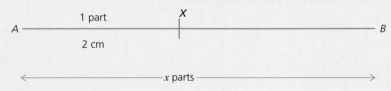

$AX : XB = 1 : x$

$\qquad = 2 : 2x$

$2 + 2x = 8$

$\qquad 2x = 6$

$\qquad\quad x = 3$ Check: $XB = 2x = 6$ cm and also equals 8 cm − 2 cm = 6 cm

> As you have multiplied 1 by 2 you must multiply x by 2

> The two parts added together equal $AB = 8$ cm

(ii) A line AB is 10 cm long. A point X divides AB such that $AX : AB = 1 : x$

If $AX = 2$ cm, form an equation and solve it to find the value of x

A —— 1 part / 2 cm —— X —————— B

$\longleftarrow$ ———— x parts ———— $\longrightarrow$

$AX : AB = 1 : x$

$\qquad = 2 : 2x$

$2x = 10$

$\quad x = 5$ Check: $2 : 10 = 1 : 5$

When answering these questions it is important that you read the question carefully and make sure that you understand which part of the line is in the ratio. Drawing a diagram may help.

1 A line AB is 12 cm long. A point X divides AB such that $AX : XB = 1 : x$

If $AX = 2$ cm, write an equation and solve it to find the value of x

2 A line PQ is 12 cm long. A point X divides PQ such that $PX : PQ = 1 : x$

If $PX = 3$ cm, write an equation and solve it to find the value of x

3 A line CD is 15 cm long. A point X divides CD such that $CX : XD = 1 : x$

If $CX = 3$ cm, write an equation and solve it to find the value of x

4 A line AB is 20 cm long. A point X divides AB such that $AX : XB = 1 : x$

If $AX = 5$ cm, write an equation and solve it to find the value of x

5 A line PQ is 10 cm long. A point X divides PQ such that $PX : PQ = 2 : x$

If $PX = 4$ cm, write an equation and solve it to find the value of x

6 A line CD is 15 cm long. A point X divides CD such that $CX : XD = 3 : x$

If $XD = 6$ cm, write an equation and solve it to find the value of x

7 A line AB is 20 cm long. Point X divides AB such that $AX : XB = 3 : x$

If $BX = 14$ cm, write an equation and solve it to find the value of x

8 A line XY is 20 cm long. A point Z divides XY such that $Z : XY = 2 : x$

If $ZY = 12$ cm, write an equation and solve it to find the value of x

9 A line PQ is 110 cm long. A point X divides PQ such that $QX : PQ = 7 : x$

If $PX = 40$ cm, write an equation and solve it to find the value of x

10 A line AB is 120 cm long. Point X divides AB such that $BX : AB = 11 : x$

If $AX = 10$ cm, write an equation and solve it to find the value of x

Summary Exercise 16.9

1 Write the ratio of white squares to grey squares in these patterns in their lowest terms.

(a) 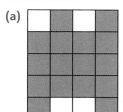 (b) 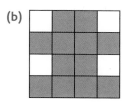 (c)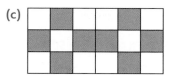

2 (a) Draw a line *AB* 10 cm long. On it mark a point *X* so that *AX* : *XB* = 2 : 3

  (b) Draw a line *PQ* 10 cm long. On it mark a point *X* so that *PX* : *PQ* = 2 : 5

3 White gold is an alloy of nickel and gold in the ratio 1 : 9. If 300 g of nickel is used, how much gold is needed?

4 In a school the teacher-to-pupil ratio is 1 : 8

  (a) If there are 20 teachers, how many pupils are there?

  (b) The following term there are 200 pupils, how many extra teachers are needed to keep the teacher-to-pupil ratio the same?

5 (a) A compound X in made from Chemical A mixed with Chemical B in the ratio 2 : 7. How much of each chemical will I need to make 36 g of Compound X?

  (b) As an experiment, I mixed Chemical A and Chemical B in the ratio 4 : 5 and made Compound Y. How much of each chemical did I need to make 36 g of Compound Y?

6 You are given that a capacity of 10 litres is approximately equal to 17 pints.

  (a) What capacity, in litres, is approximately equal to 25 pints?

  (b) What capacity, in pints, is approximately equal to 70 litres?

7 These are the ingredients for a recipe that will make 8 pancakes
100 g plain flour
2 eggs
300 ml milk

  (a) How much flour will I need to make 10 pancakes?

  (b) How much milk will I need to make 20 pancakes?

  (c) How many eggs will I need to make 2 pancakes?

8 A model boat is built to a scale of 1 : 24

    (a) If the model boat is 8 inches long, what is the length of the actual boat?

    (b) If the actual boat is 5 feet wide, how wide is the model?

    (c) If there are 12 windows on the boat, how many windows are there on the model?

9 This map is drawn to a scale of 1 : 50 000

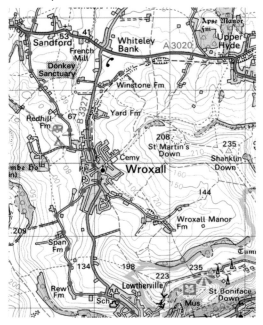

    (a) Measure the distance, by road, from the church with the spire in Wroxhall to the phone box to the north.

    (b) How far is that, in kilometres?

10 Draw this plan of a square field accurately, to a scale of 1 cm to 10 m.

    Measure the bearing of:

    (a) C from A

    (b) D from A

    (c) A from B

    (d) B from D.

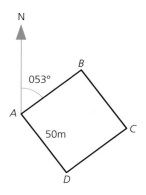

Activity: Proportional patterns

In some of the questions you made patterns with coloured tiles. In this activity you are going to design some patterns of your own.

Look at these two patterns. The ratio of red squares to white squares is 2 : 3 in both of them, but which is more attractive?

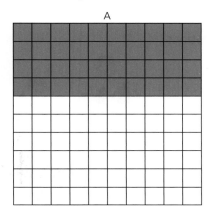
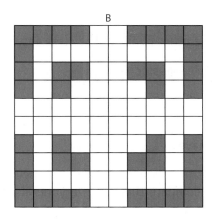

Pattern A has one line of symmetry and no rotational symmetry.

Pattern B has four lines of symmetry and rotational symmetry of order 4.

Generally, people find patterns attractive when they have some intricacy to them, and this often involves symmetry. When you design the patterns below, remember to try and make them as beautiful as possible, and then see what symmetry you have achieved.

1 Design a pattern on the grid with a ratio of red squares to white squares of 1 : 3
   Write down the number of lines of symmetry and the order of rotational symmetry.

2 Design a pattern on the grid with a ratio of blue squares to yellow squares of 3 : 2
   Write down the number of lines of symmetry and the order of rotational symmetry.

3 Design a pattern on the grid with a ratio of red squares to yellow squares of 1 : 5
   Write down the number of lines of symmetry and the order of rotational symmetry.

4 Discuss the patterns you have drawn with your partner. Have you drawn the same? Which do you think is the most attractive? Can you explain why?

17 Charts, tables and graphs

How would you and the other pupils in the class answer these questions?

● 'What is your favourite music?'

● 'How many brothers and sisters do you have?'

● 'How do you get to school?'

● 'What pets do you have?'

The individual answers may be interesting, but they are most interesting when you compare them to everyone else's. You can do this in a variety of ways.

○ Frequency tables

A teacher asked her class the question: 'How many brothers and sisters do you have?'

These are the answers, in the order that she recorded them.

1   0   2   1   1   2   3   1   0   2

3   1   2   1   0   0   1   4   0   1

To make sense of these answers, she put them in a frequency table (or tally table), like this.

Number of brothers and sisters	Tally	Frequency
0	JHT	5
1	JHT III	8
2	IIII	4
3	II	2
4	I	1
	Total	20

Note that the tallies are grouped in fives, making it easier to check the total – as long as you can count in fives!

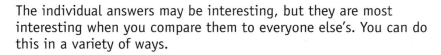

1	2	3	4	5	6	7
I	II	III	IIII	JHT	JHT I	JHT II

◯ Frequency diagrams

Another way to display the results is on a **frequency diagram**. It is easy to draw this diagram if you have done the frequency table first.

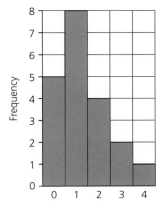

Number of brothers and sisters

The frequency diagram, drawn here as a **bar chart**, shows very clearly that 1 is the most **frequent** answer, and that very few people have three or more brothers and sisters.

If you did not have the frequency table, you could find out the total number of people in the survey by adding up the frequencies for all the bars.

$$5 + 8 + 4 + 2 + 1 = 20$$

Exercise 17.1

1 These are the answers to the question: 'How many pets do you have?'

0, 1, 3, 0, 1, 3, 5, 8, 2, 0, 2, 0, 1, 0, 2, 0, 1, 3, 2, 0

(a) Draw and complete a frequency table to show this information.

(b) Illustrate the information on a frequency diagram.

2 Ask your class the same question and collect their responses. Show the information first on a frequency table and then on a bar chart.

(a) What differences are there between your bar chart for this question and the one from question 1?

(b) Try to explain them.

3 This frequency diagram shows the results of a survey that Ms Scott's class carried out about what types of pets people had. The vertical axis shows the frequency of the number of pets.

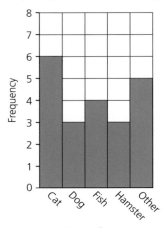

Type of pet

(a) What was the most common pet?

(b) How many more cats were there than dogs?

(c) How many pets were there altogether?

(d) There are 24 pupils in my class. Explain why the total number of pets is not 24

4 As part of a geography project George did a survey of the number of pupils who came to school by car. He wanted to know how many pupils there were in each car. This bar chart shows the results of the survey.

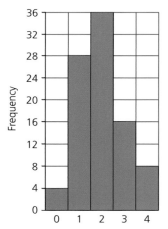

Number of children in each car

(a) How many cars were there in the survey?

(b) How many pupils came to school by car?

(c) Why do you think four cars arrived with no pupils at all?

(d) George thought it would be better if there were fewer cars arriving at school each morning. What ideas could he suggest, in order to achieve that?

5 This frequency table records the answers to the question: 'Which is your favourite pop group?'

(a) Copy and complete the frequency table, filling in all the missing values.

Favourite group	Tally	Frequency
Hotplay	JHT JHT JHT III	
Fridays		23
Club 9	JHT II	
The What	IIII	
Other		
	Total	60

(b) Draw a bar chart to illustrate this information.

6 Carry out your own survey about something that interests you. Illustrate your results in both a frequency table and a bar chart.

Pictograms

Diagrams such as bar charts can make information easier to understand. Another method of displaying information is a **pictogram**. These use the same idea as bar charts, but you can choose an image that is related somehow to the **data** you are displaying. Essentially, you use pictures instead of bars.

This is an example of a pictogram.

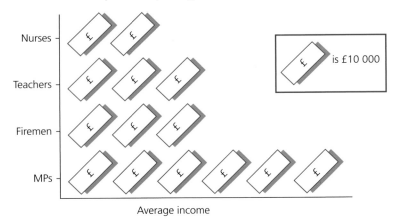

Average income

This shows very clearly that MPs get paid much more than nurses, teachers or firemen. Although the information is not very accurate, as the amounts are only to the nearest £10 000, it is very clear.

The **key** to a pictogram can be adjusted to allow for smaller amounts.

1 This pictogram shows how many house points each house won last week.

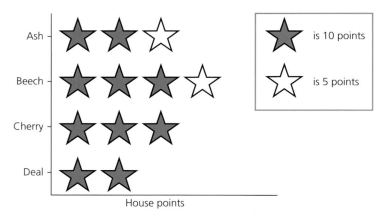

(a) How many points did each house win, to the nearest five?

(b) The following week the house points were:

Ash 45, Beech 30, Cherry 25, Deal 40

Draw a pictogram to show this information.

2 A cheese shop records its sales in a pictogram.

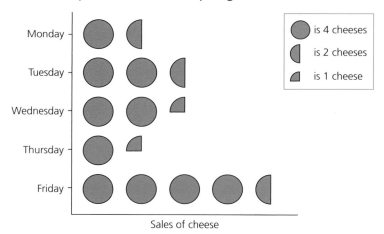

(a) How many cheeses were sold on Wednesday?

(b) How many more cheeses were sold on Friday than on Tuesday?

(c) How many cheeses were sold over the week?

(d) Why might more cheeses be sold on Friday than on the other days?

(e) Design a symbol for three cheeses and draw the row for Saturday, when 11 cheeses were sold.

Pie charts

You could display information in a **pie chart**. Like a pie, these diagrams are circular and are divided into slices or **sectors**.

This pie chart shows the result when a class was asked: 'What is your favourite sport?'

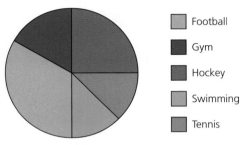

☐	Football
■	Gym
■	Hockey
☐	Swimming
■	Tennis

■ Favourite sports

You can see from this that one quarter of the people who were asked chose hockey as their favourite sport. If you know that 24 people took part in the survey, you can find out how many liked hockey by doing a calculation.

> Remember there are 360° in a full circle.

The angle for the slice representing hockey is 90°

$$\frac{90}{360} \times 24 = \frac{1}{4} \text{ of } 24$$
$$= 6$$

So six people chose hockey.

To find out how many people liked the other sports, you need to measure the angles at the centre of the pie and do similar calculations. For example, the angle at the centre of the tennis segment is 45°. (Measure it, to check.)

$$\frac{45}{360} \times 24 = \frac{1}{8} \text{ of } 24$$
$$= 3$$

So three people chose tennis.

Exercise 17.3

This pie chart compares the numbers of boys and girls in Forest Green School.

(a) What fraction of the total number of pupils are girls?

(b) If there are 120 pupils in the school, how many are boys?

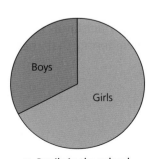

■ Pupils in the school

2 This pie chart shows how the pupils at Norbury Hill School travel to school.

(a) What fraction of the pupils come to school by car?

(b) What fraction of the pupils walk to school?

(c) One-sixth of the pupils come by bus. What angle is at the centre of this slice of the pie?

(d) The angle showing the number of pupils who come by train is 30°. What fraction of the pie is this?

(e) If there are 240 pupils in the school, work out how many come to school by car, train and bus and how many walk.

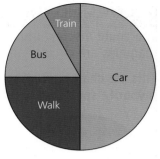

■ How pupils travel to school

3 This pie chart shows the result when 120 pupils were asked to name their favourite lunch.

(a) The angle of the slice representing pizza is 120°. How many pupils like pizza best?

(b) How many pupils chose spaghetti as their favourite?

(c) If 15 pupils chose fish fingers as their favourite, how many chose sausages?

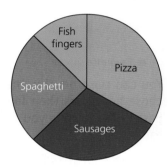

■ Favourite lunches

4 In our last science lesson we had to go outside to look for minibeasts. This pie chart shows those that I found.

(a) I found 20 beetles. How many minibeasts did I find altogether?

(b) One-eighth of the minibeasts I found were woodlice. How many did I find?

(c) What fraction of the total number were centipedes? How many is this?

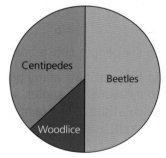

■ Minibeasts

Drawing pie charts

When you are drawing a pie chart, you need to work out the fraction of the whole pie that each slice will represent and then work out the angle.

This is the frequency table from the beginning of the chapter, with two extra columns: 'Fraction' and 'Angle'. You calculate the fraction as the fraction of the total. Then you can work out the angle, remembering that there are 360° in a full circle.

Number of brothers and sisters	Tally	Frequency	Fraction	Angle
0	JHT	5	$\frac{5}{20} = \frac{1}{4}$	90°
1	JHT III	8	$\frac{8}{20} = \frac{2}{5}$	144°
2	IIII	4	$\frac{4}{20} = \frac{1}{5}$	72°
3	II	2	$\frac{2}{20} = \frac{1}{10}$	36°
4	I	1	$\frac{1}{20}$	18°
	Total	20		360°

Always make sure that the numbers in the final column add up to 360°

Use your **protractor** to draw the pie chart. If you have drawn it correctly, the pie will be full; there should be no empty spaces and no overlap. This is the pie chart for the numbers of brothers and sisters.

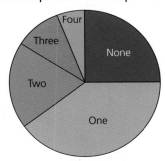

■ Numbers of brothers and sisters

Exercise 17.4

1 Copy and complete this frequency table. Then draw a pie chart to show the information.

Favourite lesson	Frequency	Fraction	Angle
Games	10		
ICT	5		
Art	3		
Drama	2		
Total	20		360°

2 Copy and complete this frequency table. Then draw a pie chart to show the information.

Favourite colour	Frequency	Fraction	Angle
Blue	18		
Red	12		
Green	6		
Total	36		360°

3 Copy and complete this frequency table. Then draw a pie chart to show the information.

Holiday destination	Frequency	Fraction	Angle
France	8		
Britain	6		
USA	4		
Spain	3		
Other	3		
Total	24		360°

4 In geography we did a survey on the colours of the vehicles that drove past the school. This is what I wrote down.

red	blue	white	silver	yellow	red
white	red	red	white	white	white
yellow	white	white	white	red	silver
red	white	white	red	white	red
yellow	white	silver	yellow	silver	red
white	white	red	white	red	white

Record this information in a frequency table. Then draw a pie chart.

5 Our class went into the woods and looked at the trees. We were given a list and had to make a tick each time we identified a tree. This is what I wrote down.

Tree	Number seen
Beech	✓✓✓✓ ✓✓✓✓
Oak	✓✓✓
Fir	✓✓✓✓ ✓✓✓✓ ✓✓✓
Pine	✓✓✓✓ ✓
Other	✓✓✓

Record this information in a frequency table, adding any extra rows or columns that you need. Then draw a pie chart to show the varieties of tree in the wood.

6 In science we did a survey of the eye colour of the pupils in my class. This is the result.

Eye colour	Frequency
Blue	8
Brown	6
Grey	3
Green	1

Copy the frequency table, adding any extra rows or columns that you need.
Then draw a pie chart to represent the results of the survey.

Line graphs

Sometimes you may need to draw a graph to show how two quantities are related. One way of doing this is to use a **line graph**.

Conversion graphs

In Chapter 15, you learnt about some amounts that were in proportion to one another. If your chart values are in proportion then the graph is a straight line.

When Winston went to Europe, the currency conversion was £1 to €1.40

This can be shown on a **conversion graph**, like this.

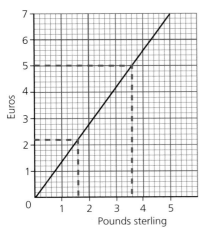

Look carefully at the scale on the graph.

● On the horizontal axis, one small square represents £0.20 or 20p.

● On the vertical axis, one small square represents €0.20 or 20 cents.

You can use the graph to convert amounts of money between pounds and euros, by drawing dotted lines on the graph. These help you to read the values accurately.

- £1.60 is equal to €2.20

- €5 is equal to £3.60

You could also draw a conversion graph to convert other quantities that are in proportion to one another, as long as you know two equivalent values, for example:

- 8 km = 5 miles

- 1 gallon = 4.5 litres.

Exercise 17.5

1 1 kilogram = 2.2 lb (pounds weight)

(a) What are these masses, in pounds?

    (i) 0 kg   (ii) 1 kg   (iii) 5 kg

(b) Draw a pair of coordinate axes on graph paper. Label the horizontal axis as kilograms and number it from 0 to 7, using a scale of 1 cm to 1 kg. Label the vertical axis as pounds and number it from 0 to 14, using a scale of 1 cm to 2 lb.

(c) Plot the three points from part (a) on your graph. Then draw a long, straight line through the points.

(d) Write the title of your graph: 'Graph to show the conversion of kilograms to pounds'.

(e) Rule lines on you graph to find:

    (i)   1.4 kg in pounds   (iii) 4.5 kg in pounds

    (ii) 3.0 lb in kilograms   (iv) 10.5 lb in kilograms.

2 1 litre = 0.22 gallons

(a) What are these capacities, in gallons?

    (i)   0 litres   (ii) 5 litres   (iii) 20 litres

(b) Draw a pair of coordinate axes on graph paper. Label the horizontal axis as litres and number it from 0 to 30 litres, using a scale of 1 cm to 5 litres. Label the vertical axis as gallons and number it from 0 to 12, using a scale of 1 cm to 2 gallons.

(c) Draw a conversion graph of litres to gallons and use your graph to find:

    (i)   12 litres in gallons   (iii) 25 litres in gallons

    (ii) 3 gallons in litres   (iv) 7.2 gallons in litres.

3 £1 = J$185 (Jamaican dollars)

(a) How many Jamaican dollars are there in:

(i) £10   (ii) £100?

(b) Use this information to draw a conversion graph for pounds sterling to Jamaican dollars. Label the horizontal axis as pounds sterling and number it from 0 to 200, using a scale of 4 cm to £50. Label the vertical axis as Jamaican dollars and number it from 0 to 40 000, using a scale of 1 cm to J$ 4000

(c) Use your graph to calculate:

(i) J$800 in pounds sterling   (iii) J$35 000 in pounds sterling

(ii) £150 in Jamaican dollars   (iv) £90 in Jamaican dollars.

4 £1 = US$1.60 (United States dollars)

Use this information to draw a conversion chart for pounds sterling to United States dollars. Use the horizontal axis for pounds sterling, from £0 to £500, drawn to a suitable scale.

Use your graph to find the value of:

(a) £450 in US dollars   (c) £225 in US dollars

(b) US$700 in pounds sterling   (d) $425 in pounds sterling.

5 The cooking time for a joint of lamb is calculated as '45 minutes per pound, plus 45 minutes'.

(a) How long would it take to cook:

(i) a 2 lb joint   (ii) a 5 lb joint?

(b) Draw a conversion graph for cooking time against mass. Use the horizontal axis for time, from 0 to 5 hours, with a scale of 2 cm to one hour. Use the vertical axis for mass, choosing a suitable scale. Think carefully about what happens to your line between 0 hours and 1 hour!

(c) Use your graph to find the time taken to roast a joint weighing:

(i) 3 lb   (ii) 4 lb

(d) How heavy is a joint that takes 2 hours to roast?

6 10 km = 6.2 miles

Draw a conversion graph to convert kilometres, from 0 to 100, into miles. Let the horizontal axis represent kilometres. Use your graph to find:

(a) 25 miles in kilometres

(b) 70 kilometres in miles

(c) the equivalent of the 60 mph speed limit, in km/h

(d) the equivalent of the French speed limit of 60 km/h, in mph.

7 The summer maths exam has two parts. The written paper is marked out of 70. The mental arithmetic paper is marked out of 20. The final mark has to be a percentage, that is out of 100. The mental arithmetic score is halved to

make it out of 10. The written paper is scaled up to make it out of 90 and then the scores are added together.

(a) (i) What will 0 marks out of 70 be as a mark out of 90?

   (ii) What will 70 marks out of 70 be as a mark out of 90?

(b) Use these two pieces of information to draw a conversion graph of the original mark to the new mark.

Travel graphs

Line graphs can show journeys.

A **travel graph** shows the relationship between distance travelled and time taken. You do not need to calculate the **speed** if you are using a graph. The speed is the distance travelled in one hour. You can read that from the graph.

This graph shows that Alan travelled 15 km in 5 hours, Betty travelled 40 km in 4 hours and Chan travelled 60 km in one hour.

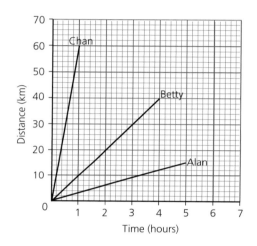

Reading the distance after one hour, you can see that as Alan's speed was 3 km/h, so he was probably walking. Betty was travelling at 10 km/h, so was possibly riding a bicycle. Chan was travelling at 60 km/h, so he was probably in a car.

Exercise 17.6

1 Look at this graph.

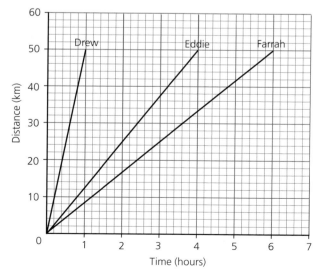

Drew, Eddie and Farrah have all travelled 50 km but in different times.

From the graph, read:

(a) Drew's speed (b) Eddie's speed (c) Farrah's speed.

How do you think each was travelling?

2 This graph is drawn to a different scale from the one in question 1

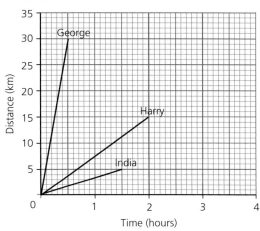

From the graph read:

(a) George's speed (b) Harry's speed (c) India's speed.

3 Here is a graph showing a car journey.

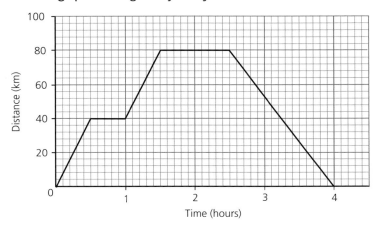

(a) At what speed was the car travelling for the first half hour?

(b) What did the car do after half an hour?

(c) What speed did the car travel after that?

(d) What speed did the car do for the last hour of the journey?

(e) Describe what you think the purpose of this car journey might have been.

4 This is the graph of another journey in four parts.

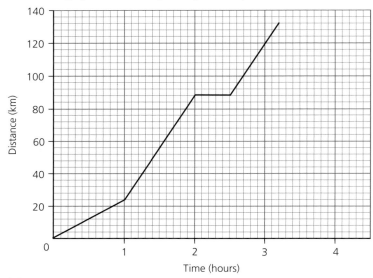

(a) Describe this journey, including the time and speed for each part of the journey.

(b) What do you think the purpose of this journey might have been?

5 A car travels along the motorway at an average speed of 70 miles an hour for one and a half hours. It stops at the Happy Muncher restaurant where the driver spends 30 minutes having a meal.

The car then travels at an average speed of 50 mph for an hour and a half to its destination. Draw a travel graph to show the journey. Take 2 cm to represent 30 minutes on the horizontal axis and 1 cm to represent 20 miles on the vertical axis. How far was the journey?

6 A delivery van travels along the motorway at an average speed of 100 km/h for one and a half hours. It stops at the Transport Café where the driver spends 40 minutes having an All Day Breakfast.

The van driver then gets back into the van and continues his journey, travelling at an average speed of 80 km/h for one hour and a quarter to his destination. Draw a travel graph to show the journey. Take 2 cm to represent 30 minutes on the horizontal axis and 1 cm to represent 20 km on the vertical axis. How far was this journey?

Extension Exercise 17.7

This exercise is like the previous ones, in that you are given some information about a collection of data. In most of the questions some of the information is missing and you need to fill it in.

1 There are 24 pupils in my class. One-quarter of them have blonde hair and two of them are redheads. Of the rest, three-quarters have brown hair and the rest have black hair. Show this information in a frequency table.

2 This frequency table records pupils' answers to the question: 'What colour is your bicycle?' Copy and complete the frequency table, filling in all the missing values. These clues will help.

(a) One-third of the total had silver bicycles.

(b) There were half as many blue bicycles as yellow ones.

(c) Twice as many children had red bicycles as had no bicycle at all.

Colour	Frequency
Red	
Yellow	6
Silver	
Blue	
No bicycle	
Total	36

3 I want to draw a pie chart to illustrate the results of a survey about how many people live in each house in my street. Unfortunately, I was so pleased when I had finished it that I opened a can of cola and it sprayed all over my table. Now I cannot read some of it. Can you fill in the missing values?

Number of people	Tally	Frequency	Fraction	Angle
1		2	=	
2	III		=	
3	⊔⊓⊤		=	60°
4	⊔⊓⊤ ⊔⊓⊤		=	120°
5		6	$= \dfrac{1}{5}$	72°
More than 5	I		$= \dfrac{1}{10}$	
Total				360°

The tallies might not all be there.

4 I carried out a survey of how many people there were in each car that went past the school in a day. I need to draw a bar chart to show my results. I have lost my survey but can remember this information.

● There were 40 people in all and there were never more than four in a car.

● Most cars had two people in them.

● Five cars had one person in them and three cars had three people.

● The number of cars in each group was always odd.

Copy and complete this table to give my results.

Number of people in car	Cars	Total number of people
1		
2		
3		
4	1	4

Summary Exercise 17.8

1 The pupils in my class were all asked how many brothers and sisters they had,
These were their answers.

2	1	2	1	3
none	3	1	4	2
3	none	2	none	1
2	1	1	none	1

(a) Copy this frequency table and use the above information to complete it.

Number of brothers and sisters	Tally	Frequency
0		
1		
2		
3		
4		
Total		

(b) Draw a bar chart to illustrate the information.

2 Here are the answers to the question: 'Do you have a garden?'

Yes	No	No	Yes	No
No	Yes	Yes	Yes	No
Yes	No	Yes	No	Yes
No	Yes	No	Yes	Yes

(a) Copy and complete this frequency table to show the information.

Garden?	Tally	Frequency	Fraction	Angle
Yes				
No				
Total				

(b) Draw a pie chart to illustrate the results of the survey.

3 This bar chart shows what everyone in my class chose to do as an evening activity.

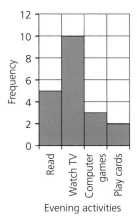

(a) How many people are in my class?

(b) What fraction of them read?

(c) How many more of them watched television than played cards?

4 This pie chart shows how I spent my day.

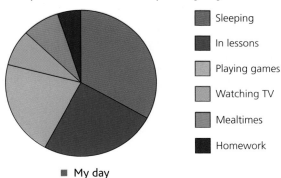

Sleeping
In lessons
Playing games
Watching TV
Mealtimes
Homework

■ My day

(a) There are 24 hours in a day. The angle at the centre of the slice for sleeping is 120°. How many hours did I spend asleep?

(b) What fraction did I spend in lessons?

(c) I spent twice as much time watching TV as I spent doing homework. How much time did I spend on my homework?

(d) How many hours did I spend playing games?

> Look at the chart to deduce more information.

5 £1 = A$1.8 (Australian dollars)

Use this information to draw a conversion chart for pounds sterling, from £0 to £500, to Australian dollars. Use the horizontal axis for pounds sterling. Choose a suitable scale.

Use your graph to find the value of:

(a) £450 in Australian dollars

(b) A$700 in pounds sterling

(c) £225 in Australian dollars

(d) A$425 in pounds sterling.

Activity: Statistical surveys

The work you have done in this chapter will be much more useful if you can relate it to a survey that you have done yourself.

There are some simple surveys you can do in your class. They each only involve one answer.

- How many brothers and sisters do you have?

- How many people live in your house?

- What is your height?

There are other surveys that look at the comparison of two values.

- What are your height and your mass?

- What are your height and your shoe size?

You would expect to find some relationship between the above data, but you may wish to carry out other surveys to support a theory of your own. This is called a hypothesis.

For example, your hypothesis might be that everybody who wears glasses is a computer wizard. You could ask: 'Do you wear glasses? How many hours a week do you spend on the computer?'

To try to show that revision helps people pass exams, you might ask: 'How many hours revision did you do? What was your average exam mark?'

Decide on your survey.

Word your questions so that you get a fair answer, for example, you could ask: 'What is your favourite subject?' rather than 'Do you like school?'

Ask at least 30 people to take part in your survey. Use the information in this chapter to help you to write and illustrate a report on your findings.

18 Time and travel

You studied time in Chapter 14

Time of travel

When you are travelling, you will often see times displayed in a
timetable telling you when your bus, train or aeroplane will depart
and when it should arrive at its destination.

From these two values you can work out the **duration** of a journey,
which is the time it takes from start to finish.

Examples

Leaving	Destination	Departure	Arrival
London Euston	Birmingham	11:12	13:50
London Kings Cross	Edinburgh	11:44	16:15

(i) How long does it take to travel from London to Birmingham?

The time taken to travel from London to Birmingham is from 11:12 to 13:50

Method 1: Use a timeline

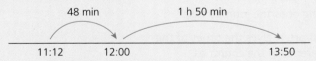

Total time is 48 m + 1 h 50 m = 2 hours 38 minutes

> Use a time line to break the journey into parts. It does not have to be drawn to scale.

(ii) How long does it take to travel from London to Edinburgh?

The time taken to travel from London to Edinburgh is from 11:44 to 16:15

Method 2: Subtraction

	h			m	
1	5̶6̶		7̶1̶	5	
1	1		4	4	
	4		3	1	

The journey time is 4 hours 31 minutes.

> You cannot take 44 from 15 so you must take 60 minutes from the hours column to make 75 minutes.
>
> 75 − 44 = 31

1 (a) A coach leaves London at 07:00 and arrives in Southampton at 08:50
    What is the journey time?

  (b) A coach leaves London at 10:55 and arrives in Southampton at 13:10
    What is the journey time?

  (c) Why do you think the first journey was quicker?

2 (a) A train leaves Bristol at 11:37 and arrives in London at 13:45. What is
    the journey time?

  (b) The next train is a slow one. It leaves Bristol at 11:48 and arrives in
    London at 14:22. What is the journey time?

3 We leave home at quarter past nine and reach the ferry terminal at Dover at
  eighteen minutes to eleven. What is our journey time?

4 An aeroplane takes off from Heathrow at 11:25 and lands in Washington at
  18:12 UK time. How long does the journey take?

5 I am using the internet to look up information about trains to Plymouth.

Depart	Arrive
11:57	15:27
12:47	16:17
13:37	17:10
15:07	18:31
16:17	19:56
17:27	20:50

  (a) What is the fastest train and how long does the journey take?

  (b) What is the slowest train and how long does the journey take?

6 This is part of a departure board at the airport. It gives the times of the
  flights but does not tell you the time difference in the countries.

Flight	Destination	Departure	Arrival
BA 345	Paris	09:35	11:55
BA1234	New York	11:30	14:30

  (a) If Paris is one hour ahead of the UK, what is the flight time to Paris?

  (b) If New York is five hours behind the UK, what is the duration of the
    flight to New York?

Time as a fraction

When you are working on problems involving time, it can be helpful to think of minutes as fractions of an hour. You are used to saying: 'half past...', 'quarter past...' and 'quarter to...' and you can work these out easily. As there are 60 minutes in an hour, other fractions are not very difficult to work out.

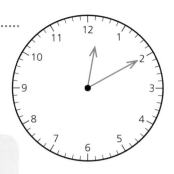

Example

Write 10 minutes as a fraction of an hour.

10 minutes = $\frac{10}{60}$ hours

$\qquad$ = $\frac{1}{6}$ hour

Exercise 18.2

1 Write each of these as a fraction of an hour.

(a) 2 minutes

(c) 20 minutes

(b) 5 minutes

(d) 55 minutes

2 How many minutes are there in each fraction of an hour?

(a) $\frac{3}{10}$ hour

(c) $\frac{7}{12}$ hour

(b) $\frac{2}{5}$ hour

(d) $\frac{9}{20}$ hour

3 How many minutes are there in $2\frac{1}{15}$ hours?

4 Write four and three-twentieths of an hour in minutes.

5 I travel by train for 2 hours and then I have to wait 25 minutes for a taxi. The taxi journey takes 40 minutes. How long has my journey time been in:

(a) hours only (use fractions)

(b) hours and minutes?

6 I travel to school by bus, with a walk at the end. The whole journey takes 55 minutes. The bus journey takes four-fifths of an hour. How long do I walk for?

7 One-tenth of my time at school is spent in general organisation, such as getting my books out and putting them away. If I am at school from 9 a.m. to 4 p.m., how many minutes do I spend organising myself?

8 A ferry crossing took 5 hours. For half that time we watched a film, for a sixth of the time we ate a meal, for a quarter of the time I read my book and the rest of the time I was bored. How long was I bored for?

Distance, speed and time

Travelling is an important part of most people's lives, from short journeys, such as travelling to school, to long ones, such as going abroad on holiday.

Every journey has a starting point and a finishing point. It also has a starting (or departure) time and a finishing (or arrival) time. The time taken on a journey depends on the speed of travel.

Calculating speed

Speed is a **compound unit**, usually expressed as kilometres per hour (km/h) or miles per hour (mph). The simplest way to calculate speed is to work out the distance that is travelled in one hour.

- If you travel 60 km in one hour, your average speed is 60 km/h.

- If you travel 60 km in two hours, then you travel 30 km in one hour and your average speed is 30 km/h.

- If you travel 60 km in 30 minutes, you travel 120 km in one hour and your average speed is 120 km/h.

Note that you refer to **average speed** when you are discussing speeds over a distance. This is because the actual speed varies during the course of the journey. It would be impossible to start instantaneously at 90 km/h, maintain this speed until you reach your destination and then stop instantaneously.

Example

A van travels 60 km in an hour and a half. What is its average speed?

It travels 60 km in an hour and a half.

It travels 20 km in half an hour.
$$(\div 3)$$
It travels 40 km in an hour.
$$(\times 2)$$
Its average speed is 40 km/h.

> Work these out just as you worked out quantities in proportion in Chapter 16. You want to end up with time as one hour.

Exercise 18.3

Use the same method as in the example above to work these out.

1 A car travels 50 km in one hour. What is its average speed?

2 A boy runs 5 km in one hour. What is his average speed?

3 An aircraft travels 1500 km in five hours. What is its average speed?

4 A train travels 35 miles in 20 minutes. What is its average speed?

5 A cyclist travels 25 km in two and a half hours. What is his average speed?

6 A boat travels 66 miles in five and a half hours. What is its average speed?

7 A car travels 2 km in 5 minutes. What is its average speed?

8 Which is faster, a car that travels 15 km in 10 minutes or a coach that travels 200 km in two hours?

9 Who is faster, a boy who walks 15 km in 3 hours or a girl who cycles 3 km in 15 minutes?

10 Which is faster, a train that travels 150 km in an hour and a half or a coach that travels 25 km in 30 minutes?

Calculating distance

If you know the speed at which something is travelling, then you know how far it will travel in one hour. From that you can work out how far it will travel in a multiple or fraction of an hour.

Example

A car travels at a constant speed of 40 miles per hour (mph).
How far does it go in:

(i) 3 hours

(ii) 15 minutes?

(i) It travels 40 miles in one hour.
     It travels 120 miles in 3 hours.   (× 3)

(ii) It travels 40 miles in one hour.
      It travels 10 miles in 15 minutes.   (÷ 4)

> This time you need to multiply or divide the values in order to reach the same time as in the question.

Exercise 18.4

1 A car travels at a constant speed of 50 mph. How far does it go in two hours?

2 A train travels at a constant speed of 100 km/h. How far does it go in 30 minutes?

3 A bus travels at a constant speed of 30 mph. How far does it go in ten minutes?

4 A man walks at a constant speed of 8 km/h. How far does he go in 15 minutes?

5 A car travels at a constant speed of 50 km/h. How far does it go in an hour and a half?

6 A boat travels at a constant speed of 30 km/h. How far does it go in two and a half hours?

7 A coach travels at a constant speed of 60 mph. How far does it go in four hours?

8   A car travels at a constant speed of 40 km/h. How far does it go in 45 minutes?

9   A train travels at a constant speed of 120 km/h. How far does it go in two hours 15 minutes?

10 An aeroplane travels at a constant speed of 850 km/h. How far does it go in four and a half hours?

Calculating time

If you know the speed at which something is travelling, then you know how far it will travel in one hour. If you also know the distance travelled, then you know if the journey takes more or less than one hour. You can use the same method of multiplying or dividing to find the time taken.

Example

A car travels at a constant speed of 40 mph.
How long does it take to travel:

(i)   80 miles

(ii) 10 miles?

(i)   The car travels 40 miles in 1 hour.
      The car travels 80 miles in 2 hours.   ($\times 2$)

(ii) The car travels 40 miles in 1 hour.
      The car travels 10 miles in $\frac{1}{4}$ hour.   ($\div 4$)

      The car travels 10 miles in 15 minutes.   Turn the fraction of an hour into minutes.

> Multiply or divide the values to get the same distance as in the question.

Exercise 18.5

1   A car travels at a constant speed of 50 km/h. How long does it take to travel 100 km?

2   A train travels at a constant speed of 80 km/h. How long does it take to travel 40 km?

3   A bus travels at a constant speed of 30 km/h. How long does it take to travel 10 km?

4   A man jogs at a constant speed of 5 mph. How long does it take him to travel 3 miles?

5   A car travels at a constant speed of 45 km/h. How long does it take to travel 30 km?

6   A boat travels at a constant speed of 25 km/h. How long does it take to travel 75 km?

7   A bicycle travels at a constant speed of 16 mph. How long does it take to travel 6 miles?

8 A car travels at a constant speed of 50 mph. How long does it take to travel 60 miles?

9 A plane travels at a constant speed of 300 km/h. How long does it take to travel 200 km?

10 A coach travels at a constant speed of 56 mph. How long does it take to travel 70 miles?

Exercise 18.6

Now that you have learnt the basics, you can use them to solve these problems. Remember to write down your working and to check your answers to make sure that they look sensible.

1 It is 330 miles from London to Edinburgh. My plane leaves at 10:15 and arrives at 11:45. What is the average speed of the aeroplane?

2 It is 350 miles from London to Glasgow. A train travels at an average speed of 70 mph. If the train makes four stops of 10 minutes each on its journey from Glasgow to London, what will the total journey time be?

3 If a cheetah runs at 100 km/h and a top Olympic sprinter runs at 12 metres per second (m/s), how far will each travel in one minute? Which is faster? How long do you think each will take to run 10 km? Are you sure? Think about it!

4 We leave home at half past eight. We drive at an average speed of 60 km/h for an hour and a half, then we stop for 30 minutes. We then drive at an average speed of 50 km/h for 75 km. What was the length of the journey and at what time did we arrive?

5 It is 110 miles from London to Bristol and a coach driver claims to do this in two and a half hours. What is the average speed of the coach?

6 The London Marathon is a race on a course that is 26.2 miles long. The race was won in 2014 by Wilson Kipsang Kiprotich with a world-record breaking time of 2 hours 4 minutes. Estimate the average speed of the record-breaking runner.

7 It is 110 miles from Dover to Newbury and 65 miles from Dover to London. Two cars leave Dover at the same time: one travels to Newbury at an average speed of 50 mph and the other travels to London at an average speed of 30 mph. Which car arrives home first?

8 The northernmost tip of Britain is John O'Groats and the southernmost is Lizard Point. The distance between the two by main roads is 1350 km and this took a car 18 hours. However, the overall shortest route using minor roads is 1311 km and this took a jeep 19 hours. Which car was going faster?

For this exercise, use the last two digits only for the year. Thus, think of 1999 as 99 and 2009 as 09 (or 9)

These are European dates and go DD/MM/YY (Day/Month/Year), not US dates that are written as MM/DD/YY

1 Look at the date 03/03/12

   3 divides exactly into 12 so both the day (03) and the month (03) are factors of the year (12)

   (a) What was the next date in March when this would be true?

   (b) On what dates in April that year would the day and the month both have been factors of the year?

2 30/11/03 is a palindromic date. It reads the same backwards and forwards.

   (a) Have there been any other palindromic dates this century so far? If so, write them down.

   (b) Write down the next three palindromic dates this century.

3 On 05/03/15 the year is a multiple of the day and the month.

   (a) On which dates this year has this been true?

   (b) On which next three dates will this be true?

   (c) Give the last three dates in the last century when this was true.

4 On 05/03/15 the product of the day and the month equals the year.

   (a) What was the next date when this was true?

   (b) What was the previous date when this was true?

   (c) List all the dates in 2016 when this is true.

   (d) What will be the next year to have more dates when this is true than 2016?

5 Mrs Smith brought her son Tommy for a trial day in the nursery on 10 March. She gave his date of birth and we thought he was exactly 3 years and 2 months old. We then found that Mrs Smith is American and had given us his birthday with the months before the days. How old was little Tommy on 10 March? Show all your working.

Summary Exercise 18.8

1 This is a river bus timetable.

Greenwich	11:15
Westminster	12:10
Victoria Embankment	12:55
Chelsea Harbour	13:20
Putney	13:50

(a) How long does the whole journey from Greenwich to Putney take?

(b) Which part of the journey took the shortest time?

(c) Boats run on a similar timetable, leaving Greenwich at a quarter past each hour. What is the latest boat I can catch to get back to Putney in time for tea at half past four?

2 Write each of these times as a fraction of an hour.

(a) 5 minutes   (b) 25 minutes   (c) 36 minutes

3 How many minutes are there in these numbers of hours?

(a) $1\frac{1}{4}$ hours   (b) $3\frac{2}{5}$ hours   (c) $2\frac{5}{12}$ hours

4 A train leaves Paddington at 13:23. The journey to Bristol takes 2 hours and 45 minutes. What time does it arrive in Bristol?

5 (a) A train travels at 120 mph for 2 hours. How far does it go?

(b) How far does the same train go in 40 minutes?

6 It took us 4 hours to travel the 372 km from Paris to Lyon. What was our average speed?

7 (a) On the way to Portsmouth to catch a ferry I drive for 125 miles at an average speed of 60 mph. What is my journey time?

(b) I take the ferry to France and, after a four-hour crossing, I then drive for 135 km at 90 km/h. What is my total journey time?

8 (a) An aeroplane leaves Heathrow at 21:26 and arrives at San Antonio at 00:45. How long does the journey take?

(b) That does not seem correct. When I look at my ticket again I find that the times given are local times. The time in San Antonio is two hours behind UK time. What is the correct length of time for my journey?

19 Perimeter and area

◯ Perimeters and areas of squares and rectangles

Look at this shape.

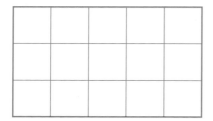

The **perimeter** is the distance all the way round the outside of a plane shape. It is measured in metric units of length: metres (m), centimetres (cm), millimetres (mm), or, in imperial units, feet and inches.

The **area** is the space enclosed inside the shape and is measured in square units. You can write:

- **square metres** as m^2 or, less usually, as sq. m
- **square centimetres** as cm^2 or as sq. cm
- **square millimetres** as mm^2 or as sq. mm
- **square kilometres** as km^2 or as sq. km.

As the shape above is drawn on a grid of centimetre squares, it is easy to calculate its perimeter and area.

For the perimeter, you add the lengths of all the sides together.

Perimeter = 5 + 3 + 5 + 3 = 16 cm

For the area you simply count up the squares.

Area = 15 cm^2

You can also calculate the area by multiplying the number of centimetres in the length by the number of centimetres in the width.

Area = length × width

It is important to make a rule for which side is the length and which is the width.

Imagine the rectangle standing upright. The side on the ground, the horizontal side, is known as the base and the upright (or vertical) length is the height. Then the formula for calculating the area is:

Area = base × height   or $A = b \times h$

The sides of a rectangle are sometimes called **length** and **width** and sometimes **base** and **height**. It does not matter which words you use in your formula. It is best to use the same words as in the problem.

In textbooks, letters that represent unknown quantities are usually italic or curly letters.

Returning to the perimeter, you add the lengths of all the sides.

Perimeter $= b + h + b + h$

$\qquad\quad = 2b + 2h$

Remember that, whenever you have a formula in which a value is unknown, you follow these steps.

1 Write out the formula.

2 Fill in or substitute the amounts you do know.

3 Calculate the answer.

4 Write the answers with the correct units.

Example

A rectangle has a base of 1.4 m and a height of 70 cm. Find: (i) the perimeter   (ii) the area.

Give your answers in metres and square metres.

$b = 1.4\,\text{m}$

$h = 70\,\text{cm} = 0.7\,\text{m}$ Turn the 70 cm into metres.

0.7 m

1.4 m

It helps to draw a quick sketch to make sure that you have the correct dimensions.

Remember BIDMAS. Multiply before you add.

(i) $P = 2b + 2h$ Formula

$= 2 \times 1.4 + 2 \times 0.7$ Substitute

$= 2.8 + 1.4$ Calculate

$= 4.2\,\text{m}$ Write the answer, with correct units.

(ii) $A = b \times h$ Formula

$= 1.4 \times 0.7$ Substitute

$= 0.98\,\text{m}^2$ Calculate and write the answer, with correct units.

Exercise 19.1

Find: (a) the perimeter (in cm)

(b) the area (in cm²) of each of these rectangles.

1 6 m by 20 cm

2 4 cm by 50 mm

3 400 cm by 4 m

4 10 cm by 0.5 m

5 0.4 m by 80 cm

6 1.2 m by 400 cm

7 10 mm by 7 cm

8 30 cm by 6 m

9 50 mm by 0.4 m

10 0.4 m by 400 cm

Longest and largest

Suppose you have a rectangle of area 12 cm².
It could have several different dimensions.

(a) base = 1 cm   height = 12 cm

(b) base = 2 cm   height = 6 cm

(c) base = 3 cm   height = 4 cm

(d) base = 4 cm   height = 3 cm

(e) base = 6 cm   height = 2 cm

(f) base = 12 cm   height = 1 cm

(a) and (f) have the longest perimeter of 26 cm.

(c) and (d) have the shortest perimeter of 14 cm.

Exercise 19.2

1 Find the area and perimeter of each of these shapes. Write down which has the largest area and which the longest perimeter.

(a)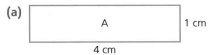

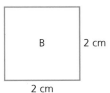

(b)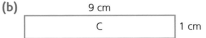

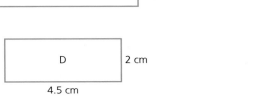

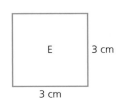

(c)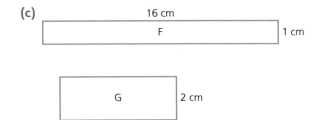

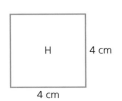

> Use whole or half centimetres for the lengths.

2 Draw as many rectangles as you can with an area of 24 cm². Which has the greatest perimeter and which the shortest?

3 Draw as many rectangles as you can with an area of 36 cm². Which has the greatest perimeter and which the shortest?

4 A farmer has 100 sheep and every sheep needs 1 m² of field on which to graze. He wants to make a rectangular field, using the smallest amount of fencing possible. What dimensions should he choose?

5 I have 16 square tiles, each measuring 10 cm × 10 cm. I want to put them together to make a chopping board. What shape will give me a chopping board with the smallest border?

6 I have 42 square photographs, each measuring 5 cm by 5 cm. How can I arrange them all into a rectangular picture collage with the shortest possible length of picture frame?

7 A farmer has 100 fencing units, each 2 m long. How can he arrange his fences to enclose the largest possible rectangular area?

8 The pupils in my class have knitted squares, each measuring 30 cm by 30 cm. We are going to stitch them together to make blankets for refugees. We have to sew tape around the border of each blanket when we have stitched the squares together. The border tape comes in lengths of 7.2 m.

What size should we make our blankets so that we waste as little tape as possible?

◯ Finding the unknown dimension

If you know the area or perimeter of a rectangle or square and one other **dimension**, you can find the unknown one.

Examples

(i) The area of a photograph is 35 cm² and the width is 5 cm. What is the length?

$A = l \times w$	Formula
$35 = l \times 5$	Substitute
$l = \dfrac{35}{5}$	Calculate
$(\div 5)$	
$= 7\,cm$	Write the answer, with correct units.

The length is 7 cm.

> Always start by writing the formula. You have used $A = b \times h$ but in this example, the terms are 'length' and 'width', so use $A = l \times w$

(ii) The perimeter of a rectangular field is 4 km and the length is 1.5 km. What is the width of the field?

$P = 2l + 2w$	Formula
$4 = 2 \times 1.5 + 2w$	Substitute
$4 = 3 + 2w$	Calculate
$(\div 3)$	
$2w = 1$	
$w = 0.5\,km$	Write the answer, with correct units.

Exercise 19.3

1 These tiled floors all cover an area of 36 m² but, as you can see, they have different widths. What length must each room be?

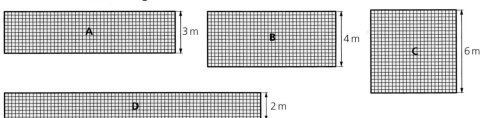

2 I have enough bricks to make a wall of area 144 m². Each one will have a different base length, as shown. How tall will each of the walls be?

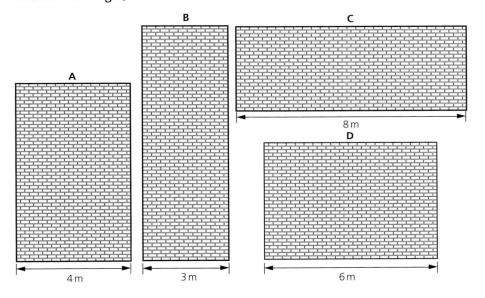

3 A rectangle of area 45 cm² has a height of 5 cm. How long is the base?

4 A rectangle of perimeter 36 cm has a base of 12 cm. What is its height?

5 I have exactly the right amount of ribbon to trim a rectangular tablecloth that has a perimeter of 10 m and a width 2.5 m. How long is the tablecloth?

6 I have a piece of string measuring 1 metre. I can put it around the edge of my maths file once exactly. If my file is 20 cm wide, how long is it?

7 I am ordering carpet for my bedroom. I know the total perimeter is 16 m and the width is 3.5 m, but what is the area of my bedroom?

8 A rectangular field has an area of 6.5 km². Its southern border is a hedge that is 2.6 km long. The farmer has to put a fence around the other three sides. How long is his fence?

Area of a parallelogram

Look at this rectangle.

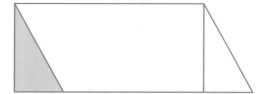

A right-angled triangle has been cut off one end and added to the other. Look at the shape this has made.

It is a parallelogram.

This word formula shows what has happened.

Area of parallelogram = area of rectangle − area of triangle + area of triangle

= area of rectangle

$= b \times h$

As the area of the triangle has been added and taken away it cancels out.

Then the formula for the area of a parallelogram is the same as the area of a rectangle with the same base and height.

Area of parallelogram = base × height

$= b \times h$

Just as for a rectangle, the base and the height are at right angles to each other.

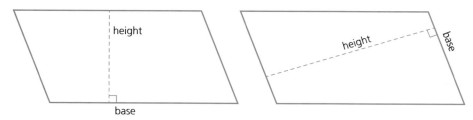

It does not matter which side you take as the base but the height must be at right angles to it.

Example

Find the area of this parallelogram.

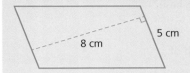

Area of parallelogram = $b \times h$ Write the formula.

                = 5×8 Substitute what you know.

                = 40 cm²   Calculate, then write the answer, with correct units.

Exercise 19.4

1 Find the area of each parallelogram.

(a)

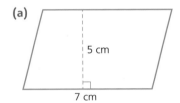

(d)

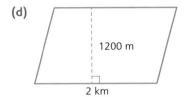

(b)

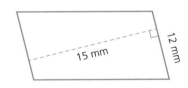

(e)

(c)

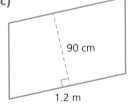

(f)

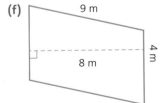

2 Find the area of a parallelogram of base 5 cm and height 8 mm.

3 Find the area of a parallelogram of base 2.4 m and height 80 cm.

4 Find the area of a parallelogram of base 0.8 m and height 1.2 m.

5 A parallelogram has area 48 cm² and base 6 cm. What is its height?

6 A parallelogram has area 3.6 cm² and height 0.9 cm. What is the length of its base?

7 A parallelogram has area 1.44 cm² and base 9 mm. What is its height?

8 A parallelogram has area 1.2 m² and height 600 cm. What is the length of its base?

◯ Area of a triangle

You have seen that the area of a rectangle and the area of a parallelogram have the same formula.

Area = base × height   or $A = b \times h$

What happens if you divide a rectangle or a parallelogram in half?

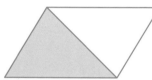

You can see that cutting a rectangle in half produces two congruent right-angled triangles.

Half a parallelogram is generally a scalene triangle. It may be an **acute-angled triangle** or an **obtuse-angled triangle**.

Therefore:

area of a triangle = $\frac{1}{2}$ × base × height

$= \frac{1}{2} \times b \times h$

If you are not working with a right-angled triangle, then you must find its height, which is **perpendicular** to its base. If you have an obtuse-angled triangle, you will have to find its height by extending the base until it is under the top of the triangle.

Remember that the little square symbol shows the base and height are perpendicular.

Examples

(i) Find the area of triangle *ABC*, with *AB* = 5 cm, *BC* = 7cm and ∠*B* = 90°

Always draw a small sketch of the triangle to make sure that you have the dimensions in the correct place.

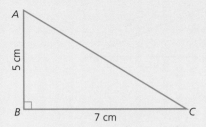

Follow the steps as before.

Area of a triangle = $\frac{1}{2} \times b \times h$ Formula

                  = $\frac{1}{2} \times 7 \times 5$ Substitute

                  = $\frac{35}{2}$ Calculate

                  = 17.5 cm²   Answer, with correct units.

(ii) Find the area of triangle *PQR*.

PQR is not a right-angled triangle so you must draw in the height, perpendicular to the base.

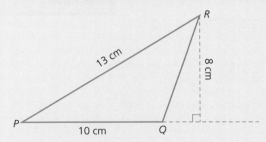

Area of a triangle = $\frac{1}{2} \times b \times h$ Formula

                  = $\frac{1}{2} \times 10 \times 8$ Substitute

                  = $\frac{1}{{}_1 2} \times 10 \times 8^4$ Calculate the common factor 2

                  = 40 cm²   Answer, with correct units.

Exercise 19.5

1 Calculate the area of each triangle.

(a)

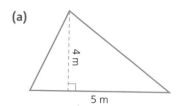

5 m, 4 m

(c)

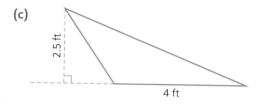

2.5 ft, 4 ft

(b)

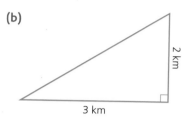

3 km, 2 km

(d)

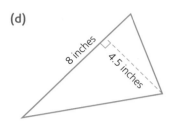

8 inches, 4.5 inches

2 Calculate the area of each triangle.

(a)

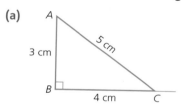

A, 5 cm, 3 cm, *B*, 4 cm, *C*

(c)

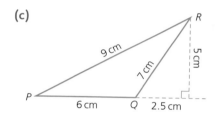

R, 9 cm, 7 cm, 5 cm, *P*, 6 cm, *Q*, 2.5 cm

> When deciding which length is the base and which is the height make sure they are perpendicular to each other.

(b)

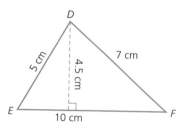

D, 5 cm, 4.5 cm, 7 cm, *E*, 10 cm, *F*

(d)

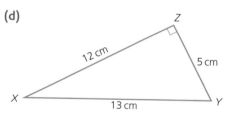

Z, 12 cm, 5 cm, *X*, 13 cm, *Y*

When there is no drawing, make a small sketch of the triangle to make sure that you get the dimensions in the correct place.

3 Find the area of triangle *ABC* with base *AB* = 10 cm and height 12 cm.

4 Find the area of triangle *DEF* with base *DE* = 70 mm and height 50 mm.

5 Find the area of triangle *GHI* with base *GH* = 1.4 m and height 80 cm.

6 Find the area of triangle *JKL* with base *JK* = 50 mm, ∠*K* = 120° and height *LX* = 30 mm.

7 Find the area of triangle *PQR* with base *PQ* = 4 cm and height 28 mm.

8 Find the area of triangle *STU* with base *ST* = 1 ft 2 in, ∠*T* = 105° and height *UX* = 9 in.

Finding unknown lengths in a triangle

Just as you did for rectangles and parallelograms, you can use the **formula** to calculate an unknown length in a triangle. It always helps to sketch the shape first.

When working with the triangle formula, remember that the area is half the base × the height. You will therefore need to double the area before dividing.

Example

A triangle has area 12 cm² and base 6 cm. What is its height?

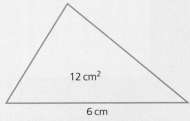

Area of triangle $= \frac{1}{2} \times b \times h$ Formula

$12 = \frac{1}{2} \times 6 \times h$ Substitute

$(\times 2)$

$24 = 6 \times h$ Calculate

$(\div 6)$

$h = \frac{24}{6}$ Calculate

$= 4\,\text{cm}$ Answer, with correct units.

Exercise 19.6

1 Find the height of each triangle.

(a)

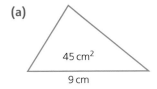

45 cm²
9 cm

(b)

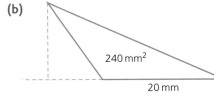

240 mm²
20 mm

> Before you start make sure that you are working in the correct units. Take the units of the area as your guide.

2 Find the length of the base in each triangle.

(a)

150 cm
3 m²

(b)

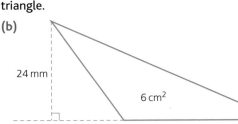

24 mm
6 cm²

3   A triangle has area 144 cm² and base 48 cm. What is its height?

4   A triangle has area 40 cm² and height 8 cm. How long is the base?

5   A triangle has area 2.4 km² and base 800 m. What is its height?

6   A triangle has area 5 cm² and height 25 mm. How long is the base?

◯ Composite shapes

Look at this room plan.

To find the total area of the room, the first thing to do is to fill in the missing lengths. Then you can divide the shape into rectangles and name them A, B, C... .

In this case, divide the room into two rectangles and label them A and B.

Do not be tempted to find the perimeter of each shape and add them together. You would include extra lengths that are not part of the perimeter of the whole shape.

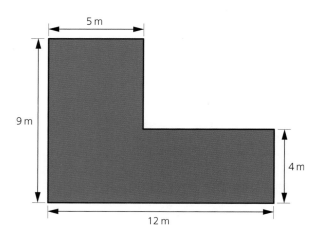

Perimeter = 9 + 12 + 4 + 7 + 5 + 5

$\qquad$ = 42 m

Area of A = $b \times h$

$\qquad$ = 9 × 5

$\qquad$ = 45 m²

Area of B = $b \times h$

$\qquad$ = 7 × 4

$\qquad$ = 28 m²

Total area = area of A + area of B

$\qquad$ = 45 + 28

$\qquad$ = 73 m²

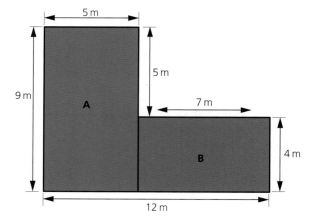

Exercise 19.7

In questions 1–4, find: **(a)** the perimeter **(b)** the area of the shape.

For each question, draw a diagram and fill in any missing lengths before you start.

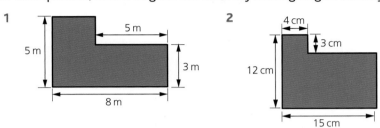

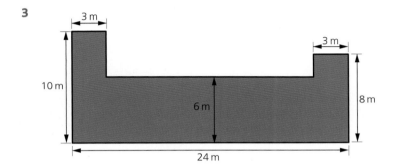

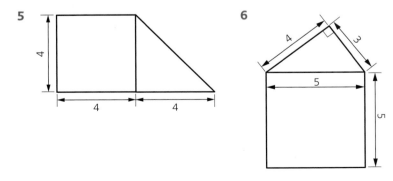

Find the area of each of these combined shapes. Take care! They include triangles.

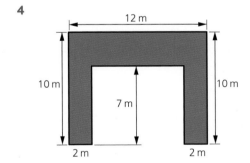

7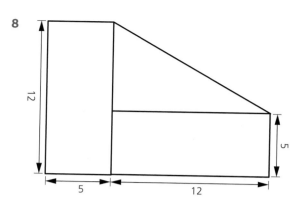

8

Shapes with holes in them

Sometimes you will need to find the area left when part of a shape is
removed or unwanted. You can use the same principle as before, to
subtract areas.

Example

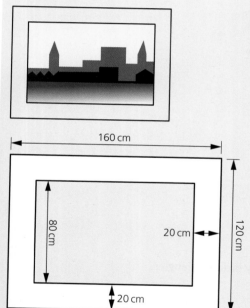

The visible part of this picture is 120 cm by
80 cm. Its picture frame is 20 cm wide all the
way round it. Find the area of the frame.

First draw a diagram, marking on it all the
dimensions. Then fill in the missing ones.

Total area of picture frame and picture
$= b \times h$

$= 120 \times 160$

$= 19\,200\,\text{cm}^2$

Area of picture $= b \times h$

$= 80 \times 120$

$= 9600\,\text{cm}^2$

Area of picture frame $= 19\,200 - 9600$

$= 9600\,\text{cm}^2$

Exercise 19.8

1. This garden is 25 m by 30 m. In the garden is a paved terrace 20 m by 5 m. The rest of the garden is grass. What is the area of grass?

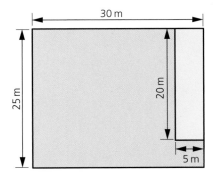

2. My quilt is 3 m by 2 m overall. The quilt has a 10 cm wide border all round it. What is the area of the border, in square centimetres?

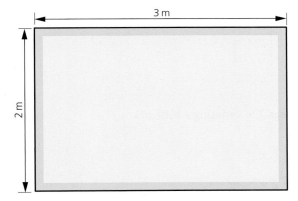

3. In my garden there is a wall measuring 2.6 m by 8 m. I have decided that I would like to make a doorway in the wall. The doorway will be 2 m tall and 90 cm wide. What will be the area of wall remaining?

4. Rebecca's swimming pool is 30 m by 10 m and has a tiled walkway 2 m wide all the way around it.

   (a) What is the area of the tiled walkway?

   (b) The tiles measure 20 cm by 20 cm. How many tiles did Rebecca need?

   (c) The tiles cost £15 for a box of ten. How much did all the tiles Rebecca needed cost?

How many squares of any size are there on a chessboard?

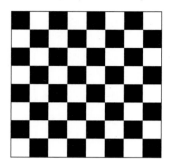

Before you think about the 8 × 8 chessboard, start with smaller arrays of squares.

 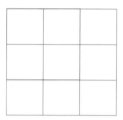

With a 1 × 1 square there is only 1 square.

With a 2 × 2 square there is 1 square 2 × 2 and 4 squares 1 × 1 making a total of 5 squares.

1   Look at the 3 × 3 square above.
    Copy and complete this sentence.
    In a 3 × 3 square there is 1 square 3 × 3, ... squares 2 × 2 and
    ... squares 1 × 1 making a total of ... squares.

2   Investigate a 4 × 4 square. How many squares of different sizes can you find?

3   Draw up this table for whole squares of side S and fill in your results so far.

S	Number of 1 × 1 squares	Number of 2 × 2 squares	Number of 3 × 3 squares	Number of 4 × 4 squares	Number of 5 × 5 squares	Number of 6 × 6 squares	Total number of squares
1	1						1
2	4	1					5
3	9		1				
4							
5							
6							

4   Continue your table for a 5 × 5 square. Can you see a pattern?

5   Use your pattern to complete the table.

6   How many squares of any size are there on an 8 × 8 chessboard?

Summary Exercise 19.10

1 Use the correct formula to find the perimeter of each of these rectangles.

(a)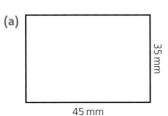

35 mm

45 mm

(b)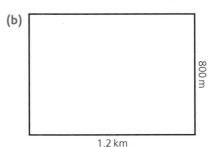

800 m

1.2 km

2 Use the correct formula to find the area of each of these shapes.

(a)

2.5 m

4 m

(d)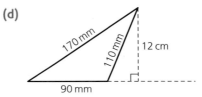

170 mm

110 mm

12 cm

90 mm

(b)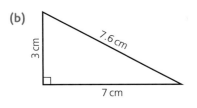

3 cm

7.6 cm

7 cm

(e)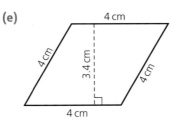

4 cm

4 cm

3.4 cm

4 cm

4 cm

(c)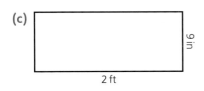

9 in

2 ft

(f)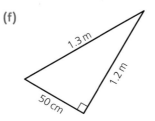

1.3 m

1.2 m

50 cm

3 What is:

(a) the perimeter

(b) the area of a square of sides 0.7 m?

4 What is the area of a parallelogram of height 1.2 m and base 50 cm?

5 What is the height of a rectangle of area 144 cm² and base 12 cm? What is special about the rectangle?

6 What is the base of a parallelogram of area 36 cm² and height 90 mm?

7 What is the height of a triangle of area 60 cm² and base 40 cm?

8 What is the base of a triangle of area 2.4 m² and height 1.6 m?

9 Find the perimeter and the area of each of these shapes.

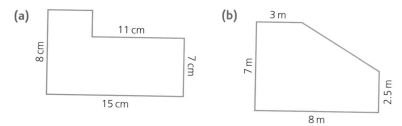

(a)
11 cm
8 cm
7 cm
15 cm

(b)
3 m
7 m
2.5 m
8 m

Activity: Do people with large feet have large hands?

When you are thinking about this sort of question, the way to answer it is to do a survey.

Before you look at how to conduct the survey, first decide exactly what you mean by 'large'.

Look at your hands, look at your feet, look at your friends' hands and feet. Put your hand against your neighbour's hand. You will see that some hands are longer than others and some are wider.

So you could measure 'largeness' by length and width, but a better measure would the areas of the hands and feet. It is quite easy to see how big feet are, because everyone has a shoe size with measurements such as 35, 36, 37, 38

For this survey, use these measurements.

• Hands: length, width and area

• Feet: length, width, area and shoe size.

Before you actually do the survey, make sure that everyone knows their own statistics. Lengths and shoe sizes are quite straightforward but calculating areas is not so simple.

First, take a piece of centimetre-squared paper and put your hand on it, with your fingers together. Draw around your hand and look at the sheet of paper. The whole squares are easy to count, but you will also have parts of squares of different sizes. There are two ways you could count these.

Method 1

Count all the whole squares. Then count each square that is less than whole but more than half a square as one whole too. Then add the two totals together and record this as the area of the hand.

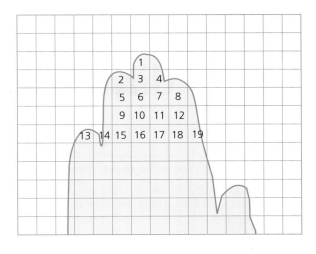

Method 2

Count all the whole squares, then try to combine incomplete squares to make whole squares.

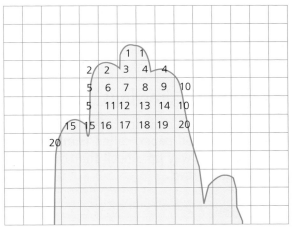

Choose which method you are going to use. Make sure you use the same one throughout the whole survey. Collect the data for hands and feet from the whole class and fill in a **data sheet** with all the statistics. The sheet should be designed to give everybody a number, not a name, so no one need be embarrassed by their large feet and small hands!

The larger the sample included in the survey, the more representative the results will be.

When the data sheet is complete, you will need to decide which aspects of the survey you wish to look at in detail. You could draw:

● a **bar chart** representing the data

● a **pie chart** representing the data

● a **scatter graph** to compare one set of data against another.

If you have a spreadsheet program on your computer, you could enter the data and let the computer draw the diagrams for you.

> When you have completed your diagrams, you must write a conclusion to your report. Do people with large hands have large feet?

20 Shapes in three dimensions

Look around you. What do you see? It is likely that you are surrounded by solid objects: they have **three dimensions.** However, the shapes that you have studied so far have all been in **two dimensions.** It is easier to draw in two dimensions and to study angles and lengths in two dimensions.

Think about a three-dimensional (3D) cuboid.

In the picture, only the front looks like a rectangle but you know that the top and the sides are also rectangles. This cuboid has been drawn to show the three dimensions.

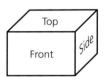

Isometric drawings

When you need to draw in three dimensions it can be helpful to use triangular spotted paper, called **isometric paper.** Make sure that you use it the right way up. Check that the dots are in vertical columns, not horizontal rows.

Example

Draw a cuboid 3 cm by 2 cm by 2 cm.

First, choose which dimension will be the height.

Let it be 2 cm.

Then just draw the lines of the correct lengths, by counting the dots.

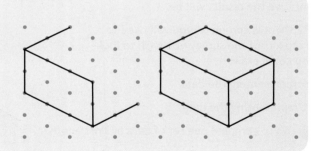

Exercise 20.1

For this exercise, you will need isometric and centimetre-squared paper and some centimetre **cubes**.

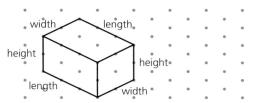

Draw these cuboids on isometric paper. Make the first dimension the height and the second the length. Then the third is the width.

1 4 cm by 5 cm by 2 cm

2 3 cm by 1 cm by 4 cm

3 2 cm by 3 cm by 5 cm

4 1 cm by 2 cm by 3 cm

5 3 cm by 3 cm by 3 cm

> Remember to make sure that your isometric paper is positioned correctly.

> All of the sides of the last cuboid are the same length so therefore it is a cube.

Drawing more complex solid shapes

When architects draw solid shapes or buildings they draw a **plan**, which is the outline the building will make on the ground, and the **elevations**, which are how the sides will appear.

Exercise 20.2

Here are some architect's drawings of a solid shape.

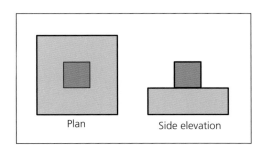

Plan   Side elevation

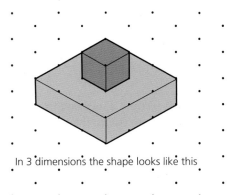

In 3 dimensions the shape looks like this

1 Make the above shape from centimetre cubes. Then draw it on isometric paper.

2 Make this shape from centimetre cubes. Then draw the view from above and from the front. Use centimetre-squared paper.

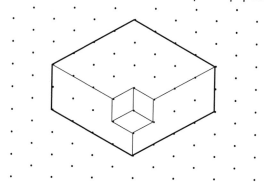

3 These are the views from above and from the sides of a three-dimensional (3D) shape. Make this shape in centimetre cubes. Then draw it on isometric paper.

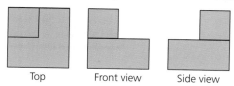

Top   Front view   Side view

4 Make this shape from centimetre cubes. Then draw the view from above and from the front. Use centimetre-squared paper.

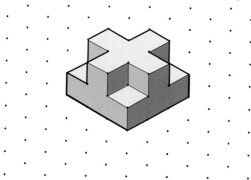

5 These are the views from above and from the sides of a 3D shape. Make this shape from centimetre cubes. Then draw it on isometric paper.

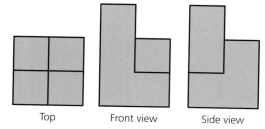

Top   Front view   Side view

Nets

It is often easier to identify the three dimensions if the faces of the 3D shape are painted different colours.

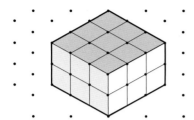

If you were to flatten out the shape above into its **net**, it would look like this.

	SIDE			
FRONT	BOTTOM	BACK		TOP
	SIDE			

Think about some numbers associated with the cuboid and its net as shown above.

● The cuboid is made from 18 centimetre cubes.

● It has 6 faces.

● The top and the bottom faces each show 9 squares.

● The side faces each show 6 squares.

● The front and back faces each show 6 squares.

Altogether that makes 9 + 9 + 6 + 6 + 6 + 6 = 42 squares.

From this, you can say that the **surface area** of this net is 42 cm².

Example

Find the surface area of a cuboid measuring 2 cm by 3 cm by 4 m.

```
                      2 cm          2 cm
                  ┌─────────┐   ┌─────────┐
              2 cm│  SIDE   │2 cm
                  │  4 cm   │
     2 cm    4 cm │         │   2 cm       4 cm
  ┌──────┬────────┼─────────┼──────┬────────────┐
  │      │        │         │      │            │
3 cm│FRONT │ BOTTOM │3 cm     │ BACK │3 cm  TOP    │
  │      │        │         │      │            │
  └──────┼────────┼─────────┼──────┴────────────┘
     2 cm │        │    2 cm        4 cm
          │2 cm    SIDE   │2 cm
          │        4 cm   │
          └────────────────┘
```

Area of top and bottom	$= 2 \times 3 \times 4$	$= 24\,cm^2$
Area of two sides	$= 2 \times 2 \times 4$	$= 16\,cm^2$
Area of front and back	$= 2 \times 2 \times 3$	$= 12\,cm^2$
Total area	$= 24\,cm^2 + 16\,cm^2 + 12\,cm^2$	
	$= 52\,cm^2$	

Exercise 20.3

Use centimetre-squared paper for this exercise. Draw the net of each of these cuboids. Then calculate the surface area.

1 4 cm by 5 cm by 2 cm

2 3 cm by 1 cm by 4 cm

3 2 cm by 3 cm by 5 cm

4 1 cm by 2 cm by 3 cm

5 3 cm by 3 cm by 3 cm

Exercise 20.4

Here are some puzzles to help you think more about shapes in three dimensions.

The outside faces of the cubes and cuboids have been painted. Try to solve the problems by imagining what the solids would look like.

If you really need to, make the shapes out of centimetre cubes, but try without, first.

1 This 3 cm by 3 cm by 3 cm cube is made from centimetre cubes and has all its faces painted orange.

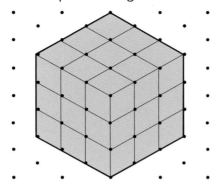

   (a) How many centimetre cubes are used to make this cuboid?

   (b) How many centimetre cubes have exactly three faces painted orange?

   (c) How many centimetre cubes have exactly two faces painted orange?

   (d) How many centimetre cubes have only one face painted orange?

   (e) How many centimetre cubes have no faces painted orange?

   (f) Check that your answers to parts (b)–(e) add up to your answer to part (a). If not, make up a cuboid and check!

2 This 2 cm by 3 cm by 3 cm cuboid is made from centimetre cubes and has all its faces painted orange.

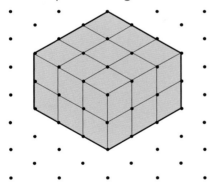

   (a) How many centimetre cubes are used to make this cuboid?

   (b) How many centimetre cubes have exactly three faces painted orange?

   (c) How many centimetre cubes have exactly two faces painted orange?

   (d) How many centimetre cubes have only one face painted orange?

   (e) How many centimetre cubes have no faces painted orange?

   (f) Check that your answers to parts (b)–(e) add up to your answer to part (a).

3 This 3 cm by 3 cm by 3 cm cube is made from centimetre cubes and has a hole through its middle. All its outside faces are painted orange.

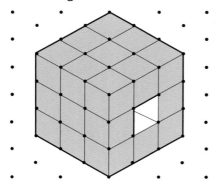

(a) How many centimetre cubes are used to make this cuboid?

(b) How many centimetre cubes have exactly three faces painted orange?

(c) How many centimetre cubes have exactly two faces painted orange?

(d) How many centimetre cubes have only one face painted orange?

(e) How many centimetre cubes have no faces painted orange?

(f) Check that your answers to parts (b)–(e) add up to your answer to part (a).

4 This 3 cm by 3 cm by 3 cm cube is made from centimetre cubes. It has three holes that go through the middle from one side to the other. All the remaining outside faces are painted orange.

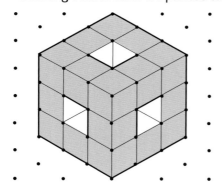

(a) How many centimetre cubes are used to make this solid?

(b) How many centimetre cubes have exactly three faces painted orange?

(c) How many centimetre cubes have exactly two faces painted orange?

(d) How many centimetre cubes have only one face painted orange?

(e) How many centimetre cubes have no faces painted orange?

(f) Check that your answers to parts (b)–(e) add up to your answer to part (a).

◯ Volumes of cubes and cuboids

Think again about some of the cubes and cuboids you have been making.

You can think of a cube or cuboid as layers of cubes.

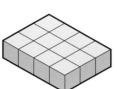 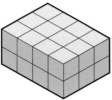 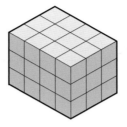

1 layer
$V = 4 \times 3 \times 1$
$V = 12$ centimetre cubes

2 layers
$V = 4 \times 3 \times 2$
$V = 24$ centimetre cubes

3 layers
$V = 4 \times 3 \times 3$
$V = 36$ centimetre cubes

You can see that you can calculate the volume of a cuboid by multiplying the length by the width (or breadth) and then multiplying by the height.

The formula for calculating the volume of a cuboid is:

$V = $ length × width × height

$V = l \times w \times h$

> Volume is a cubic measurement. It is written in terms of (unit)^3. For example, you write cubic centimetres as cm^3 and cubic metres as m^3.

Example

Find the volume of a cuboid of length 4 m, width 2 m and height 3 m.

$l = 4\,m \qquad w = 2\,m \qquad h = 3\,m$

$$V = l \times w \times h$$
$$= 4 \times 2 \times 3$$
$$= 24\,m^3$$

Exercise 20.5

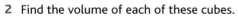

1 Find the volume of each of these cuboids.

(a) 3 cm by 5 cm by 2 cm

(b) 15 m by 10 m by 3 m

(c) 40 cm by 1.2 m by 80 cm

2 Find the volume of each of these cubes.

(a) length of side 4 cm

(b) length side 40 cm

(c) length side 0.4 cm

3 Which has the greater volume, a cube with sides of 4 cm or a cuboid with sides 13 cm, 5 cm and 1 cm?

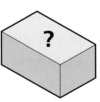

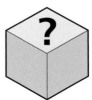

Finding the third dimension

If you know the volume and two dimensions of a cuboid, you can find the third dimension. You do this by substituting values into the formula, just as when you found unknown lengths when you knew the area of a two-dimensional shape.

Examples

(i) Find the height of a cuboid of length 4 cm, width 3 cm and volume 60 cm³.

$l = 4\,cm$ $\qquad w = 3\,cm$ $\qquad V = 60\,cm^3$

$V = l \times w \times h$		Formula
$60 = 4 \times 3 \times h$		Substitute
$60 = 12 \times h$	$(\div 12)$	Calculate
$h = 5\,cm$		Write the answer, with correct units.

(ii) Find the height of a cuboid of volume 6 m³ with length 2 m and width 80 cm.

$l = 2\,m$ $\qquad w = 80\,cm = 0.8\,m$ $\qquad V = 6\,m^3$

$V = l \times w \times h$	Formula
$6 = 2 \times 0.8 \times h$	Substitute
$6 = 1.6 \times h$	Calculate
$h = \dfrac{6}{1.6} = \dfrac{60}{16} = \dfrac{15}{4}$	Calculate
$h = 3.75\,m$	Write the answer, with correct units.

> Remember that if measurements are given in different units, you must put them all into the same units before doing any calculations.

Exercise 20.6

1 Find the height of each of these cuboids.

(a) Base area 8 cm², volume 56 cm³

(b) Base area 10 cm², volume 180 cm³

(c) Length 5 cm, width 2 cm, volume 24 cm³

2 Find the missing length, width or height for each of these cuboids.

(a) Volume 4.8 m³, length 5 m, height 80 cm

(b) Volume 6 cm³, width 6 mm, height 2 cm

(c) Volume 480 000 cm³, length 1.5 m, width 40 cm

Units of volume

You may wish to do the end-of-chapter activity before this exercise.

Here is a 10 cm by 10 cm by 10 cm cube.

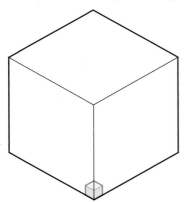

The volume of the whole cube is 10 × 10 × 10 = 1000 cm³.

In one corner is a single cube of volume 1 cm³.

> 1000 cm³ = 1 litre
>
> 1000 ml = 1 litre
>
> Therefore
>   1 cm³ = 1 ml

Exercise 20.7

1 (a) How many cubic centimetres are there in a litre?

 (b) How many cubic centimetres are there in 10 litres?

 (c) How many cubic centimetres are there in 0.5 litres?

 (d) How many cubic centimetres are there in 1.2 litres?

2 Work out the capacity of the following cuboids, in litres.

 (a) 20 cm × 25 cm × 40 cm

 (b) 1.2 m × 60 cm × 50 cm

 (c) 5 m by 4 m by 1.2 m

3 Work out the heights of these cuboids.

 (a) Volume = 1 litre, length = 10 cm, width = 10 cm

 (b) Volume = 5 litres, length = 25 cm, width = 8 cm

 (c) Volume = 300 litres, length = 2.5 m, width = 1.2 m

4 (a) How many millilitres are there in a litre?

 (b) How many millilitres are there in 400 cubic centimetres?

 (c) How many cubic centimetres are there in 30 millilitres?

5 What is better value, a 1.5 litre pack of bath essence costing £1.95 or a 5 cm by 12 cm by 10 cm cuboid container of bath essence costing 75p?

Look for some patterns in square numbers and cube numbers.

1 Calculate these products.

(a) 1×1

(b) 2×2

(c) 3×3

(d) 4×4

2 Find the difference between the two numbers.

(a) 2^2 and 1^2

(b) 3^2 and 2^2

(c) 4^2 and 3^2

(d) 5^2 and 4^2

3 Calculate these products.

(a) $1 \times 1 \times 1$

(b) $2 \times 2 \times 2$

(c) $3 \times 3 \times 3$

(d) $4 \times 4 \times 4$

4 Find the difference between the two numbers.

(a) 2^3 and 1^3

(b) 3^3 and 2^3

(c) 4^3 and 3^3

(d) 5^3 and 4^3

5 The difference between the squares gives a very obvious pattern, while the difference between the cubes gives an unfamiliar pattern. Try taking the second difference, which is the difference between your answers to 4(b) and 4(a), between 4(c) and 4(b) and between 4(d) and 4(c).

Can you see a pattern now?

6 This is the start of the pattern of odd numbers that Fibonacci produced. You looked at these numbers in the activity at the end of Chapter 7

1			
3	5		
7	9	11	
13	15	17	19 ...

$1 = 1 \times 1 \times 1$

$3 + 5 = 8 = 2 \times 2 \times 2$

$7 + 9 + 11 = 27 = 3 \times 3 \times 3$

Continue this for three more rows.

From the pattern of squares (Chapter 6) you know that consecutive odd numbers give squares, but in Fibonacci's triangle the sum of certain odd numbers gives the series of cubes. Now look at this more closely.

7 Copy this pattern and complete the next three rows:

$1 = 1^2$

$1 + 3 + 5 = 9 = 3^2$

$1 + 3 + 5 + 7 + 9 + 11 = 36 = 6^2$

$1 = 1^2$

$1 + 3 + 5 = 9 = 3^2$

$9 - 1 = 8$

$36 - 9 = 27$

8 From your pattern you should see that:

$1^2 - 0^2 = 1 = 1^3$

$3^2 - 1^2 = 8 = 2^3$

$6^2 - 3^2 = 27 = 3^3$

$10^2 - 6^2 = 64 = 4^3$

Where have you seen the pattern 1, 3, 6, 10 before?

Investigate the pattern further. Does it always work? What difference of squares gives you 1000 or 10^3?

9 Draw a series of cubes on triangular spotted paper. Here are the first two for you.

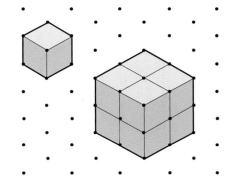

How many dots are there in each drawn cube?

1^3 needs 7 dots

2^3 needs 19 dots

3^3 needs ? dots ...

Have you seen this sequence of numbers before?

10 Here is the same dot pattern but some of the lines have been taken away.

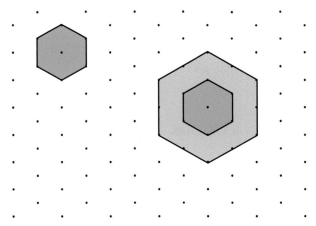

Instead of looking at cubes, you are now looking at hexagons.

Investigate this pattern of hexagonal numbers.

It is closely associated to the cube numbers. Can you compare the two series?

For this exercise, you will need isometric paper and centimetre-squared paper.

1 On isometric paper, draw a cuboid measuring 3 cm by 2 cm by 4 cm.

2 On centimetre-squared paper, draw the net of the cuboid in question 1 and calculate its surface area.

3 Calculate the volume of a cuboid measuring 3 cm by 2 cm by 4 cm.

4 Here is a solid shape drawn on isometric paper.

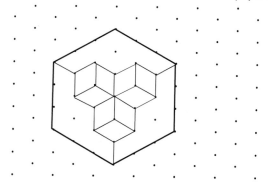

(a) On centimetre-squared paper, draw the view from the top and one of the sides. Mark the side you are drawing on the top view.

(b) How many cubes are there in the shape?

5 If a cube has a volume of 8 cm³, what is the length of one side?

6 (a) A cuboid has length 8 cm, width 5 cm and height 9 cm. What is its volume, in cubic centimetres (cm³)?

(b) What is the volume in litres?

7 Another cuboid has width 50 cm, length 2.5 m and height 4 m. What is its volume in:

(a) cubic centimetres (cm³)

(b) cubic metres (m³)

(c) litres?

8 A cuboid has a base area of 12 cm² and a volume of 168 cm³. What is the height of the cuboid?

Activity: Make a litre cube

How big is a litre?

You are used to seeing a centimetre and a metre, and you have an idea about grams and kilograms, but how big is a litre?

You will need scissors and glue for this activity.

1 Cut out 12 strips of paper, each 10 cm by 2 cm.

2 Score each strip as shown. Use a ballpoint pen.

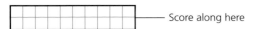 Score along here

3 Now crease each of your strips.

 Crease firmly

4 You now have twelve long, thin L-shaped strips to make into a cube. Take four and stick them together to make the base like this.

Glue here  Glue here

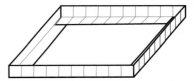

5 Now take four more strips for the uprights.

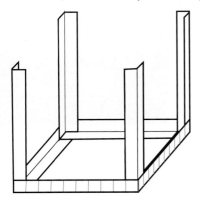

6 Finally take the last four strips and put the top on.

The space inside your frame has capacity one litre which is equivalent to 1000 cm³

Work with your classmates and put your cubes together to make larger cubes and cuboids.

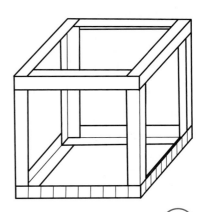

Probability

You know that some things will **definitely** happen and others will **definitely not**, but there are other things that **could** happen. It is useful to know how **likely** it is that some things could happen. After all, you will want a **good chance** of sunshine tomorrow if you are planning to go to the beach.

The study of probability is all about chance – how likely things are to happen. It is based on trials or **events**. An event may be tossing a coin, or picking a pair of socks from a drawer. Every event has one or more possible **outcomes**.

Two more important words that relate to probability are:

- **fair**, which means that every outcome has an equal chance of occurring
- **random**, which means picking 'without looking', so the outcome happens 'by chance'.

Consider these statements. Are they true?

- It is **impossible** that pigs will fly.
- It is **certain** that the sun will rise tomorrow.
- If I flip a coin, there is an **even chance** that it will show up as heads (or tails).

The probability scale

If an outcome is impossible, it has a probability of 0

If an outcome is certain, it has a probability of 1

All other outcomes have probabilities between 0 and 1

If an outcome has an even chance, then it has a probability of 1 in 2 or $\frac{1}{2}$

These values can be shown on a probability scale.

Impossible	Possible	Evens	Probable	Certain
0	$\frac{1}{4}$	$\frac{1}{2}$	$\frac{3}{4}$	1

Exercise 21.1

1 Write down three things that are **impossible**.

2 Write down three things that are **certain**.

3 Write down three things that have an **even chance** of happening.

4 Write down three things that are **possible**, they could happen but have a less than evens chance.

5 Write down three things that are **probable**; they have more than an even chance of happening.

6 Make a copy of the probability scale and mark on it the probability of the outcomes listed below. The first two are done for you.

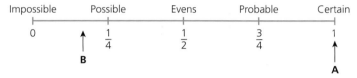

A: The sun will set tonight.

B: I will throw a six with a normal die.

C: I will get heads when I toss a coin.

D: There will be chips for lunch tomorrow.

E: There is life on Jupiter.

F: Chelsea will win the FA cup next year.

G: I will clean my teeth tonight.

H: There will be somebody in my class away on Monday next week.

You could put the types of outcome in the last question into three groups.

(i)   Those you have control over (e.g. I will brush my teeth).

(ii)   Those for which you can have a sensible guess (e.g. there will be chips for lunch).

(iii) Those for which you can calculate the **theoretical probability**.

Theoretical probability

Theoretical probability is used to **predict** the likelihood of something happening by chance, such as:

● tossing a coin and scoring a head

● drawing a card from a pack and it being the knave of hearts

● picking two socks from a drawer and getting a pair.

Tossing a coin has two possible outcomes. Drawing a particular card from a pack has 52 possible outcomes. Picking a pair of socks from a drawer depends on what is in the drawer.

Any event will have an outcome. The total of the probabilities of all the possible outcomes for an event is 1

The probability of a particular outcome

If you flip a coin you can either get a head or a tail.

So there are two possible outcomes, one of which is a head.

You write the probability of flipping a head as $P(head) = \dfrac{1}{2}$

You might say to yourself: 'There is a one in two chance,' but in mathematics you write $\dfrac{1}{2}$ or sometimes 50% or 0.5

To calculate the probability of a particular outcome, follow three steps.

1 Identify how many possible outcomes there are in total.

2 Identify how many of those should be considered.

3 Write the probability as a fraction:

$$\dfrac{\text{number of possible outcomes being considered}}{\text{total number of possible outcomes}}$$

This will become clear, with an example.

Example

What is the possibility of rolling a die with:

(i)   the number 6

(ii) an odd number?

On a normal die there are the numbers 1, 2, 3, 4, 5, 6

(i)   There are six possible outcomes, one of which is 6

$P(6) = \dfrac{1}{6}$

(ii) There are three possibilities for scoring an odd number: 1, 3, 5

$P(\text{odd number}) = \dfrac{3}{6} = \dfrac{1}{2}$

> The word **die** is considered the correct singular form of dice, although some people use the word dice to describe one die – they shouldn't!

Exercise 21.2

1 What is the probability of rolling a 1 with a normal die?

2 When a 10p coin is tossed, what is the probability of its landing tails up?

3 When you roll a normal die, what is the probability of throwing an even number?

4 When one card is chosen at random from a normal pack of cards, what is the probability of taking an ace?

5 When a letter is chosen at random from the letters of the alphabet, what is the probability of choosing a vowel?

6 If a letter is chosen at random from the word 'MATHEMATICS', what is the probability that it will be a letter M?

7 When a normal die is rolled, what is the probability that it will give a prime number?

8 I have three folded pairs of socks in my drawer: one pair of white socks, one pair of black socks and one pair of yellow socks. I take out one pair at random. What is the probability that it will be the yellow pair?

9 I offer a bag containing six yellow sweets and three orange sweets to my little brother. If he takes a sweet at random, what is the probability that it will be yellow?

10 There are 24 people in my class. If the headmaster selects one of us at random to run an errand, what is the probability that he will choose me?

11 What is the probability that the last digit of a three-digit number chosen at random will be a 5?

12 In my garage there are four pots of white paint and two pots of magnolia paint. However, the labels have come off the pots.

   (a) If I choose one pot at random, what is the probability that it will be white?

   (b) How many pots would I have to take to be sure of having one pot of white paint?

The probability of an outcome not happening

If I roll a normal die, the probability of getting a 6 is $\frac{1}{6}$ because there are six possibilities, one of which is 6

There are five other possibilities, which means the probability of **not** throwing a six is $\frac{5}{6}$

Notice that $\frac{1}{6} + \frac{5}{6} = 1$, and 1 is the probability that an event must have an outcome.

This is because an outcome must either happen or not happen, so you can say:

P (outcome) + P (not that outcome) = 1

which is another way of writing:

The probability of an outcome not happening = 1 – probability of that outcome happening

> **Example**
>
> If the probability of rain tomorrow is $\frac{3}{4}$, what is the probability that it will not rain tomorrow?
>
> $$P \text{ (no rain)} = 1 - \frac{3}{4}$$
> $$= \frac{1}{4}$$

Exercise 21.3

1 If a number is chosen at random from the first ten positive integers {1, 2, 3, 4, 5, 6, 7, 8, 9, 10}, what is the probability of that number:

(a) being odd

(b) being prime

(c) being a square number

(d) not being prime?

2 If a card is chosen at random from a standard pack of 52 cards, what is the probability of that card being:

(a) a ten

(b) a spade

(c) the ace of spades

(d) a royal card (i.e. king, queen or knave)?

3 A B C D E F G H I J K L M N

List the letters above that have line symmetry.

List the letters above that have rotational symmetry.

If a letter of the alphabet from A to N is chosen at random, what is the probability of it having:

(a) only one line of symmetry   **(d)** rotational symmetry

(b) more than two lines of symmetry   **(e)** no rotational symmetry?

(c) rotational symmetry of order 3

4 If a normal die is rolled, what is the probability of throwing a number that is not:

(a) less than three   **(b)** 6   **(c)** a square number?

Just one thing can change the situation

Sometimes one thing can change the whole situation. For example, if I have a bag of sweets of various colours and I eat the sweet that I choose at random, there is one fewer sweet in the bag, which means one fewer of that colour. The probability of my choosing another sweet of that colour will therefore have decreased.

Example

In a bag there are five red sweets and four yellow sweets. If I offer the bag to my friend, what is the probability that she chooses a red sweet?

$$P\,(red) = \frac{5}{9}$$

My friend did choose a red sweet. I now offer the bag to my teacher. What is the probability that he chooses a yellow sweet?

There are now four red sweets and four yellow sweets in the bag.

$$P\,(yellow) = \frac{4}{8} = \frac{1}{2}$$

Exercise 21.4

1 There are seven sweets in a bag; three lemon ones and four orange ones. I offer the bag to my little sister who takes one at random.

What is the probability that she takes:

(a) a lemon sweet   **(b)** an orange sweet?

If my little sister took an orange sweet, and then took a second sweet, what is the probability that the second sweet was:

(c) lemon   **(d)** orange?

2   We bought 12 tins of cat food: 4 tins of liver flavour, 3 tins of beef flavour, 2 tins of chicken and the rest rabbit. I took the labels off to enter a competition and now I do not know which flavour each tin contains.

If I select one tin at random, what is the probability that it is:

(a) liver flavoured

(b) chicken flavoured

(c) either beef or rabbit

(d) not rabbit?

The first tin that I opened was liver flavour. What is the probability that the next tin will be:

(e) liver

(f) beef?

3   Socks are often a mystery. I have six pairs of grey socks, two pairs of black socks and four pairs of white socks. When I send them all to be washed, one sock always vanishes. What is the probability that the missing sock is:

(a) white

(b) black or grey

(c) not grey?

I checked my socks and found that the missing sock was grey. When I next put all my remaining socks through the wash, what is the probability that the sock that goes missing this time will be:

(d) grey

(e) not black?

Extension Exercise 21.5

Sometimes you have to look at the possible outcomes of events and put them into a table before you can work out the probability.

1   Four teams, Alpha, Beta, Charlie and Delta, are going to play in a tournament in which each team plays the others. You can record the matches like this...

Team	D	C	B
A			
B			
C			

or like this:

Team 1 vs Team 2	
A	B
A	C
A	D
B	C
B	D
C	D

From either table you can see there are six matches or six events.

(a) If I were to select one match at random, what is the probability that A would be playing?

(b) If I were to select one match at random, what is the probability that C would be playing?

2 Repeat question 1 with five teams: A, B, C, D and E. Start by drawing a table to find the total number of matches.

3 My friend and I are playing a game. I pick a number from 1 to 10 and then he doubles it and adds the result to my number.

(a) Copy, extend and complete this table to show all of our possible pairs of numbers.

My number	My friend's number	Sum of our numbers
1	2	3
2	4	6
3	6	
4		
5		
6		

(b) If one of our pairs of numbers were selected at random, what is the probability that the sum would be an even number?

(c) If one of our pairs of numbers were selected at random, what is the probability that the sum would be a multiple of 3?

4 My friend and I are playing a new game. We each have to pick a card from a pile of four cards, numbered 1, 2, 3 or 4

(a) Copy, extend and complete this table to show all of our possible pairs of numbers.

First number	Second number	Sum of our numbers
1	2	3
1	3	4
1	4	5
2	1	
2	3	
2		

(b) If one of our pairs of numbers were selected at random, what is the probability that the sum would be 7?

(c) If one of our pairs of numbers were selected at random, what is the probability that the sum would be an odd number?

(d) Which sum is the most likely? What is the probability of getting this total?

5 Look at this hexagonal spinner.

(a) What is the probability of spinning a 2?

(b) What is the probability of spinning a 4?

(c) What is the probability of spinning an odd number?

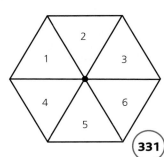

6 Now look at this hexagonal spinner.

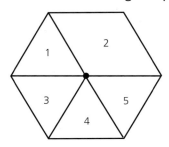

(a) What is the probability of spinning a 2?

(b) What is the probability of spinning a 4?

(c) What is the probability of spinning an odd number?

Summary Exercise 21.6

1 Draw a probability scale. Show the probability of these events on the scale.

(a) You will go to bed tonight.

(b) Men will land on Mars this week.

(c) You will have homework tomorrow night.

(d) You will not come to school tomorrow.

(e) Next Christmas will be a white Christmas.

2 Write down an example of something that is:

(a) probable

(b) impossible

(c) likely.

3 If I choose a letter at random from the word MAGIC, what is the probability that it will be:

(a) a vowel

(b) a consonant?

4 If a normal die is rolled, what is the probability that the number will be:

(a) a six

(b) a prime number

(c) at least 3

(d) less than 4?

5 If a card is chosen at random from a normal pack of cards, what is the probability that it will be:

(a) a red card

(b) either a nine or a ten

(c) a king

(d) a red ace?

6 I have a bag of sweets. In this bag there are six lemon sweets, three orange sweets and one blackcurrant sweet.

If I take one sweet at random, what is the probability that it will be:

(a) lemon

(b) orange

(c) not blackcurrant?

I decide to eat the blackcurrant sweet first. If I then take a sweet at random, what is the probability that it will be:

(d) orange

(e) blackcurrant?

Activity: Probability experiments

In this chapter you have been using theory to calculate probabilities. But does it work in practice? Try these experiments and compare the experimental results with your calculations.

1 Toss two coins one after the other. Draw up a tally table like the one below to record your results.

Throw	Tally	Total
H H		
H T		
T H		
T T		

First toss the two coins one after the other 20 times and check your results.

Then repeat this another 80 times, making 100 times in all.

What fraction of your throws gave two heads?

2 Roll a normal die 20 times. Record how many times you roll a six and how many times you roll another number. Your tally table will look like this.

Roll	Tally	Total
a six		
not a six		

Throw the die another 80 times to make 100 times in total. What fraction of your throws gave a six? Is this the answer you would expect?

3 In the first two experiments you knew what the theoretical probability should be. However, there are some situations in which you do not know what the likely outcome might be. In these situations you can only find the probability by experimentation. The more experiments you do, the more accurate your calculated probabilities will be.

In science lessons, you have learnt that any test must be fair, that you keep all the things that can change the same, and only allow one of them to change. The idea of fairness in probability is similar, but it also includes the idea, for example, that a die or a coin is well balanced, and is no more likely to land on one face than any other.

Try one of these experiments. Make sure that you make the experiment fair by dropping or throwing the object in the same way every time.

(a) Toss your shoe. The shoe could land sole up or sole down, or on its left side or on its right side. Are there any other positions that it could land in?

(b) Throw a small plastic model animal. It could land on its right side, or left side, or on its feet or on its back. Is there any other position in which it might land?

(c) Drop a piece of bread and butter on the floor. What is the probability that it will land butter-side down?

22 Working with data

These are the maths exam results, as percentages, for Aidan's class.

45	67	89	34	72	81
75	83	72	93	69	84
68	85	83	77	72	91
76	83	70	84	90	77

The pupils do not find it very useful just to get their results. They always ask questions such as:

- 'Who got the best mark?'
- 'Who was the worst?'
- 'What was the average?'

The answers to these questions help them to see how well they did in the exam. Were they near the top or near the bottom? Did they do better than average? How can they tell?

Range

The range is the difference between the highest mark and the lowest mark. Therefore, for the set of marks above, as the highest mark was 93 and the lowest was 34:

Range = 93 − 34

= 59

Averages

An **average** is a typical value that can represent a set of **data**.

When you mention an average, most people will assume that you are talking about the **mean**. However, there are times when it is appropriate to use a different average, which could be the **median** or the **mode**.

The mean

The mean is the total of all the numbers, divided by the number of numbers. This is also called the **arithmetic average**.

$$\text{Mean} = \frac{\text{the total of all the data values in the set}}{\text{the number of values in the set of data}}$$

Example

Find:

(i) the range

(ii) the mean of these six numbers.

     9   11   18   4   10   14

(i)   Range = 18 − 4   highest number − lowest number

              = 14

(ii) Mean = $\dfrac{9 + 11 + 18 + 4 + 10 + 14}{6}$

            = $\dfrac{66}{6}$

            = 11

Exercise 22.1

1 Find the range and mean of each set of numbers.

     (a)   1   3   6   8   2

     (b)   24   99   36

     (c)   101   213   42   84

     (d)   13   14   13   13   14   11

     (e)   0.2   0.6   1.2   21   8

2 Mrs Collins measured the heights of all the pupils in the class. The range is 70 cm. If the tallest pupil is 1.90 m tall, how tall is the shortest pupil?

3 Mrs Collins weighed all the teachers in the staff room and the range of their masses is 21 kg. If the lightest teacher weighs 49 kg, how much does the heaviest weigh?

4 I have to find the range and mean of a set of numbers, but I have spilt ink over one of them.

     8   5   2   7   9   4

     (a) My friend tells me that the range is 7 and the mean is 6. What number is hidden by the blot?

     (b) My friend was wrong! The range was 9 and the mean was 5. What number was really under the blot?

5 We have been growing bean plants from seeds and these are the heights of the plants, measured in centimetres.

14   15   12   13   16   15

17   17   13   16   15   14

15   15   14   15   16   18

(a) What is the range of heights?

(b) What is the mean height of the plants?

Frequency tables

It is easier to solve problems such as question 5 if you put the results in a **tally** or **frequency table**.

Height (cm)	Tally	Frequency	Total
12	I	1	12
13	II	2	26
14	III	3	42
15	JHT I	6	90
16	III	3	48
17	II	2	34
18	I	1	18
Total		18	270

You can calculate the total for each height by multiplying the height by the corresponding frequency.

To find the mean, you divide the total of all the heights by the total frequency.

Example

Find the mean height of the plants in the frequency table above.

Total height = 270

Divide this by the total frequency, which is 18

Mean = 270 ÷ 18

   = 15 cm   Write the answer with the correct measurements.

> You can write your division like this or you may prefer to put it in a fraction and cancel to the lowest terms.

1 The council did a survey to find out how many people lived in each house in our road. Their results are shown below. Put their results into a frequency table like the one above. Calculate the mean number of people per household.

6	5	1	2	4
3	4	2	7	1
2	4	6	2	3
3	2	4	1	5

2 These are the marks for a French vocabulary test. Put these into a frequency table like the one above. Calculate the mean mark.

18	13	19	18	18	18
12	15	14	14	14	17
20	13	18	17	16	14
17	15	17	19	15	13

Finding the total

Do you remember how to calculate the mean?

$$\text{Mean} = \frac{\text{the total of all the data values in the set}}{\text{the number of values in the set of data}}$$

Sometimes you know the mean and the number of items but not the total.

You can still calculate the total from the information you have.

Example

The mean mass of the 11 players in the football team was 45 kg. What was their total mass?

$$\text{Mean} = \frac{\text{the total of all the data values in the set}}{\text{the number of values in the set of data}}$$

Write out the formula for calculating the mean.

$$45 = \frac{\text{the total mass of the team}}{11}$$

Then put in the numbers you know.

$45 \times 11 = \text{total mass}$

Total mass = 495 kg

Write the answer with the correct units.

> This is just like substituting values into a formula, as you did in Chapters 11 and 19

Exercise 22.3

1   There are 18 people in the class. Last week the average number of house points was 12. How many house points did we collect in total?

2   I have three sisters. Their average mass is 35 kg. What do they weigh altogether?

3   We have to bring in bottles for the bottle stall at the school fair.

   (a)   There are 16 people in the class and we need at least 200 bottles. How many should we each bring in?

   (b)   On average, we brought in 14 bottles each. How many more bottles did we have than we needed?

4   I baked four cakes for the village fête. Their mean mass was 6.5 kg.

   (a)   What was the total mass of the four cakes?

   (b)   I baked a fifth cake that weighed 7.2 kg. What is the mass of all five cakes?

   (c)   What is the mean mass of the five cakes?

5   Our cricket team has a mean average mass of 45.8 kg.

   (a)   What is the total mass of the team?

   (b)   The 12th man weighs in at 48.2 kg. What is the total mass of the team, including the 12th man?

   (c)   What is the mean mass of the team if we include the 12th man?

6   There are 20 people in my class and our mean mark in the English exam was 72.5%.

   (a)   What was the total of all our marks?

   (b)   Mr Chips has marked my paper wrongly. He gave me 64% instead of 74%. What does this now make the mean mark for the class?

7   Last week was Charity Week at our school. My class decided that we would contribute a fifth of our pocket money. There are 24 of us in my class. The total amount contributed was £41.40

   (a)   What was the mean amount of pocket money contributed?

   (b)   What we didn't realise was that Smith was ill that day and didn't make his contribution of £2 until the following day. We had therefore worked out our calculations incorrectly as only 23 people had originally contributed. What was the new total and what was the correct mean amount of pocket money before and after Smith made his contribution?

The median

These are the marks Tom achieved in his recent exams.

27%   67%   73%   81%   75%   69%   91%

Tom calculates his mean mark as 69%. However, he did really badly in French because he was late to school that day. How can he show his average is really better than 69%?

A different way of looking at the average of the marks is to look at the **median**. This is the actual middle mark, when they are listed in order.

First, put the marks in order.

27   67   69   73   75   81   91

As there are seven marks, the middle mark will be the fourth, which is 73%.

These are the steps to find the median.

1 Put the data values in order, smallest first.

2 Count the data values.

3 If there is an odd number of values, the median is the middle one.

4 If there is an even number of values, then the median is the mean of the middle two. For example, if you have 12 items the median will be the mean of the sixth and seventh.

Examples

(i) Find the median of 3, 9, 8, 5, 1, 5, 7, 6

1, 3, 5, (5, 6), 7, 8, 9   Put the eight numbers in order.

The median is the mean of the 4th and 5th = $\dfrac{5+6}{2}$

The median is 5.5

(ii) Find the median of 3, 6, 2, 5, 7, 9, 4, 6, 8, 3, 7

2, 3, 3, 4, 5, (6), 6, 7, 7, 8, 9   Put the 11 numbers in order.

The median is the 6th (middle) number.

The median is 6

The mode

The **mode** is another average of a sample of the data. It is the value that occurs most frequently or most often.

A set of data may have no mode, if no two values are the same.

> The number of times each value appears is called the frequency.

A set of data may have two or more modes. Look back at the two examples above. In the first, the mode is 5. In the second, the numbers 3, 6 and 7 all appear twice, so the modes are 3, 6 and 7

The mode is particularly useful when you are analysing measurements such as shoe size, when there is no halfway value between one size and the next (for example between 6 and $6\frac{1}{2}$).

The mode is the only average that can be found for a set of non-numerical data, such as favourite sports.

Exercise 22.4

1 Find the median for each set of numbers.

(a)	1	3	6	8	2
(b)	24	99	36		
(c)	101	213	42	84	
(d)	13	14	13	13	14	11
(e)	0.2	0.6	1.2	21	8

2 Find the median and mode for each set of numbers.

(a) 1 1 1 2 2 2 3 4 5 5 6 6 7 7 8

(b) 15 18 17 12 14 15 16 13

(c) 7 8 9 10 8 7 6 8 9

3 Find the range, the mean, the median and the mode for each set of numbers.

(a) 1.2 3.2 5.6 3.2 7.3

(b) 13.2 15.6 17.0 14.8 17.5 18.1 15.6 17.0 13.2 17.0

(c) 10.14 9.18 4.25 5.65 9.18 7.58 4.25 9.18

(d) 8.08 8 8.8 0.8 0.08

(e) 12 1.2 2.1 21 2.12 21.2

4 (a) Fred played 20 games of cricket last season. His batting average was 5 and his range of scores was 100. However, both his median and his modal scores were 0. Explain.

(b) Fred's sister Freda also played 20 games of cricket last season. Her mean score was also 5, and so too were her median and modal scores. However, the range of her scores was 0. Explain.

(c) Who would you rather have batting on your side, Fred or Freda? Explain why you made the choice you did.

Displaying data: frequency tables and bar charts

It is often easier to read a picture than to read a list of data. In mathematics the images you can use to display data are known as **tables**, **diagrams** and **charts**.

The simplest image to use is a **bar chart**. The height of each bar tells you the frequency of each item of data. Before you can draw a bar chart, you need to sort the data into useful groups. You can do this by using **tallies** in a **frequency table**.

Exercise 22.5

1 These are marks for a French vocabulary test that Mrs Hopwood's class has just completed. The marks are out of 25

16	20	19	23	18	24	18	17
20	21	18	16	22	24	19	16
22	19	17	17	20	25	21	16

(a) Copy and complete this frequency table to show the distribution of the marks.

Mark	Tally	Frequency
16		
17		
18		
19		
20		
21		
22		
23		
24		
25		
Total		

(b) What is the range of the marks?

(c) Work out the mean, the mode and the median.

(d) What, if anything, does this tell you about the marks?

(e) Draw a bar chart to illustrate the marks.

2 We did a traffic survey for prep. I stood outside my house for 20 minutes and filled in a frequency table to show how many vehicles passed me. Here are my results.

Vehicle	Tally	Frequency
cars	JHT JHT JHT JHT JHT JHT JHT I	
vans	JHT JHT JHT III	
bikes	JHT JHT JHT II	
lorries	JHT III	
buses	JHT IIII	
Total		

(a) Copy the table and complete the frequency column. What was the modal group?

(b) Why can you not work out a median and a mean?

Grouped data

Suppose you were to measure the height of every pupil in your class. The result could be different for every pupil. Therefore it would be sensible to group your data together in a range of values.

In the next exercise, there are two groups of data about rainfall. There would be little point in having a frequency for each value, to the nearest millimetre. You must decide how you are going to group your data.

Exercise 22.6

1 These figures show the daily record of rainfall during April in centimetres.

2.2	0	3.4	0.2	0	2.8	1.6	2.5	3.5	2.4
3.1	3.7	1.7	2.9	0	1.5	2.6	3.1	1.7	0.6
2.7	0.6	3.2	1.1	3.6	3.4	2.3	0	2.4	1.3

Copy and complete this frequency table. Then draw a bar chart to show the rainfall over the month of April.

Rainfall (cm)	Tally	Frequency
0–0.9		
1–1.9		
2–2.9		
3–3.9		
Total		30

2 Draw a frequency table, and then a bar chart, to show this data for the amount of rainfall (in centimetres) over the month of June. Put the data into the same groups as you did for question 1

1.6	0	3.1	0	0.2	2.8	1.6	2.5	3.2	2.5
1.4	0	0.6	2.6	1.4	1.9	2.3	0	0	0.4
2.3	0	0.3	1.2	0.8	3.1	2.3	0	1.7	1.3

3 Refer to the information in questions 1 and 2. Find the range and the mean rainfall for each of the months of April and June. What do all your results tell you about the two months?

Average age

Calculations involving time always need care. Unlike decimal numbers, you cannot easily carry a digit into the next column.

● There are not 10 seconds in a minute but 60

● There are not 10 minutes in an hour but 60

● There are not 10 hours in a day but 24

● There are not 10 months in a year but 12

Ages used in problems are generally stated in terms of years and months.

When you need to add ages, put the years and the months in separate columns. Remember that, when you carry, you must carry twelve because there are twelve months in a year.

Example

These are the ages of four children.

10 years 10 months, 11 years 5 months, 10 years 5 months, 10 years 8 months

What is the total age of the four children?

	Years	Months	
	10	10	The total for the months is 28
	11	5	28 months is 2 years and 4 months
	10	5	
+	10	8	Put 4 in the 'months' column and carry 2 to the years column.
Total	43 years	4 months	
	2		

To find the average age you must divide the total of all the ages by the number of children. If the division does not work out exactly, then you need to carry the remainder. You must remember that, when going from years to months, you turn the years into months by multiplying by 12

Example

Find the average age of the four children in the previous example.

Average age = $\dfrac{43 \text{ years } 4 \text{ months}}{4}$

Take the years first. $43 \div 4 = 10 \text{ r } 3$

3 years is 36 months

Add it to the 4 to make 40 $40 \div 4 = 10$

The average age is 10 years 10 months.

Extension Exercise 22.7

1 (a) Find the total ages of these three children.

   11 years 4 months, 13 years 9 months, 7 years 11 months

   (b) Find the average age of the three children.

2 (a) Find the total age of this family.

   Dad: 32 years 6 months

   Mum: 30 years 8 months

   Gareth: 10 years 11 months

   Leonie: 7 years 3 months

   Abigail: 2 years 5 months

   (b) Find the average age of the family members.

3 (a) Find the total ages of two sets of twins.

   One pair are both 11 years 9 months old.

   The other are both 13 years 5 months old.

   (b) Find the average age of the four children.

4 (a) The average age of the pupils in our class of 20 is 11 years 9 months.

   What is the total of all our ages?

   (b) A new boy arrives. He is only 10 years 5 months old.

   What is the total age of all 21 of us?

   (c) What is the new average age of the class?

5 The mean age of my four best friends and me is 12 years 4 months.

   (a) What is the sum of our ages?

   (b) My mother insisted that I included my little brother in our calculations.
   With his age added, the mean came to 11 years 10 months.

   What is my little brother's age?

Summary Exercise 22.8

1 Here are the heights of six children, measured in metres.

   1.42   1.35   1.41   1.50   1.38   1.46

   What is the mean height of the children? What is the range?

2 Work out the mean, median and mode of each set of numbers.

   (a) 3   4   4   4   5   6   7   7   8

   (b) 2.1   1.8   1.6   2.3   1.8   2.1   1.4   2.1   1.9

   (c) 14.1   12.4   13.2   14.1   12.8   13.8

3 These are the ages of five children, in years and months.

   11 years 6 months, 10 years 4 months, 10 years 6 months,
   11 years 4 months, 10 years 11 months

   (a) What is the mean age of the children?

   (b) A sixth child joins the group and the mean age of the six children is
       11 years and 1 month. What is the age of the sixth child?

4 Here are the marks for the recent mental arithmetic test. The marks were
  given out of 20

   15   16   14   13   15   17

   11   15   17   12   16   14

   13   19   14   16   18   15

   (a) Draw a tally table to show the results.

   (b) Find the mean, mode and median of the marks.

   (c) Show the results on a frequency diagram.

Activity: It's time to go!

Why do you have to learn mathematics? You should have seen many practical
examples in this book that will answer that question, but now you are about to
enter a very special time when maths is truly important – the holidays.

1 Take a map. Where do you want to go?

   Use whatever maths you have learnt to work out the distance to your chosen
   destination. How will you get there? How fast will you travel? When will you
   arrive? Is it in the same time zone?

   Draw up a travel itinerary, giving the details of your departure time, method of
   travel and arrival.

2 What will you do when you get there?

Find out more about your destination.

What do you want to see? How will you get to those places? How long will it take?

Draw up a holiday timetable, giving the details of the days when you are sightseeing.

3 How much is it going to cost?

You might need a bit of help with this. Perhaps a travel agent will give you some brochures.

First compare different travel companies, then work out the total cost of the holiday at different times of year. Why is it cheaper in May than in August? Look carefully at the cost for children and the sharing a room options. These can save you money!

4 How much money do I need to take with me?

First find out the currency you will need, then find out some prices. You will need to know the cost of:

- meals

- drinks

- ice cream

- any trips or visits you want to make.

5 What will I take with me?

How much can you carry? If your suitcase is too heavy you will not be able to carry it. What will you put in it? Shoes and books are heavy, so you may have to cut down on those. T-shirts are light but coats are not.

Make a list of everything that you want to take and check the total mass.

6 Did I enjoy the holiday? Was it worth it?

How do you measure fun? Can you work out some scale of fun versus cost and make a graph? What questions could you ask yourself and other members of the family?

Whatever the answers – have a great holiday!

Glossary

2D Two-dimensional – a flat (plane) shape such as a rectangle or circle.

3D Three-dimensional – a solid object such as a cube or sphere.

Acute angle An angle that is between 0° and 90°

Acute-angled triangle A triangle in which all the angles are less than 90°

Alternate angles Angles inside parallel lines, in a Z-shape, that are equal.

Area The amount of space inside a flat (two-dimensional) shape such as a rectangle or circle. It is measured in square units, such as cm^2.

Axis (plural: axes) One of the two numbered lines on the coordinate grid; they cross at the origin where both values are zero.

Bisect Divide a line or an angle into two equal halves.

Cancelling The process of dividing the top and bottom of a fraction by one or more common factors to reduce it to its lowest terms.

Co-interior angles Angles inside a pair of parallel lines that add up to 180°

Common factors Numbers that are factors of two or more other numbers; for example, 5 is a common factor of 20 and 25

Common multiples Numbers that are multiples of two or more other numbers; for example, 100 is a common multiple of 20 and 25

Conversion graph A straight-line graph that can be used to convert between standard units of measurement or currencies.

Coordinate grid A grid of squares with a pair of axes (x and y).

Coordinates The horizontal and vertical dimensions used to plot a point on a grid; for example, the point (3, 5) is 3 along and 5 up from the origin.

Corresponding angles When two lines are crossed by another line, the angles in matching corners are called corresponding angles.

Cube A 3D shape with six identical square faces.

Cube number A number produced by another number multiplied by itself and by itself again; for example, 3^3 is $3 \times 3 \times 3 = 27$

Cuboid A 3D shape with six faces that are all rectangles or squares.

Data A piece of information, such as a highest daily temperature. Data usually refers to a group of such values that can then be analysed and/or plotted on a chart or table.

Decimal fraction The fraction part of a decimal number, less than one, written after the decimal point.

Decimal place The position of the digits in the fractional part of a decimal number, written to the right of the decimal point. They stand for tenths, hundredths, thousandths, ...

Denominator The bottom number on a fraction, telling you how many equal parts there are in the whole.

Diagonal A line joining non-adjacent corners on a 2D shape.

Difference The result of a larger number take away a smaller number; the difference between 5 and 11 is $11 - 5 = 6$

Digit A numeral, from 0 to 9, representing a number; 45 is a two-digit number.

Equilateral triangle A triangle in which all sides are equal and all angles are 60°

Equivalent fractions Fractions that have the same value although their numerators and denominators are different, for example, $\dfrac{3}{4} = \dfrac{9}{12}$

Equivalent units   The approximate comparison between metric and imperial units.
   1 foot ≈ 30 cm, 1 metre ≈ 3 ft 3 in or 3.25 feet
   8 kilometres ≈ 5 miles
   1 lb ≈ 450 g, 1 kg ≈ 2.2 lb
   1 pint ≈ 600 ml, 1 gallon ≈ 4.5 litres, 1 litre ≈ 1.7 pints
   10 litres ≈ 2.2 gallons

Estimation   Making an approximation, often by calculating with rounded numbers.

Factor   A number that divides into another number; for example, 1, 2, 3 and 6 are factors of 6

Factor pair   Two factors that, when multiplied together, equal the number; for example, 6 = 2 × 3 = 1 × 6, so the factor pairs of 6 are 2 and 3, 1 and 6

Formula   A rule used to calculate a specific value, often written in letters or words; for example, the formula for the volume of a cuboid is length × width × height or $l \times w \times h$

Fraction   A number less than one written like this: $\frac{3}{4}$

Highest common factor   The largest factor that will divide two or more numbers exactly.

Imperial units   Non-metric units in common usage in Britain and America.
   Mass (weight):
   16 ounces (oz) = 1 pound (lb)
   14 pounds (lb) = 1 stone (st)
   1 ton (t) = 2240 pounds (lb)
   Length:
   12 inches (in) = 1 foot (ft)
   3 feet (ft) = 1 yard (yd)
   1760 yards (yd) = 1 mile (m)
   Capacity:
   2 pints (pt) = 1 quart (qt)
   8 pints (pt) = 1 gallon (gal)

Improper fraction   A fraction in which the numerator (top number) is larger than the denominator (bottom number), such as $\frac{7}{3}$; its value is greater than one.

Integer   A whole number, may be positive or negative; 4, ⁻3 and 17 are all integers.

Inverse   An opposite calculation. Addition is the inverse of subtraction. Division is the inverse of multiplication.

Isosceles triangle   A triangle with two equal sides and two equal angles.

Line graph   A line that represents the relationship between two variables, such as distance and time; it may be straight or curved.

Linear sequence   A sequence of numbers in which the difference is constant.

Long division   Division by a number with two or more digits, that shows each stage of the calculation and works down the page.

Long multiplication   Multiplication by a number with two or more digits, that shows each stage of the calculation and works out multiplication by first the units, then the tens, ... in each line of a frame, and then adds the products together.

Lowest common multiple   The smallest number that appears in the multiplication tables of two or more numbers.

Lowest terms A fraction in which the numerator and denominator have no common factors.

Mean A value equal to the sum of numbers divided by the number of numbers, often referred to as the 'average'; for example, the mean of 3, 5, 7 and 9 is:

$$\text{mean} = \frac{3+5+7+9}{4} = \frac{24}{4} = 6$$

Median The middle value in a row of numbers listed in numerical order. If there is an even number of numbers, the median is the mean of the middle two numbers.

Metric system The decimal system of measurement based on units that are related to their subunits by powers of ten.

Metric units Units of mass (weight), length and volume that are in use in Britain and in Europe as well as many other countries.

1000 milligrams (mg) = 1 gram (g)   1000 grams (g) = 1 kilogram (kg)
1000 kilograms (kg) = 1 metric tonne (t)
10 millimetres (mm) = 1 centimetre (cm)   100 centimetres (cm) = 1 metre (m)
1000 millimetres (mm) = 1 metre (m)   1000 metres (m) = 1 kilometre (km)
1000 millilitres (ml) = 1 litre (l)

Mixed number A combination of a whole number and a fraction, such as $2\frac{3}{4}$

Mode The value that occurs most often in a set of data; the only average that can be applied to non-numerical data such as favourite colours.

Multiple A number that is a product (i.e. multiplication) of a factor; for example, 6 is a multiple of 2

Negative numbers Numbers less than 0; for example. ⁻4, called 'negative 4'

Net A 2D shape that can be folded up and made into a 3D shape.

Numerator The top number on a fraction; how many parts of the whole there are; for example, in $\frac{3}{4}$ there are 3 parts out of 4

Obtuse angle An angle between 90° and 180°

Obtuse-angled triangle A triangle in which one angle is obtuse.

Order of operations The order in which a calculation should be done: brackets, index numbers or other calculation, then divide, multiply, add, subtract (BIDMAS).

Parallel Lines that are the same distance apart and will never meet however long they are.

Parallelogram A quadrilateral with two pairs of equal and parallel sides.

Percentage A fraction written in hundredths of a whole, with a percentage sign:

for example, $25\% = \frac{25}{100}$

Perimeter The line around the outside of a 2D shape.

Pie chart A circular chart in which quantities can be compared by the angle at the centre of each sector.

Polygon A flat shape with sides that are straight lines.

3 sides – a triangle	8 sides – an octagon
4 sides – a quadrilateral	9 sides – a nonagon
5 sides – a pentagon	10 sides – a decagon
6 sides – a hexagon	12 sides – a dodecagon
7 sides – a heptagon	20 sides – an icosagon

Power   The number of 'lots' of a number multiplied together, such as 3^4, 7^2, 10^4

Powers of 10   Ten multiplied by itself; 10, $10^2 = 100$, $10^3 = 1000$, $10^4 = 10\,000$, $10^5 = 100\,000$, $10^6 = 1\,000\,000$.

Prime factors   Factors of a number that are also prime numbers; for example 2 and 3 are prime factors of 6

Prime numbers   Prime numbers are numbers that only have two factors, themselves and 1 (e.g. 2, 3, 5 and 7; 1 is NOT a prime number).

Product   The answer to a multiplication (e.g. the product of 3 and 4 is 12).

Proper fraction   A fraction in which the numerator is less than the denominator, such as $\frac{3}{4}$; the value of a proper fraction is less than one.

Protractor   A transparent circular or semicircular scale used to measure angles.

Radius   A line from the centre to the circumference of a circle. All radii are the same length in any one circle.

Ratio   A relationship between two numbers of the same kind, expressed as 'a to b' or $a : b$

Rectangle   A quadrilateral with four right angles and two pairs of equal sides.

Reflection   How a shape would appear if it were seen in a mirror. The resulting shape is its image.

Reflex angle   An angle between 180° and 360°

Remainder   The number left over after a division calculation; for example, $25 \div 2 = 12$ remainder 1

Rhombus   A quadrilateral with four equal sides but no right angles.

Right angle   An angle that is equal to 90°

Right-angled triangle   A triangle in which one angle is 90°

Rotation   A turn of an object through a number of degrees, clockwise or anticlockwise, about a centre of rotation.

Rounding   Writing a number so that it is not exact but retains its approximate value. A number may be rounded to the nearest ten, hundred thousand, ..., to a number of significant figures or decimal places.

Scalene triangle   A triangle with three sides of different lengths and three angles of different sizes.

Sector   Part of a circle between two radii.

Simplifying   The process of reducing a fraction to its lowest terms.

Speed   A compound unit of distance and time, written as km/h or mph.

Square number   A number that results from a number being multiplied by itself; for example, $4 \times 4 = 16$, 16 is a square number.

Sum   The answer to an addition calculation; for example, the sum of 3 and 4 is 7

Symbols   Numbers or operations (+, ×, ÷, −) written as letters or simple shapes.

Three-dimensional   A solid object such as a cube or sphere.

Top-heavy fraction   See improper fraction.

Translation   How an object is moved, first along and then up or down, to its image.

Two-dimensional   A flat or plane shape such as a rectangle or circle.

Unit fraction   A rational number written as a fraction where the numerator is one and the denominator is a positive integer. For example, $\frac{1}{2}$, $\frac{1}{3}$, $\frac{1}{4}$ etc.

Vertically opposite   The angles formed when two straight lines cross. At every such point, there are two pairs of equal vertically opposite angles.

Index